Rules For Entering The Horse Business

1) Learn about the business. Foolishly, many people go into the business without really understanding what they're getting into. Study horse magazines and other sources of information.

2) Obtain sound, honest advice. The person you choose as your advisor in the horse business will make the difference between a pleasant and an unpleasant experience; between profit, loss and ruin. You must find a competent, knowledgeable and, most importantly, honest counselor—someone who is compatible with you and your needs. There's absolutely no way that a person who is not spending a majority of his or her time in the business can do justice to an investment without good advice.

3) Work out a plan for your investment. Establish your goals and determine how much you want to spend toward obtaining them. You should make a complete assessment of the tax and other financial ramifications of your plan. Then stick to your plan.

4) Emphasize quality. You don't necessarily have to pay a million dollars for a horse or invest a million in the business to become a success. However, you should buy the best-quality stock available for your price range. Probably the leading cause of failure in the horse business is that the investor attempts to buy a bunch of cheap horses and hopes to get lucky. Forget it! Cheap horses cost as much to keep as expensive ones—maybe more—and don't produce nearly the return.

5) Be patient. Don't become discouraged when you don't win the Kentucky Derby with the first horse you buy. That has happened only once (Hoop, Jr., 1945) and may not happen again for a long time!

Successful
Thoroughbred
Investment

Successful Thoroughbred Investment

In A Changing Market

by Jack Lohman
and Arnold Kirkpatrick

Thoroughbred Publishers, Inc.
Lexington, Kentucky, U.S.A.

Library of Congress Catalog Card Number
84-52504

Published in the United States by

Thoroughbred Publishers, Inc.
P.O. Box 4240
Lexington, Kentucky 40544

Acknowledgements

There are so many people to whom we owe so much, both of us, that we had initially decided not to include acknowledgements in this book, because it would be absolutely impossible to express proper thanks to all our friends and loved ones who have stood by us and supported us both through hard times over the years. You know who you are, though, and we hope you know how much we appreciate your love and loyalty.

For the purposes of this book, there are a few people who do deserve acknowledgement. Some of them are people who qualify for the mention, above, and others have simply put in a great deal of effort in the publication of this work.

Primary among the latter are Mark Simon and Pat Terry of *The Thoroughbred Record,* who, along with a great deal of *The Record* staff, among them David Dink, Prudy Libby, Kelly McCoy, and Jean Broida, put in many long hours checking on us and supporting us. Similar expressions of appreciation go to Lucille Bevis, Suzanne LaRue, and Marian Wahlgren, who typed, fixed coffee, ran errands, and listened to endless complaints during the writing of this book, to Bob Stokhaug, who helped with pedigree research, and to Bill Johnson of the Thoroughbred Press, who ramrodded the printing to make sure it came out on time.

Then there were people who gave of their own time to read and make suggestions on the chapters in their particular areas of expertise. They include Rich Rolapp of the American Horse Council; John Kropp, attorney, Cincinnati; Jay

Hickey of the Horse Council's general counsel; Mike Walz of Citizen's Fidelity Bank in Louisville; and Charlie McIntosh, racing secretary at Latonia. Finally, there are two acknowledgements which we need to make.

With respect to charts, past performances, and other information from the *Daily Racing Form*:

With respect to computer pedigrees, race records, and statistics reprinted herein:

Table Of Contents

About The Authors

Jack Lohman

Jack Lohman is a practical horseman, and a good one.

He was born in Two Rivers, Wisconsin, but, in 1939, moved with his parents to New Orleans, where he attended school and developed a feeling of home for Louisiana which lasts to this day.

He attended Tulane University on a Navy scholarship, which prevented him from studying agriculture as he would have preferred, but during his college years he held jobs as a hotwalker and an assistant in the photo-finish department at Fair Grounds race track. At that time he also bought his first racehorse, a trotter, for $400 and spent weekends touring county fairs in a dilapidated pickup truck, hauling a battered trailer which contained his one-horse stable. As a standardbred trainer, driver, and groom, Lohman never broke his maiden, but he also never failed to pick up a check.

He graduated from Tulane in 1952 with a B.A. in Business Administration and a commission as an ensign in the Navy. Following service in the Korean War, Lohman held, for varying periods of time, jobs as a manufacturer's agent, an aircraft salesman, and an accountant, before he met and married his wife, Alice, who convinced him to return to his first love—horses.

They moved to Kentucky, where Lohman got a job teaching in the Mercer County High School, rented an old farmhouse, and purchased his first two broodmares. One of them was an old Spendthrift castoff, Phanatam, whom Lohman bought for $300. For him, she produced five good winners, including

Jacks Again, a *Sensitivo colt who won 25 races and $164,010, which today would be worth three times that amount.

In 1961, the Lohmans purchased 161 acres of unimproved land south of Lexington, named it Alpha Omega Farm, and began turning it into a horse farm. By 1965, the farm was progressing well and Lohman had approximately 50 boarders on the farm when, on Kentucky Derby Weekend, he became infamous when some 20 horses died on his farm from food poisoning. Always a progressive thinker, he had been using an advanced, airtight silo for feeding the horses and the system had been working very successfully for two years. But, through human error, some air was allowed into the silo, and botulin formed.

In the face of that disaster, it probably would have been easier to turn to another form of making a living, but Lohman renamed the farm Clear Creek Stud and continued to operate the farm successfully until 1969.

At that time, the Louisiana breeding program was beginning to make a great deal of progress and, since Lohman never could seem to get used to the Kentucky winters (his wife says he did nothing but complain from Thanksgiving to Easter), they returned home to Louisiana, where they purchased 78 acres 15 miles north of Covington, keeping the name Clear Creek Stud. Today, Clear Creek Stud has grown to 350 acres, with nine stallions and approximately 200 broodmares.

Lohman has been very active in organizations relating to the horse business in Louisiana. For 12 years, he was a member of the board of directors of the Louisiana Thoroughbred Breeders Association and, for ten years, was editor of the Louisiana Horse magazine. Through the latter position he was one of the founding members of American Horse Publications. He was the original publisher of the excellent newsletter Racing Update, now published out of Lexington, Kentucky, by Bill Oppenheim, and was also original publisher of Equine Sportsmedicine News, now published out of Cincinnati, Ohio, by Tom Ivers and Esprit Racing Team, Ltd.

He has been president and chairman of the Louisiana Horse Council, and was the president of the Louisiana Breeders Sales Company, which is the forerunner of Fasig-Tipton Louisiana, Inc.

In 1975, under the corporate name of Lakefront Turf Club, Inc., Lohman obtained a lease from Jefferson Downs to operate a 32-day "breeders" race meeting in the fall, emphasizing two-year-old and Louisiana-bred racing. That meeting recently completed its eighth year of operation.

He has also formed and operates several successful partnerships among his friends to purchase and race thoroughbreds in Louisiana.

In 1978, with the help of several friends, Lohman wrote and published the first edition of his very successful book How To Make Money Investing In Thoroughbreds. A second and a third printing in January of 1979 and February of 1982, respectively, have sold out, prompting the publication of this book, Successful Thoroughbred Investment In A Changing Market.

11

Arnold Kirkpatrick

Arnold Kirkpatrick is the only man in the history of the thoroughbred business to win significant industry awards as both a writer and a breeder.

In 1983 he won the Eclipse Award for Outstanding Magazine Writing on Thoroughbred Racing. Five years earlier, he received one of Keeneland's coveted Consignors Gold Cups as co-breeder and consignor of Taisez Vous, the best filly sold at the 1975 Keeneland July yearling sale. Taisez Vous, incidentally, won the Grade I Santa Margarita Invitational Handicap and La Canada Stakes, the Grade II Milady Handicap, plus eight other races, and earned $372,185, being the second-leading money winner for her sire, Silent Screen.

Both awards are the results of long years of experience in the horse business. While he was growing up in Florida, Kirkpatrick worked on a ranch, when he wasn't spearfishing, and, during his occasional summers in Kentucky, worked in the press room and composing room of the Thoroughbred Press, which until 1980 owned and published *The Thoroughbred Record*.

Upon his graduation from Tulane University in 1965, numerous years after Jack Lohman was there, Kirkpatrick went to work as an editorial assistant for *The Thoroughbred Record*, where he would continue for 11 years and serve in practically every capacity on the magazine, from research assistant, to managing editor, to president and publisher, which were the titles he held in 1976, when he resigned to join the American Horse Council in Washington, D.C. During his tenure with *The Record*, he was the founding president of American Horse

Publications, which is now an international organization with more than 80 member publications; he worked extensively on research and editing of William H. P. Robertson's definitive *History of Thoroughbred Racing in America*; he was a director of the National Turf Writers Association; and he was elected secretary-treasurer of the Thoroughbred Club of America.

In Washington, Kirkpatrick served as director of research and executive secretary to the Racing Advisory Committee of the American Horse Council. In that capacity he handled all matters pertaining to racing—including thoroughbred, standardbred, quarter horse, Arabian, and appaloosa racing and breeding—in addition to the preparation and delivery of testimony on behalf of the horse industry before numerous governmental bodies.

In December of 1980, Kirkpatrick returned to Kentucky to become vice president of Spendthrift Farm, one of the world's largest thoroughbred operations. There he participated in the acquisition and syndication of a number of stallions, including the champion two-year-old Lord Avie, the last champion retired to the farm. He also assisted in the private placement of 32% of the stock in Spendthrift in August of 1983 which, at $32-million, is believed to be the largest single private placement in history.

In May of 1982, Kirkpatrick was elected president of the Kentucky Jockey Club, which operates Latonia Race Course near Cincinnati. Since that time, Latonia has consistently set new records for attendance and handle, while the Jim Beam Stakes, Latonia's showcase event, has grown from a nongraded stakes with $150,000 in added money, to a graded event with a purse of $300,000 in 1984.

Kirkpatrick resigned from Spendthrift in March of 1984 to open Kirkpatrick & Company, a full-service consulting firm which specializes in consultation in most facets of the thoroughbred business.

Kirkpatrick was highly instrumental in the formation of the Breeders' Cup Series, and he also either currently serves or has served as a director of the Thoroughbred Racing Associations of North America, the organization which sets standards for and represents the majority of the major race tracks in the U.S. and Canada; as president of Friends of the Equine, Inc., and a trustee of the Morris Animal Foundation, both of which raise and distribute funds for equine research; as an advisor to the American Association or Equine Practitioners; and as an officer or director of numerous other civic and charitable organizations.

He has become a speaker of international renown at seminars and symposiums on the thoroughbred business and is listed in the *International Who's Who of Authors and Writers*, and *International Men of Achievement*.

Preface

There's a story which has been circulating throughout the thoroughbred world as long as we both can remember:

A wealthy industrialist came down to Kentucky, with a notion of getting into the horse business. "I've got plenty of money," he told a number of people, "what I need is someone in the horse business with some experience to help me out." Sure enough, as you might expect would happen to anyone going around advertising that he had plenty of money, the wealthy industrialist found someone with experience in the horse business. It also wasn't much more than a year before the industrialist had to admit to a friend, "It wasn't too long before *he* had the money and *I* had the experience."

This story is prophetic, unfortunately, but it certainly needn't be. The horse business is the most exciting, emotionally rewarding activity either of us has ever pursued professionally, and it can be very, very profitable. In our combined experience in the business, however, we have seen dozens of people, smart people, successful business people, who have taken a bath in the horse business because, when they entered it, they checked their brains at the door.

That is what this book is all about. It is intended to acquaint you with the vast and complex world of thoroughbred racing and breeding, to help you avoid—or, at least, ease your trip over—some of the bumps we've experienced.

You'll grow to like the horse business; we'll almost guarantee it, if you've got any spirit, any gamble, in you at all; and, if we can help you to avoid some of the pitfalls, you'll like it much better.

We believe that publication of this book will help the horse business, because happy and successful participants make for a healthy industry, and vice versa. A recent study done for the White House Office of Consumer Affairs showed that the average unhappy customer will share his story with at least nine other people, while 13% will share their tale with at least 20 people. We want you to be a happy participant in the business, and having you start out with a sound basis of knowledge of the business will help achieve this goal.

When we were primarily involved in publishing, both of us would receive numerous books on how to become successful betting the horses and, to be honest, most of them went into the wastebasket, because we felt, basically, if the author was so successful, why is he writing about it instead of doing it? This book does not fit into that mold. If you read the sections on the authors, you'll realize we have both been actual—and, we immodestly say, successful—participants in the horse business. We both have race track experience and, in fact, are at the present operating race track executives. Additionally, we both have considerable experience on the breeding farm. As mentioned, we hope that you, our readers, can benefit from that experience.

This book has arisen from a crusade that both of us have carried on through our long years of friendship. We are dedicated to the proposition that there is money to be made in the horse business, as you will see shortly, and that it can be a profitable and exciting field for investors of all levels and backgrounds. The crusade is that we want people who come into the business to know what they're getting into, to recognize the risk factors as well as the emotional and fiscal benefits of participation in the horse business.

Whether it's the thrill of standing in the winner's circle, seeing a newborn foal, the Kentucky Derby, a serene morning on a farm, or the heat of battle, racing holds many attractions, and diverse investment possibilities.

As with any business, the rewards in the thoroughbred business are commensurate with the amount of risk you want to take. There are some relatively safe—and we must emphasize that they are only "relatively safe"—ways of investing in thoroughbreds and then, again, there are some exciting ways to participate. We'll discuss them all, but there's one admonition we'd like to make here. If you're looking for a totally risk-free place to invest your money; if you don't feel a rush when a closely bunched pack of horses strains with every last ounce of their being for the finish line; if you don't get a thrill out of watching a foal romp and jump and buck his way across a spring pasture; then put your money in municipal bonds and forget about the horse business. If you like the feel of a muzzle pushing at you looking for something good to eat; if you care at all about the wonders of nature; if you would be thrilled by standing in the winner's circle of a race track; then, baby, this is it.

And, as mentioned, if you're careful, this can, and will, be a financially rewarding experience. As you can see from the accompanying charts from *The Thoroughbred Record,* the past decade has seen the Keeneland July sales average outperform the Dow-Jones Industrial average by 32-to-1 and the Saratoga sales average outperform the Dow-Jones by 20-to-1 (see chart on opposite page). The overall yearling market has not risen as fast and has "only" outperformed the Dow-Jones by about 10-to-1 and the Consumer Price Index by about 3-to-1. The chart below is illustrative of the fact that the thoroughbred business is not much different from any other business in that it pays to deal at the top.

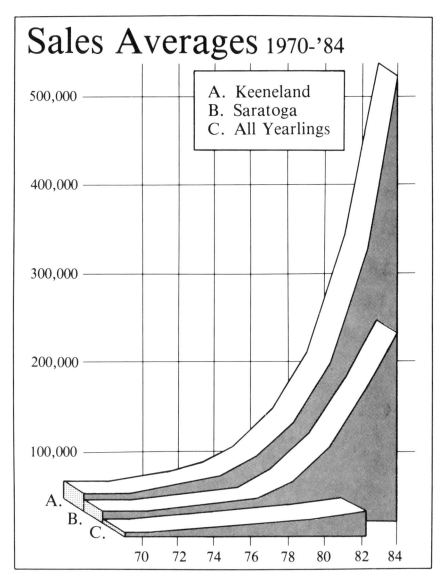

Sales Averages 1970-'84

A. Keeneland
B. Saratoga
C. All Yearlings

500,000

400,000

300,000

200,000

100,000

A.
B.
C.

70 72 74 76 78 80 82 84

		DOW-JONES INDUSTRIAL AVERAGES vs. SUMMER SALES AVERAGES vs. INFLATION RATE					
Year	Dow-Jones[1]	% Change	Keeneland	% Change	Saratoga	% Change	Inflation Rate[2]
1960	641	−1.5	11,844	1.5	11,082	−0.6	1.6
1961	690	7.6	14,178	19.7	10,612	−4.2	1.0
1962	574	−16.8	12,993	−8.4	12,265	15.6	1.1
1963	701	22.1	14,191	9.2	12,815	4.5	1.2
1964	838	19.5	17,505	23.3	17,763	38.6	1.3
1965	872	4.1	17,973	2.7	17,549	−1.2	1.7
1966	877	0.6	18,206	1.3	19,535	11.3	2.9
1967	860	−1.9	20,812	14.3	22,145	13.4	2.9
1968	896	4.2	30,671	47.4	24,425	10.3	4.2
1969	876	−2.2	25,699	−16.2	18,353	−24.8	5.4
1970	688	−21.5	30,152	17.3	26,803	46.0	5.9
1971	893	29.8	31,775	5.4	30,541	13.9	4.3
1972	929	4.0	37,100	16.8	28,930	−5.3	3.3
1973	881	−5.2	56,814	53.1	42,718	47.6	6.2
1974	806	−8.5	53,489	−5.9	37,219	−12.9	11.0
1975	877	8.8	53,637	0.3	37,068	−0.4	9.1
1976	1,003	14.4	66,575	24.1	44,349	19.6	5.8
1977	913	−9.0	85,343	28.2	57,310	29.2	6.5
1978	813	−10.9	121,654	42.6	80,246	40.0	7.7
1979	834	2.6	155,567	27.9	98,096	22.2	11.3
1980	876	5.0	196,863	26.6	111,159	13.3	12.4
1981	968	10.5	250,113	27.0	160,597	44.4	8.5
1982	803	−17.0	337,734	35.0	176,730	10.0	6.9
1983	1,225	52.5	501,495	48.4	210,790	19.3	2.6
1984	1,130	−7.8	548,609	9.4	249,089	18.2	4.2

[1] Dow-Jones Average, as of July 1 of year indicated, is rounded off to nearest dollar, and does not reflect splits or stock dividends.
[2] Inflation Rate as determined by the Bureau of Labor Statistics derived from the change in the Consumer Price Index.

This applies to the race track, as well as the sales. In 1982, the top 2% of the runners in North America earned precisely 25% of all the purses offered for the year. By 1983, the gap had widened to the point where the top 1.9% of the horses had earned 26.6% of all the purse money offered for the year. The equation will be skewed even further toward the top horses in 1984, as the Breeders' Cup program pours an additional $20-million into the North American purse structure, all for top horses.

It should also be noted that, as this book is being written, the thoroughbred business is in an extremely volatile period of change. We feel it is probably in the second year of a four- to six-year shakeout. A study by the excellent publication *Racing Update* in March of 1984 concluded, ". . . the commercial yearling market is in poor health as things stand now. . . . In our opinion, certainly no more than two of every seven 1983 Kentucky auction yearlings showed a profit, and the figure is probably closer to one in four." This proved to be prophetic at the 1984 September yearling sales when only about 10% of the stallions represented by yearlings at the sales achieved a median of three times their retail stud fees, which has traditionally been the rule of thumb for determining whether or not a breeder makes money on a yearling.

As we write this book, we feel that many stud fees will drop in 1985 and subsequent years to a rate of about half to one-third of what they had been in the late '70s and early '80s. This, of course, will be reflected in the syndication value of good horses at the race track, and, unfortunately, we feel that a number of people will be disappointed with the stud value of horses they had been expecting to make them rich.

19

Further, since the price of broodmares is also a function of yearling prices, we expect an adjustment in the overall broodmare market during this shakeout period.

There is one very important point to dispel this ominous note. Throughout history, in times of market fluctuation, in times of recession or depression, there have been people who continued to make money, good money. They were the people who were smart, who studied, who worked hard, and who were able to anticipate trends and capitalize on that anticipation. There are a lot of people like that in the horse business today, and, if you hook up with one or more of them, your chances of success will improve dramatically. This book, we hope, will help you find those people.

Finally, a word about the evolution of this book. Originally, in 1978, the Lohman half of the current team of authors wrote a book entitled *How To Make Money Investing In Thoroughbreds,* and the Kirkpatrick half of the team was one of the editors. That book sold out in three printings and, when the two of us got together to talk about a fourth printing with Pat Terry of *The Thoroughbred Record,* which is publishing this book, we decided the business had changed so much in just a short time that it would be necessary to rewrite the original book, expand it considerably, and completely change its thrust. Therefore, we present to you *Successful Thoroughbred Investment In A Changing Market.*

This book is organized in a sequence designed to acquaint you with the business in the order in which you would logically encounter it. For instance, after you've read the first two chapters, which we do urge you to do before going any further, you can skip to the chapter on the race track or on the farm or on the sales, whichever interests you most, but we believe that you'll enjoy each chapter. To make them more enjoyable than a strict "How To" book, we've sprinkled each chapter with anecdotes, true stories, of how people have achieved success or met with failure.

As you go through the book, you'll notice several redundancies, including, "Don't check your brains at the door," "It's better to own a piece of a good horse than all of a bad one," and "You get what you pay for." These are totally intentional, for they are among the points that, if you remember them, will make this business a better experience for you.

Another important point to remember throughout is that when we use the masculine "he" in any form it means "he or she," because the horse business is one where brains count as much as strength, so women can, and do, compete equally, and very successfully, with men.

Finally, the jargon of the business is extremely important, so we spent a lot of time and effort compiling the glossary which appears at the end of the book. We urge you to study it, because it, too, will make your entry into the business easier.

We hope you'll enjoy this book and, even more importantly, hope it will help you have fun and enjoy success in the horse business.

Chapter 1

Some Success Stories

Welcome to the horse business!

As you read this book, you'll discover, if you haven't already, that thoroughbred racing and breeding are almost always stimulating, often financially productive and, on occasion, spectacularly rewarding.

In this chapter, we'll acquaint you with some of the success stories associated with the business, and, in later chapters, we'll recount some horror stories about some ways people have been taken. For every extreme story, though, there are hundreds of ordinary stories of ordinary people making nominal sums of money with their horses. But they always seem to enjoy themselves thoroughly along the way.

There are three basic formulas success stories follow. There are tales of "lightning in a bottle," where moderate to small investments have resulted in spectacular success; there are stories of spectacular investments resulting in spectacular success; and there are stories of moderate to small investments resulting in moderate success.

There is a common thread that flows through each of these stories, though, and that is luck. It is an accepted truth that it takes a great deal of luck to be successful in the thoroughbred business. It's also true that some people are lucky in the business once or maybe twice, some people are consistently lucky, and some people never get lucky.

In our opinion, this phenomenon was probably best explained by the great trainer Hirsch Jacobs who was asked about his luck.

"The harder I work," he said, "the luckier I get."

The most spectacular success story associated with the thoroughbred business began on Saturday, July 19, 1975, when a delightful young couple named Mickey and Karen Taylor accompanied their good friend, partner, and advisor, Dr. Jim Hill, to the Fasig-Tipton Kentucky Summer Yearling Sale, held in a temporary arena on Newtown Pike in Lexington. There, for $17,500 they purchased a muscular, dark bay colt by Bold Reasoning out of My Charmer, by Poker, from the two-horse consignment of a small breeder, the late Ben Castleman, whose farm was just about two miles from the sales arena.

The colt was later named Seattle Slew—Seattle because the Taylors lived not too far from Seattle, and Slew, the story goes, for the swampy areas around Dr. Hill's home town of Fort Myers, Florida (although many knowledgeable people maintain to this day that the latter half of the name comes from the fact that he toes out somewhat in the right fore).

A $17,500 yearling, Seattle Slew won the Kentucky Derby undefeated. He was owned by Karen and Mickey Taylor, left, and Jim and Sally Hill, right.

Now that you know the name, you no doubt recall the horse. Seattle Slew was what is called a racehorse! (And, in this business when you mention the word "racehorse" in the context of one like Seattle Slew, it always comes with an exclamation point.) Slew went undefeated at two, winning the Champagne Stakes by nearly ten lengths, and won the Eclipse Award as champion two-year-old colt of 1976. He opened his three-year-old campaign by setting a track record of

1:20⅗ in a seven-furlong allowance prep for the Flamingo Stakes, which he also won with ease, followed by a 3¾-length victory in the Wood Memorial Stakes, his last prep race before the Kentucky Derby.

Slew swept through the Triple Crown the way you'd expect Ghengis Khan to sweep through a group of conscientious objectors, winning the Kentucky Derby, Preakness Stakes, and Belmont Stakes, each with increasing ease. He became the first horse in history to win the Triple Crown undefeated, and it appeared he was likely to remain that way for the rest of his racing career.

There are only two kinds of horses, though—those who have been beaten and those who are going to get beaten. Shipped to California for the Swaps Stakes, Slew finished out of the money for the first defeat of his career and the only time he would ever finish worse than second. He wound up the year with Eclipse Awards, both as Horse of the Year and champion three-year-old colt, not to mention earnings of $641,370.

At four, Slew won the Woodward Stakes, setting a track record, in addition to the Marlboro Cup Invitational and Stuyvesant Handicaps. His greatest race of the year, though, and perhaps the greatest race of his career, was a second to Exceller in the 1½-mile Jockey Club Gold Cup Stakes. In that race, Slew went to the front at the start, pressed by the likes of Triple Crown winner Affirmed and Life's Hope. On a track listed as sloppy, the three of them blistered through murderous early fractions of :22⅗ for the first quarter, :45⅕ for the half, and 1:09⅖ for six furlongs (as a point of comparison, Secretariat's fractions when he set the world record for the distance in the Belmont Stakes, on a fast track, were

Despite losing the lead to Exceller in midstretch of the 1978 Jockey Club Gold Cup, Seattle Slew battled back to drop a nose decision in what many racing people consider Slew's best race of his career.

:23⅗, :46⅕, and 1:09⅖). At that time, beginning a spectacular move on the inside, was another exclamation-point racehorse, Exceller, who blew past the other horses as though they were standing still, collared and passed Seattle Slew at the head of the stretch, and looked as though he would draw out to win by daylight, a lot of daylight, as a matter of fact. Exceller opened up a lead of about three-quarters of a length, but Slew reached down into that big heart of his and began to fight back. Stride by stride, inch by inch, he cut into Exceller's lead, but it was a dead-tired horse working against a fresh one, and a good one. At the end, Slew had failed by a short nose to catch Exceller, and many of the people who saw the race thought he would have caught the winner in another couple of jumps. But that's what makes horse racing.

Win, lose, or draw, it was one of the most courageous performances ever seen on a race track. The loss probably cost Seattle Slew a second title as Horse of the Year, but he gained the admiration of the racing world. Affirmed, incidentally, went on to be named Horse of the Year off his victories in the Triple Crown. Seattle Slew was retired with earnings of $1,208,726, a profit of $1,191,226, and a return on investment of 6,807%.

When he was retired, Slew was syndicated by Brownell Combs II to stand at Spendthrift Farm for $300,000 a share which, in a 40-share syndicate, increased his worth to the Taylors and the Hills by another $12-million, to raise the return on investment to 75,378%.

The story doesn't end there, however, either for the original owners or for the people who paid $300,000 for shares in the horse. Slew's first two crops have included champions Slew o' Gold and Landaluce, the 1984 Kentucky Derby and Belmont Stakes winner Swale, and the additional Grade I stakes winners Slewpy, Adored, and Seattle Song—probably the most fantastic early stud success in the history of the breed. Recently, two shares in the horse changed hands for sums in excess of $2-million *each*, the second one for $2.9-million, and in October of 1984 one of your co-authors was quoted a price of $3.5-million for a share. While one can't make a direct extrapolation, because the price is escalated due to scarcity, the value of the horse can safely be estimated at $80- to $90-million, a return on investment of 463,950% at the bottom figure, 521,093% at the top.

Then there's the story of another horse, small, ill-bred, and back at the knee (which is considered by most conformation experts to be the most fatal flaw a horse can have). He was bred by the highly successful Golden Chance Farm, near Paris, Kentucky. Despite the fact that the farm races most of the horses it breeds, this one was considered to be so small and badly conformed that when he was a yearling they sold him in the Keeneland January Sale, where many of the yearlings are sold because their breeders don't think it's worth carrying them until September when most yearlings are normally sold. The little colt brought a final bid of $1,100 from J. E. Calloway, who kept him for precisely a year and sold him at the same sale in 1977 for double the price he'd paid for him. The buyer at $2,200 was Hal Snowden Jr., who broke the colt, had him gelded, and sold him to a Japanese client, who "promptly returned him because of the knees."

24

Not too long afterward, Snowden found two other buyers by the name of Colleen Madere and Dortha Lingo, who apparently didn't know or care about horses being back at the knee. They took the young gelding down to Louisiana where he won a few races, including the Lafayette Futurity, and earned a little over $50,000, before Snowden bought him back from Mmes. Madere and Lingo in March of 1978. In April, Snowden entered the little gelding in an allowance race at Keeneland and after he finished fourth, Snowden sold him, sight unseen, for $25,000 to Sam Rubin, a gentleman from New York who imports bicycles and plays the races.

Sam Rubin leading in $25,000 purchase John Henry after yet another stakes triumph.

To date, the ill-bred, badly conformed, smallish gelding, named John Henry, has earned $6,591,860—almost twice as much as the second-leading money-winning horse of all time. In 1981, when he was Horse of the Year, he set an all-time seasonal earnings record of $1,798,030, and in 1984 earned $2,336,650; he won thoroughbred racing's first million-dollar race, the Arlington Million Stakes, in 1981, and repeated, in 1984, with a victory so impressive that it leads us, your authors, to speculate that he could become the first horse in history to crack $10-million in earnings. (To put that in perspective, John Henry was the first horse to reach the earnings levels of $3-, $4-, $5-, and $6-million.)

Return on investment to this point is 26,055%, and, despite all the aforementioned faults, he sure as hell looks good crossing the finish line.

If you have somewhat more substantial resources than the Taylors and Hills or Mr. Rubin, you don't necessarily have to rely so heavily on lightning in a bottle, because there is a considerable element of fashion and hype in the thoroughbred business. This hype and fashion can work to the advantage of a colt who is, for example, an extremely highly touted yearling, because he'll not need to be nearly the racehorse that Seattle Slew was in order to generate a considerable syndication price.

In 1981, Sheik Maktoum bin Rashid al Maktoum, one of several members of the Royal Family of Dubai who are interested in racing, came to the Keeneland July Sale where he purchased, among other yearlings, a good-looking bay son of Northern Dancer, the most fashionable sire in the world today. The colt was the first foal of a fairly nice racemare, Sweet Alliance, who had won the Kentucky Oaks, the Jersey Belle Handicap, four other races, and $179,219. She, herself, was also very well bred, being by the top broodmare sire Sir Ivor, out of a good stakes winner and stakes producer, Mrs. Peterkin.

The Sheik got the colt, after a heated bidding duel with a syndicate headed by Robert Sangster, paying $3.3-million, only $200,000 less than the world-record price for a yearling. The colt, named Shareef Dancer, was sent to England to be trained by Michael Stoute. As it turned out, he didn't like firm going, so he had to be placed rather carefully, lest his value be diminished by unimpressive racing performances.

In two starts at two, Shareef Dancer was able to win only a six-furlong maiden race at Newmarket, defeating an undistinguished field. Indeed, at the beginning of his three-year-old campaign, it appeared he might be a $3.3-million dud, as he finished second in his first race of the year. Nine days before the prestigious Irish Sweeps Derby, however, Shareef Dancer scored his first important victory when he won the King Edward VII Stakes over 1½ miles at Royal Ascot. In the Irish Sweeps Derby, also run at 1½ miles, Shareef Dancer swept to a three-length victory over Caerleon and Teenoso, who were regarded as two of the leaders of the division, and his reputation was made.

Shareef Dancer never raced again, but when he retired, with a total of three wins in five starts and earnings of $212,722, he was named champion three-year-old in England and Ireland, and was the highest-weighted colt in his division of the International Classification (which includes European horses only). As a

Shareef Dancer sold for $3.3-million as a yearling, and then went on to win the Irish Sweeps Derby at three, prior to being syndicated for $40-million.

racehorse, his return on investment was a net loss of 93.5%. However, due to his fashionability, when he was retired for stud duty at Dalham Hall Stud, Newmarket, England, in 1983, he was reportedly syndicated for $40-million, a net profit of $36.9-million. As a percentage return on investment, that works out to about 1,118%.

A similar story in this country, although it's not as extreme, is that of Devil's Bag, who brought a top price as a yearling, lived up to his tremendous potential, however briefly, and, through syndication, produced an exceptional profit for his owners.

A full brother to the superb racemare and champion Glorious Song, Devil's Bag was sold to the long-established Hickory Tree Farm for $325,000 at the 1982 Keeneland July Sale. When Devil's Bag was sold, his price was a little over $19,000 less than the sales average, primarily because his sire, Halo, was not particularly fashionable at the time, since Halo's other notable son, Sunny's Halo, had not yet won the Kentucky Derby, and the major portion of Halo's success as a sire had been in Canada.

At any rate, Devil's Bag came out running at two, and he was about as impressive as any horse who ever looked through a bridle. He won his first start, a six-furlong maiden race at Saratoga, by 7½ lengths and followed with a 5¼-length

Devil's Bag destroyed his competition at two, as in the Laurel Futurity, above, and was syndicated for $36-million before he ever raced at three.

victory in his second race, an allowance at the same distance. In his next start, the seven-furlong Cowdin Stakes, Devil's Bag set a stakes record of 1:21⅗ in beating Dr. Carter, a pretty fair sort himself, by three lengths. In his next start, the Champagne Stakes at a mile, Devil's Bag again defeated Dr. Carter, this time by six lengths in 1:34⅕, another stakes record, erasing that set by Seattle Slew seven years previously. After closing out the year with another impressive win in the Laurel Futurity, Devil's Bag was syndicated to race at three and retire to stud afterward for $1-million a share in a 36-share syndicate.

Devil's Bag was a considerable disappointment in 1984 as a three-year-old, as he struggled to win a prep for the Flamingo Stakes, then finished fourth in the Flamingo itself, his first loss. After winning the Forerunner Purse at Keeneland by 15 lengths, he was shipped to Louisville for the Kentucky Derby, but was hard pressed to defeat a mediocre field in the Derby Trial Stakes, a week before the Derby. Reasoning that something must be drastically wrong with the colt to cause such a reversal in form, his connections had him examined, once again, by a veterinarian, who found a bone chip in his right knee. Devil's Bag was retired with eight wins in nine starts and earnings of $445,860, not much return on investment. However, the luster of his family and his spectacular early races had made him a $36-million stallion prospect, and increased the total profit on him to $36,120,860, a return on investment of 11,114%.

Finally, we'd like to wind up with a story of a moderate investment which, to date, has produced a moderate return. This is also an example, however, of the way that one horse can carry several others and turn an otherwise unsuccessful venture into a profitable one.

In 1981, Jack Lohman put together a limited partnership called Clear Creek Bloodstock, with shares selling for $25,000 each, and he took the proceeds to various yearling sales. He purchased three colts—a son of Barrera—Miss Swoon, by Swoon's Son, for $300,000 at the Keeneland July Sale; a son of Buckfinder—Three Waters, by Water Prince, for $150,000 at the Fasig-Tipton Kentucky July Sale; and a son of Cornish Prince—Miss Quickstep, by Native Dancer, for $100,000 at the Keeneland September Sale.

The three colts were taken to Louisiana where, at the time this is being written, the Barrera colt, named Swoon de Bar, has won a maiden race and $9,370, and the Buckfinder colt, named Found the Cash, is an allowance winner of five races and $23,523, including a race in which he set a track record for $1\frac{5}{16}$ miles. The third colt, named Temerity Prince, has done enough to make the entire partnership worthwhile.

Through November 1, 1984, he has won eight stakes and seven other races; he has placed in two other stakes and has achieved total earnings of $278,122. Since all his stakes victories and placings, thus far, have been in Louisiana, they may not have increased his value as a stud by as much as winning a graded stakes, somewhere, but, with his breeding, his stud value could be estimated at around $400,000 (Kirkpatrick estimate), so he's returned about $678,000 to the partnership which owns him. They intend to race him in 1985, which should increase his earnings, as well as his stud value.

Temerity Prince, purchased as a yearling for a more modest $100,000, has earned over $275,000 through his four-year-old season for a Louisiana syndicate.

29

That gives the partnership total earnings of about $310,000, to date, plus a stallion prospect worth $400,000, for a net of about $710,000, against an investment of $550,000, so they're in the black.

Maybe the most important thing in this instance, though—even more than the $160,000 profit—is that these horses are owned by Louisiana people and they're racing in Louisiana, so they're giving their owners a little fun, and that is, after all, what it's all about.

Chapter 2

Choosing Your Advisor

This is going to be the most important step you will ever take in the horse business.

The choice of your advisor or advisors will, quite literally, make the difference between a pleasant and an unpleasant experience in this business, between profit (we hope) and loss, or between loss and ruin. This is no exaggeration! People have been ruined in this business, because it's extremely easy to get in over your head—it can happen very quickly, and it usually happens after some early success.

At the risk of being redundant, we remind you, once again.

Don't check your brains at the door

We both know highly successful business people who have taken a terrible beating in the horse business because they didn't check out their advisors. These were people who would no more think of hiring someone to drive a $50,000 tractor-trailer rig without checking him out than they would think of trying to swim the Pacific Ocean. Yet, they'll give a half-million dollars to some guy to buy and train the most expensive and fragile animals in the world, and all they know about him is they met him in a bar someplace and he said he was a horse trainer. Anyone you hire, or take on as an advisor, should be happy to give you a number of references, and you should check those references carefully.

Before going any further, it should be noted that your advisor can be any one of a number of people, a "general advisor," a bloodstock agent, a horse trainer, a farm operator, or a lawyer/accountant. We'll discuss the various choices of advisors in further detail, right after listing the qualifications we feel are most important. For the time being, though, whenever we mention "advisor," you can take your pick.

Why do you even need an advisor? For one thing the horse business, especially the thoroughbred horse business, is very complicated and, we assure you, you cannot hope to learn enough about it in any reasonable time frame to keep up with the changes which are occurring throughout it without working on it full time. This business is full of absolute fanatics, people who think about nothing but horses; they don't read books unless they're about horses; they don't see movies unless they have horses in them; they don't listen to music unless it's Dan Fogelberg's "Run for the Roses"; and you'll be competing in the same arena with those people.

As a matter of fact, many of the people who are in the business full time use experts to help them in various facets of the industry where they don't feel as strong as some others. For instance, Robert Sangster, who has enjoyed greater financial success than anyone else in the world in the thoroughbred business over the past decade, employs a team concept in his operation. When he comes to the Keeneland sales, he is accompanied by a number of people—his business managers, his trainers, several bloodstock agents, and three or four veterinarians, all of whom serve a specific purpose on the Sangster team when they select a yearling.

As you'll discover in Chapters 7 and 8, the Internal Revenue Service places considerable emphasis on your choice of advisors and experts in determining whether or not your horse operation qualifies to be treated as a business or not, while banks place a similar emphasis in determining whether or not to lend you money for your equine operations.

So your advisor is going to be one of the best investments you'll make in the horse business.

Just to emphasize this most important point, let's recount a couple of horror stories. Both of these are absolutely true and, believe it or not, neither of these is all that unusual. Some of the names have been eliminated to protect the innocent. The first is the story of how a bad advisor cost his client a great deal of money, while the second is a story of how two people got smart too fast, and that wound up costing them money, too.

On February 27, 1982, a gentleman in Louisiana paid $750,000 for a three-year-old who was the leading contender for the HITS Parade Invitational Derby, a minor stakes which is restricted to horses sold in the "HITS Parade Invitational Two-Year-Olds in Training Sale." The horse could run a little—he'd won the HITS Parade Futurity (same restrictions) the previous year and had earned nearly $140,000—so he was obviously the class of the field for the "Derby" the next day. The odd thing about the situation was that Real Dare, for that was the horse's name, was a gelding and there are not too many geldings, with the possible exceptions of Kelso, Forego, and John Henry, who are worth that sort of price tag, let alone one who is obviously several levels below a top horse.

Sure enough, the next day Real Dare returned a substantial portion of his purchase price, $60,000, as he easily won the HITS Parade Derby, and then the story came out as to why the new owner paid such a sum for a gelding. When an incredulous reporter from *The Thoroughbred Record* congratulated the owner, then asked him how he could justify paying such an exorbitant sum for a gelding, the proud owner replied, "We are researching the possibility of having microsurgery performed on Real Dare after this year. There's a urologist in California who, I understand, has performed this surgery about 200 times without a failure . . . on sheep, hogs, and horses. What the surgery does is make a gelded animal fertile again. They would take the testicles from another horse. The testicles only produce the sperm; the genetics are all in the prostate." Well, anyone who got a "C" in biology, much less passed veterinary school, knows that the genetics are contained in the sperm, but the gentleman in question didn't take the time to ask a veterinarian.

Needless to say, Real Dare is still a gelding and, as a matter of fact, he is apparently still running in moderate company, winning occasionally. At the time this book was written he was only about $630,000 short of returning his purchase price to his new owner. Once again, an agent with a sharp line had struck, and someone who failed to check out a story was left holding the bag, a rather considerable one in this case.

The second horror story involves a good advisor and two clients who refused to pay attention to him.

Bill Lockridge is about as good a person as there is in picking out a yearling which might be successful on the race track. In 1970, two fellows came up from Texas and asked Bill to find a nice filly for them. He took them out on the farm and showed them a daughter of Crimson Satan—Bolero Rose, by Bolero. After some discussion, he sold them the filly privately for $11,000.

The next year they came back for the Keeneland July Sale and asked him to pick out another filly for them. He went to the sales and paid $25,000 (you could do that in those days) for a daughter of Jacinto—Turkish Belle, by *My Babu.

By the time the two guys from Texas came back for the 1972 Keeneland July sales, the first filly, now named Crimson Saint, had won two stakes and set a track record in one of them, while the other, named Bold Liz, had won the $50,000-added Hollywood Lassie Stakes and had brought her earnings up to $168,235 by defeating colts in the $100,000-added Hollywood Juvenile Championship Stakes, two days before the sales.

Bill asked them if they'd like him to pick out another filly for them. "No thanks," they said, "we can do it ourselves."

Just for the record, the two guys from Texas wound up in bankruptcy not too long afterward, losing the two good fillies that Bill had bought for them. Crimson Saint wound up setting two track records and winning $91,770, including four stakes races. Her yearlings, as of 1984, had sold for a total of $4,350,000, helped along by a Secretariat colt who brought $1,800,000 at the 1983 Keeneland July Sale and an Alydar filly who brought $1,100,000 at the 1984 sales. Bold Liz wound up with $174,785 in earnings and three yearlings out of her have been sold for a total of $495,000.

The point we're trying to make is don't get too smart too fast.

Qualities of an Advisor

We hope, by now, you've decided to get yourself a good advisor or advisors, to check them out before you actually sign on with them, and most importantly, to listen to them once you've put your faith in them.

Before going on to list the qualities that we feel are important in the selection of an advisor, we'd like to call your attention to the list of required reading at the end of this chapter. Since you're reading this book, we have reason to assume that you're serious enough about the horse business to study it, and we'd like to urge very strongly that you study it carefully before you jump in. The list of required reading is a step in that direction. We've not put the list in at this point, because we were afraid it might interrupt the flow of this deathless prose, but the suggestion is that you go through at least a substantial part of the list before you begin to look for an advisor.

Now, when you begin to look for this superhuman being who is going to turn you into an instantaneous success, what are the qualities that make an advisor good? Following are the qualities which we feel should apply to all the people you hire in the business, whether you decide on a general advisor, a bloodstock agent, a trainer, or some other sort of help.

> *1) Honesty.* Although we hate to say it, the horse business has become a haven for quite a number of charlatans over the years, principally because it is a business so few people know about. There's an aura of mystery to it which seems to lend itself to people with less than sterling character getting ahold of new people coming into the business. Part of the problem is due to the fact that there is no licensing requirement or procedure for bloodstock advisors or agents. It is exacerbated, too, by the fact that the shysters seem to get out and spend a lot of time digging up new customers, while the legitimate types are at the office doing their homework. A lot of people do seem to wind up in the wrong hands right from the very outset, though.
>
> Honesty, in this sense, means a lot more than just personal integrity. Your advisor should be willing and even anxious to answer any questions you have, openly and honestly. And you should ask a lot of questions. Too often people who are very successful in other businesses are reluctant to appear stupid by asking a lot of questions about the horse business. Look at it this way, though. You didn't make a million dollars in the manufacture of widgets without knowing about the business, and the same thing applies to horses. Beware of someone who has *all* the answers, though; that's unnatural, also.
>
> Your advisor should try to educate you on the business, rather than keeping you in the dark. One of the best trainers in the world,

today, operates under the theory of keeping his clients "like mushrooms . . . in the dark all the time and up to their necks in manure." You don't want that, at least at first.

2) *Intelligence.* While you don't necessarily need a genius in this business, you also don't want someone who needs to get undressed to count to 21. There's a tremendous flow of information constantly in the horse business, and your advisor must be able to assimilate that information and interpret it accurately for your benefit. He should be someone who can spot trends and anticipate the market, if not before anyone else, at least early on.

3) *Knowledge and Experience.* While some people tend to think they can impress clients with an encyclopedic knowledge of the minutiae of the business, there is no substitute for experience. As one disgruntled client said of an advisor, recently, "He can tell you the fourth dam of the winner of the 1938 German Derby, but, if you ask him for a bar of soap, he'll bring you a watermelon every time."

It is preferable to have someone who has been around long enough to know *where* to find the answers to your questions, who knows the ins and outs of the business, than to have someone who has spent his entire time in an ivory tower somewhere reading about it.

4) *Compatibility.* If you are going to do things right and your advisor is going to do right by you, you will be spending a lot of time with him. Further, since one of your goals is to make this a pleasant experience, it wouldn't make sense to use someone you despise, no matter how good he is. Pick someone with whom you'd like to spend time even if it weren't for your horse business. As a matter of fact, you might want to sacrifice some small portion of the other qualities for compatibility; you'll find it works out better that way in the long run.

5) *Communications.* This ranks right along with compatibility in importance. You don't want to find out your horse is entered in a race by reading it in the *Daily Racing Form,* or that the horse has broken down by discovering a large number of veterinary charges on your monthly statement. One of the reasons you have all these people working for you is to keep you apprised of what's happening in your business.

There are occasional trainers and farm personnel— some of the "best" in the business, as a matter of fact—who seem to believe that it's really none of the client's business what's happening with their horses, as long as things are going well. That is not so! You should receive regular reports from your advisor and/or trainer as to how your horses, all of them, are progressing. Even if you have a mare who's doing little more than gestating, you should receive periodic reports, because there are critical points in her gestation period when you should know her condition.

As mentioned, this ranks in importance with compatibility and, in fact, it is a function of compatibility. If you don't really like your associates, and vice versa, you'll be reluctant to call them to find out what's happening, or they will be less likely to call you with the good news, as well as the bad.

Now that you know what qualities to look for in an advisor, it's time to decide what kind of advisor you want. This should be based primarily on the extent of your experience in the business, the size of your investment, and the extent of your involvement. You'll have to decide whether you want to hire a general advisor or a bloodstock agent; whether you want to race or breed, in which case you'll need to decide on a trainer or a boarding farm (you should do this with your advisor or bloodstock agent); and whether or not you want to hire a separate accountant and/or lawyer to work with your horse operation, or if you'd prefer, to try to educate your present lawyer and accountant in the horse business.

First, a general advisor vs. a bloodstock agent. These are not, necessarily, mutually exclusive. As a matter of fact, your "general advisor" can, and often will, be someone who functions as a bloodstock agent. The difference is in the function he serves for you.

A bloodstock agent makes his or her living from buying and selling horses, and many agents feel their responsibility to the client ends with those functions. Others, on the other hand, are very good about giving their clients additional advice about matings, trainers, farms, etc. However, since a pure bloodstock agent makes his money by buying and selling—and convincing his owners to buy and sell—he could be more likely to be interested in turning your horses over than in meeting your long-term goals.

By contrast, we view a general advisor as someone who will help you set up a complete program, who will follow along with you throughout the steps of that program, and who will look toward achieving your goals. This person will serve you on a retainer basis, or, if you really want to inspire effort on his behalf, you might want to work out a formula with a moderate retainer and a percentage of your profits. Sometime in the future, if things are really going well, you might even want to go into partnership with your advisor, if he has sufficient funds to invest at the level of your participation in the business.

In addition to working with you to set up and oversee your investment plan in the industry, he can also pick and coordinate your other people, the trainer, the farm, etc.; he can serve as a clearinghouse for your information and bookkeeping, so that you'll have to worry about only one bill per month, rather than a lot of them; he can make the necessary arrangements for you at the race track and/or sales; in short, he can sort of be a personal manager for your equine affairs.

This will, quite obviously, cost you more than having a straight bloodstock agent or trainer or farm operator handle your business, but we feel it will be money well spent and, indeed, like purchasing a fine car, might be cheaper in the long run than going second class.

If you decide to race, one of the first things you'll want to do is pick a trainer, and, as with all your people, the qualities you look for in an advisor will be important in your choice of a trainer. You'll have to make other choices, too.

Do you want someone who's up and coming or a "big name" trainer? How big is too big? Where do you want to race—near home, at a major racing center, or abroad? Are you going to be claiming horses or bringing them along?

As you're starting out, we'd suggest an up-and-coming trainer who races somewhere close to your home. That way you can go to the track in the morning to watch your horses train, and watch them run in the afternoon, all the time learning more and more of what goes on at a race track. You might call the racing secretary at your local race track for suggestions. While he won't say, "So-and-so will be perfect for you," he will give you the names of several trainers who might be likely candidates for your horses.

Generally, the young, up-and-coming trainer will have more time to spend with you, although a number of "big" trainers seem to have a great deal of time to spend with new clients. It's all a matter of organization. Some trainers who have a large stable are very well organized and, as a consequence, are able to spend their time with people, while others, less organized, don't ever seem to have any time, despite the fact they have only a couple of horses. Basically, it doesn't really matter how few or how many horses your trainer has; if he doesn't have time to spend with you, it's too many.

Also, if you start out with a few claiming horses, you're not going to get Woody Stephens to train for you, so you have to find someone on your own level. And, it is very important to inquire as to whether or not he can get stalls for your horses.

Insofar as your lawyer and accountant go, the size and complexity of your horse business are probably going to be the primary determinants of whether you use your regular people or hire specialists. Basically, racing and the horse business are pretty attractive to members of both professions and, unless you get into the business pretty deeply, your own lawyer and accountant should be able to learn enough to carry you along. That is, if they consult with some established equine specialists, if they attend one or two of the many, many seminars that are held each year on equine taxation, and if they are interested. On the subject of interest, it would be very helpful to your professionals if they could find the time to accompany you through your indoctrination into the business.

Start by buying each of them a copy of this book. Don't lend them yours; you'll never get it back.

An Indoctrination to the Business

On several occasions in this chapter, we've mentioned an indoctrination into the business. If you've shown enough interest to read this far, you probably already have some interest in the business and, perhaps, a little working knowledge of it. If you're really going to get serious and invest a substantial amount of money, though, you should also be willing to invest a little time, as well. That is why we have set up the following indoctrination course which you *should* try to accomplish before you begin to invest in the business. As with the list of "required reading" which follows it, the course can be altered, or parts of it can be postponed, but the segments of the thoroughbred business are totally interdependent and it helps to know a little bit about each one, whether you're particularly interested in it or not.

Probably the easiest place to start is where the entire equation ends—at the race track. There you'll learn how to read the *Daily Racing Form* and a condition book; you'll learn about the classification of races and the very concise way that the quality of races puts a value on racehorses. You'll learn how much it takes to train a horse and how fragile they really are; you'll learn about the training cycle and how many things can go wrong with a horse, especially a good one. You'll need to go out early in the morning during training hours and see how things work behind the scenes (many tracks have special morning programs designed for people who want to learn about training). You'll also learn how hard it is for a horse to break even at the track and how you can hit a big lick, *a la* John Henry and Seattle Slew. In short, you should expand on what you will learn in Chapter 3. If you intend for your operation to be primarily racing oriented, or if you intend to start out racing before going into breeding, we'd recommend you do this for at least a week, less if you're going into the breeding end right away.

Whether you're going to start out at the races or in breeding, your intermediate stop should probably be at the auction sales, and, nowadays, you'll have plenty of opportunity to attend a sale pretty close to home, no matter where you live. In 1983 alone, there were more than 150 auctions in North America, with more than 21,000 horses selling for gross receipts in excess of $700-million (see Chapter 4). At the sales you'll learn how to read a catalog; you'll learn something about the value of a horse and the perceived value of a horse; you'll learn about the influence of fashion on the business and about conformation. You'll meet a lot of people—happy people and discouraged people—and you'll come to the realization, perhaps at the sales more than anywhere else, that nothing is certain in the horse business. You should probably spend three or four days at the sales, if you're not ready to buy yet, just watching and listening to what goes on. You should also make it a point to attend a variety of sales: breeding stock, yearling, and two-year-olds in training.

If you're mostly interested in breeding, you should spend a day or two at a farm during several seasons of the year. For example, in the winter or spring, during the breeding/foaling season, you should spend four or five days there watching the foaling operation, observing the activities at the breeding shed, learning about teasing and the reproductive cycle of the mare. You should spend some time "riding" with the farm veterinarian or with a local veterinarian as he makes his rounds. Then you should come back prior to sales time to spend a day or so learning about sales preparation, spend another day or so during weaning season, and a couple of days when the yearlings are being broken. In all, it should take a couple of weeks to expand on the contents of Chapter 5.

Finally, we'd recommend that you attend several of the seminars that are held during the year for horsemen and equine investors. They range in format from simple introductions to the horse business to advanced taxation and accounting, so you need to choose carefully lest you be bored or overmatched. The equine publications you'll be reading generally list them, and you can pick and choose at your pleasure. A really good place to start, though, is the annual convention of the American Horse Council, which is held in Washington, D.C., each year in late May or early June. There, you will learn about a variety of subjects at a variety of levels, which offer something for almost everyone.

Now that the American Horse Council has been brought up, this is probably as good a place as any to put in a plug for it. The AHC was formed in 1969 as a stopgap measure to defeat a bill introduced by U.S. Senator Lee Metcalf of Montana which would have, in effect, killed any tax benefits enjoyed by the horse industry. In the 15 years since then, the Horse Council has far exceeded the original vision of its founders. Now, it is an effective voice for the horse industry before a large number of agencies of the government, not just the Congress; it is a clearinghouse for information on the horse business and a source of information for the government and the media, as well as members. Through a system of advisory committees, including those on racing, horse shows, and health and regulatory matters, it has created a unity within the horse industry which never, ever, could have existed without the AHC.

Finally, as you go through the bibliography at the end of this book and the list of required reading which immediately follows this chapter, you'll note that many of the publications listed there are products of the American Horse Council. Furthermore, many of them, including some of the most useful ones, are free to members. Those include the *Horse Industry Directory,* which includes the names and addresses of anyone you could possibly want to talk to in the horse business; *Tax Tips for Horse Owners,* which is an abbreviated treatment of the tax law as it applies to the horse business; the monthly *Tax Reference Service Bulletins,* which keep you informed and updated on tax cases and regulations which affect your business; and the *AHC Business Quarterly,* which contains practical information on everything from marketing to computers to preparation of a stallion service contract. The staff has remained small, but they maintain the capability of answering almost any conceivable question that might arise in your horse operation and, if they can't answer it, they know who can.

We cannot emphasize strongly enough how important it is for you to join the American Horse Council, both for your own benefit and for the future welfare of the horse business. There are three classifications of membership—sustaining, which is $1,000 a year; supporting, which is $500 a year; and subscribing, which is $100 a year. They'll take more, though, if you want to send it. Send a check, today, to:

American Horse Council
1700 K Street (Suite 300)
Washington, D.C. 20006
Phone: (202) 296-4031

Tell them Jack and Arnold sent you, and in addition to all the other useful things they'll give you, they'll send you a bumper sticker for your pickup.

Seriously, next to your investment in this book, it'll be the best money you spend in the business.

A List of Required Reading

Now on to the list of required reading. As mentioned, this is an information-intensive business, and the more you read and keep up to date, the better off you'll be. Naturally, some of these publications will be more important to you than others, and those are preceded by an asterisk. The others, though, will be very useful in providing you with an insight into the business. For sources on finding or purchasing the books and magazines listed below, refer to the first page of the Bibliography.

> ***Blood-Horse, The;** P.O. Box 4038, Lexington, KY 40544. Weekly magazine, with excellent annual supplements, including "Principal Winners Abroad," "Auctions of 19--," "Stakes Winners of 19--." *Numerous articles on current racing, breeding, and sales, complemented by other articles of interest to the industry.*
>
> ***Thoroughbred Record, The;** P.O. Box 4240, Lexington, KY 40544. Weekly magazine, with excellent annual supplements, including the "Sire Book" and the "Breeders Book" (which contains in a single volume much of the same information as is found in *The Blood-Horse*'s annual "Stakes Winners" and "Thoroughbred Stallion Records of 19--" supplements). *Numerous articles on current racing, breeding, and sales, complemented by other articles of interest to the industry, including interviews, profiles, and international coverage.*
>
> ***Horse Owners and Breeders Tax Manual;** Thomas A. Davis, Esq.; American Horse Council, Washington, D.C., updated annually. 800 pp. *Invaluable reference on taxation in the horse business.*
>
> ***Horse From Conception to Maturity, The;** Peter D. Rossdale, M.A., F.R.C.V.S.; California Thoroughbred Breeders Association, Arcadia, CA, 1972. 226 pp. *One of England's leading veterinarians describes, in lay language, the life cycle of the thoroughbred horse, with most of what you can expect to encounter along the way.*
>
> **Anatomy of the Horse;** Robert F. Way, V.M.D., M. S. and Donald G. Lee, V.M.D.; J. B. Lippincott Company, Philadelphia, PA, 1965. 214 pp. *Excellent, understandable treatment of equine anatomy.*
>
> **Great Breeders And Their Methods, The;** Abram S. Hewitt; *The Thoroughbred Record,* Lexington, KY, 1982. 390 pp. *Biographical profiles of some of the world's leading breeders and the horses that made them that way.*
>
> **Training Thoroughbred Horses;** Preston M. Burch; *The Blood-*

Horse, Lexington, KY, 1967. 130 pp. *Hints on purchase, development, and training thoroughbreds from a Hall of Fame trainer.*

Veterinary Notebook; William R. McGee, D.V.M.; *The Blood-Horse*, Lexington, KY, 1958. 180 pp. *An elementary guide for the practical horseman, written in lay style by one of the world's leading veterinarians.*

Stud Farm Diary, A; Humphrey S. Finney; J. A. Allen and Co., London, 1959. 136 pp. *As the title implies, this is a diary of the day-to-day operations of a stud farm, with anecdotes. Charmingly written by one of the industry's greats.*

Fit Racehorse, The; Tom Ivers; Esprit Racing Team, Cincinnati, OH, 1983. *Pioneer text in the new fields of equine sports medicine and internal training.*

Feeding To Win; Don Wagoner; Equine Research Publications, Grapevine, TX, 1973. 314 pp. *Textbook-type book on equine nutrition.*

*Laughing in the Hills; Bill Barich; Penguin Books, New York, NY, 1980. 228 pp. *A beautifully written book which contains a good explanation of life at the race track.*

*Book Of The Horse, The; Pamela Macgregor-Morris (Edited by); G. P. Putnam's Sons, New York, NY, 1979. 208 pp. *Outstanding encyclopedic treatment of horses, from evolution to practical horse care. Extremely readable.*

*Racing Update; P. O. Box 11052, Lexington, KY 40511. *An excellent newsletter containing statistical information about breeding, with a liberal dash of opinion.*

American Racing Manual, The; *Daily Racing Form*, Hightstown, NJ, 19--. 1754 pp. *Annual compendium of all vital statistics of U.S. (and some foreign) thoroughbred racing, breeding, and sales.*

Good reading. . . and good luck.

Chapter 3

At The Race Track

Most horse owners are racing fans, whose interest led them beyond the status of a mere spectator. As a result, most new owners get into the horse business by investing in a claiming horse or two. The advantages of this avenue of investment are the immediate action and fairly well-substantiated value of the horse.

Class of Races

Before further discussion of claiming races and other forms of races which will also be discussed later in this chapter, it would probably be worthwhile to give you an idea of where they rank in the scheme of things at the race track, i.e. explain how the various types of races offered at the track stand on the pyramid of quality. In descending order of importance, they are:

Stakes races —generally the highest quality of races offered in the business. While the majority of stakes are characterized by the requirement that owners put up some of their own money to enter (stakes money) and by the presence of "added money" put up by the tracks, the category of stakes also includes some invitational races in which the owners of horses do not have to "stake" their horses—the horses are invited based on their performance ability. While stakes races represented only 3.5% of all the races run in North America during 1983, the purses they carried represented 21% of all the money earned by horses running that year. Stakes

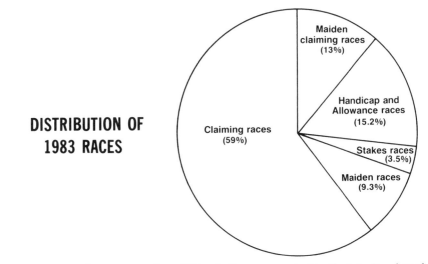

DISTRIBUTION OF
1983 RACES

Claiming races make up more than 70% of all races run in North America, but they account for only 45% of the total purse money, whereas stakes account for only 3.5% of the races, but make up 21% of the purse money.

range in value from the very low ($5,000 added, or even lower at some of the smaller tracks in the country) to the very high (the top purse for the Breeders' Cup is $3-million), but the average purse for stakes is around $50,000. Stakes can be run under allowance, handicap, or weight-for-age conditions, all of which will be explained below. As you will see in the next chapter, stakes wins are very important to the future value of a horse as a breeding animal.

Handicap races —often called "overnight handicaps," these are races in which the owners do not have to pay a fee to enter, but the racing secretary will assign weights to each horse in the race, as he does in some stakes races. The weight assignments are designed to "handicap" the better horses in the race by making them carry more weight than those deemed of lesser ability, theoretically giving all the In its purest form, the handicapper is attempting to make all the horses in the race finish in a dead heat, which, of course, never happens. (There have been 17 triple dead heats recorded since the invention of the photo-finish camera. One of those was the 1944 Carter Handicap, which is considered to be the greatest handicapping feat of all time.)

Allowance races —are sort of reverse handicap races, because all the horses which are entered start out at a set weight assignment and they are given weight off, "allowances," for failure to do certain things, such as win two races lifetime, or a race at a certain minimum class or distance since a specified date. In the general scheme of things, allowances and handicaps are about equal, except that handicaps are usually for older, more established horses, while allowances are usually for younger horses. In both handicap and allowance races, the class of race is determined by the size of the purse and, as you'll learn in the next chapter, some handicap and allowance races are actually superior to some stakes races. Allowance races can also be maiden races.

Maiden races —are races for horses who have never won a race at an official pari-mutuel meeting in their lives. They can be maiden allowance races, maiden special weights, maiden claiming, and there have even been maiden stakes races.

Claiming races —as you'll see in the remainder of this chapter, are, by definition, races in which every horse which is entered carries a price tag and is liable to be purchased, irrevocably, by any eligible buyer at the meet. Claiming prices range from less than $1,000 up to a race which Hollywood Park held on Breeders' Cup Day in 1984 for horses with a claiming price of up to $1-million (see Appendix 1). As you'll also see, claiming races are racing's great equalizer. While claiming races annually represent more than 70% of all races run in North America, they account for only 45% of the purses.

Claiming Races

Claiming races make up the bulk of any racing program in America. The majority of horses available ultimately become claimers of one price or another. The purpose of claiming races is to categorize this large population by price. If a horse is worth $20,000, it is highly unlikely that he would be entered in a race where he could be claimed for $10,000. Although he would very likely win such a race, the possibility of having to sell him for half of what he is worth usually prevents people from taking such chances. On the other hand, if he is entered for $30,000 he won't be claimed, but he probably won't win, either. The most likely place a $20,000 horse would be entered would be in a race with a $15,000 to $20,000 claiming price, depending upon his age and infirmities, and what the owner and trainer felt they could get away with.

In this manner, claiming serves as a great equalizer for the 70% of the horses that are forced to run below the top level of competition. Some trainers make their living by claiming other people's horses and trying to improve them. They are known as "haltermen." When you visit the paddock you will see several of the leading trainers marking on their program as each horse passes by on the way to the post. These marks are for future reference in case a trainer finds an owner wanting to claim a horse. These trainers know that a horse is seldom entered far below his value, and, when one drops suddenly in price, there may well be a reason for it, such as an injury that has been kept secret. If you try to enter the horse business by buying claimers, reread the chapter about advisors first.

In many states no one is allowed to claim a horse except an owner who has started at least one horse at the current meeting. Louisiana, California, and several other states now have what is known as an open claiming rule. This rule provides an opportunity for new owners to claim a horse. Anyone who can establish financial responsibility can claim a horse provided he has deposited the required amount of money (claiming price plus sales tax) with the horsemen's bookkeeper by the required time.

In states where open claiming is not available, you must purchase your first horse privately in order to become an owner. If you purchase one horse in order to claim more horses, the horse that you purchase privately is known as a "policeman."

The danger of buying a racehorse at private treaty reminds us of a story Col. Phil Chinn told years ago. Col. Chinn was a legendary figure, an excellent horseman, a heavy gambler, and an outstanding raconteur.

It seems the good Colonel had an unraced two-year-old of royal lineage that couldn't outrun a fat man. The advent of April brought a raft of wealthy Easterners to Central Kentucky to visit the farms, see the promising two-year-olds, and attend the Keeneland meeting in advance of the Kentucky Derby.

The Colonel had worked diligently with the handsome, royally bred colt that he had paid so dearly for. But, alas, it looked like this colt was a cropper. The only thing to do was to sell the colt to salvage what he could.

While eating dinner at a local restaurant, the Colonel met one of the New York gentry, who was desperately looking for a promising two-year-old. This New Yorker was a great believer in speed, and offered $50,000 (a mighty sum in those days) for a well-bred two-year-old who could work three furlongs that week in 35 seconds. Now the Colonel knew that his two-year-old couldn't work anywhere near that fast, but he had an idea!

He told the wealthy New Yorker that he had just the horse for him and to be at his barn at 6:00 the next morning so he could show him off in a work at Keeneland. Promptly at six, the Colonel's fish arrived ready for the hook. The colt, whose looks complemented his royal pedigree, pranced and showed off as he rounded the barn on the way to the track. Once on the track, he bowed his neck and looked for all the world like a stakes horse. Col. Chinn had instructed the rider to make the colt look like a champion. And that he did. With two quick pops of the whip, he broke the colt off at the three-eighths and the colt worked a very rapid :34⅗! After a hot breakfast in the track kitchen, the deal was made!

There were some comments by horsemen that the track must have been extremely fast that morning, because more than one two-year-old went three furlongs in 34 and faster! But the next day times were back to normal.

No one had even noticed that, at midnight, under the cover of darkness, Col. Chinn and his groom had gone out to Keeneland and dug up the three-eighths pole and moved it a hundred feet closer to the finish line!

Buyer beware.

If your potential trainer suggests that you put money in the account of one of his other owners, or his own account, in order to claim a horse, be wary! This is against the rules of racing and is dishonest. It is a poor way to start off in the horse business, but it is unfortunately not too rare. There have been horror stories involving trainers who convinced neophyte owners to put money in another owner's account to claim a horse. After the claim was made the trainer refused to give the owner who put up the money his horse. It is difficult to go to the authorities and tell them that you did something dishonest to get in the horse business and ask them to help you get your money back.

Once a horse is claimed, if he is to be raced, he normally must remain at the track where he was claimed until the end of the meeting. This obviously does not mean that if he is injured he cannot go to the farm, but it means that he cannot run at another race meeting until the other one ends. In Louisiana, due to the long race meetings prevalent in the state and the conflicting racing dates, the Louisiana State Racing Commission allows a claimed horse to go to other tracks within the state 60 days after being claimed, rather than being restricted to one track until the end of the meeting.

Most states provide some protection for owners of claiming horses in the form of a restriction on when the horses can be entered after they are claimed. This restriction, known as being "in jail," requires that if the newly claimed horse is entered in a race within 30 days after the claim he must be entered for a minimum claiming price 25% higher than the purchase claim price.

Claiming rules vary in different states. In Louisiana, for instance, a claim must be entered 15 minutes prior to post time, and some states require even more time, but in no case is it less than 15 minutes prior to post. In most states the horse becomes property of the new owner when the gate opens and the race starts. (In Louisiana, the horse changes ownership when the horse steps from the paddock onto the race track. This rule was changed in Louisiana because a couple of trainers who found out their horses were claimed—they weren't supposed to know until after the race—had told their jockeys to let their horse run away during the post parade causing them to be scratched, thus avoiding the claim.)

To claim a horse, a claim slip is filled out, put in a sealed envelope, time stamped, and put in the claim box. The locked claim box is in an entry booth (for privacy) in the racing secretary's office with a time clock next to it. After the claiming deadline, the box is opened and any claim slips are opened. The claim slip must be *perfectly* filled out, or the claim will be nullified. Assuming the claim slip is properly filled out (more than one claim has been voided by an incorrect date or misspelling) the racing secretary, or his representative, verifies that the proper amount of money is on deposit with the horsemen's bookkeeper, and that the owner is properly licensed. Once verified, the racing secretary notifies the stewards of the claim and gives the new owner, or his trainer, a delivery order. With this delivery order in hand the trainer goes to the paddock where the physical transfer of ownership takes place. The old owner (or his representative) takes the bridle off the horse and the new owner puts his halter on and leads the horse to his new barn. Use of the term "halterman" to describe a trainer who claims horses regularly as part of his business is the result of the practice of putting a halter on the horse at the time of transfer.

Once the claim is made, the horse is yours—win, lose, or draw, healthy or sick, dead or alive, even though any purse winnings from the race go to the previous owner. There has been more than one case of a claimed horse breaking a leg during the running of the race and having to be destroyed. In some areas, it is possible to insure your claim through the Horsemen's Benevolent and Protective Association—or a private company if they handle the rest of your business—but it is expensive.

When more than one claim has been entered for a horse, the new owner is decided by lot. One time several years ago, there was a filly named Split a Burger entered for a claiming tag of $19,000 in a race in New York. While owners are supposed to claim only for racing purposes, and breeders are not supposed to claim at all, the fact that Split a Burger was a half sister to the multiple graded stakes winner Taisez Vous may have had something to do with her apparent attractiveness, because she certainly was no runner. A few days after the race, the racing secretary of the New York Racing Association described the claim box as having looked "like a ticker-tape parade." When more than one claim is entered, the racing secretary supervises a "shake" to determine who gets the horse. The shake involves using a Kelly bottle with numbered balls, or pills, as they are known. This is the same bottle used by pool players. If there are five claims, there are five numbered balls put in the Kelly bottle. Each claim slip is then numbered on the back so that it is identified with a number on a pill. The racing secretary draws one of the numbered pills from the Kelly bottle and the winner of the shake is determined. If the horse won easily and came back sound, you may be hoping to win the shake, but if he ran poorly and came back unsound, you will be hoping that you lost the shake. Claiming can be a dangerous game.

A claiming horse will not normally change rapidly in value. There are occasional cases where claiming horses become stakes horses—Shifty Sheik, who finished second to Slew o' Gold in the prestigious Woodward Stakes, had been claimed for $35,000 only a few weeks earlier—but success stories like this are few and far between. The more solid claim prospect is the older horse (four-year-old and up) who has survived the two- and three-year-old "drop out" years and has displayed his ability and competitiveness at a certain price level in the claiming ranks. Most of these old campaigners have infirmities in the form of enlarged ankles or knees, rough tendons, or bad feet, but they run in spite of their aches and pains. They are competitors! They have the ingredient that counts the most—heart. The major downside risk in claiming horses, as it is in any horse investment, is unexpected and unanticipated injury or sickness. When we speak of two- and three-year-old "drop outs" we are referring to the many horses that get to the races, break their maidens, perhaps win a race or two more, and disappear. They either disappear because the competition overmatches their talent or they "'got to hurting'' a little and lost their will to compete.

There are three things to remember if you decide to enter the thoroughbred business with claiming horses. First, two- and three-year-olds are often over-priced. They have not demonstrated early in their careers that they cannot run, so their owners are still high on them. Second, these youngsters do not yet have in-firmities that discourage them from running. Two-year-old races generally are the truest run races of all because these horses are eager young athletes bred to race, trying to do what is asked of them. They want to run and haven't learned to "'cheat a little'' to avoid the aches and pains that come from exhaustion after total effort during a race. With these aches and pains, and with a little experience, they will learn sometimes that 90% effort produces a lot less aftereffects, and those with less heart and desire will give less effort. Third, two- and three-year-olds will normally decline in value as they get closer to being four-year-olds.

For educational purposes, look at the final times for claiming races for four-year-olds and up. Then look at the times for similar races for three-year-olds and two-year-olds. The races for young horses are won in slower times. Sure, the youngsters will mature and run a little faster, but age and conditions of the race restrict competition, too. Keep in mind that when a horse gets to be four, the competition gets tougher.

From the purchase of a claimer or two, owners who become more involved usually do so by moving on to buying younger horses in the form of two-year-olds in training or yearlings. Although in this chapter we are dealing with what goes on at the race track, we are going to reach back further to the training center where the yearling was broken, since that is an integral part of the finished racehorse. Much of the information we deal with will also be applicable to those who invest in claiming horses, since, once a young horse starts racing, the scenario for both is much the same.

Breaking and Training

Breaking yearlings is a highly individualized pursuit. There are as many methods of breaking yearlings as there are trainers who break them, but they all need two things in common—patience and attention to detail. No two yearlings are the same and each one requires individual attention, understanding, and pa-tience just like a schoolchild. Without those two basic ingredients, yearling break-ing will ultimately produce more rogues and outlaws than it will good horses.

The timing and location of yearling breaking is a matter of personal preference and economic judgment. Some yearlings go directly from the yearling sales at Keeneland across the track to the training barns of the reputable John Ward where they are put into the schooling process immediately. Other yearlings are sent back to the farm to be broken, while others are sent off to the old, estab-lished breaking centers in the Carolinas, Florida, and California. Still others go to one of the newly established full-time training centers around the country.

The technique of breaking yearlings varies from farm to farm, but patience is an essential ingredient in the educational process.

Wherever a yearling goes, he will have one thing in common with all the other yearlings—he'll have no idea of what a saddle or bridle looks like, much less what to do when the bell rings in the gate and the doors open. By virtue of his being a thoroughbred, he is bred to race, but he is nowhere near that point, because he hasn't been trained to race. When you see a horse come from the paddock and parade in front of the grandstand before a race, you take it for granted that the horse is wearing a saddle, accepts the bridle and bit, walks in a straight line, and is responsive to the jockey on his back. But he has to learn all that, and that is what the breaking process is all about.

When yearlings come to the breaking process they come with varied backgrounds and temperaments. A homebred from a one-man farm may be pampered and spoiled by a loving owner and will be an overbearing monster, while another may be a terrified introvert as a result of impatience or just plain neglect. Sales yearlings may come to the breaking farm well mannered as a result of good sales preparation, but such is not always the case. Many yearlings come away from the sales traumatized by their experience, and this can result in aggressive, overbearing behavior, or introverted, "spooky" behavior.

Think about it a minute. A yearling has been raised in a serene farm environment from the time he was born. For 14 to 16 months he has done nothing but romp and play, and, except for the couple of months of care and attention during sales preparation, he did pretty much as he pleased. Then bright and early one morning, as a sales yearling, he is loaded onto a van or trailer (he better not

esitate either) and bounced around (and if you don't think a trailer or van
ounces at 60 miles per hour, you should ride in the back with the horses
ometime). When the trailer comes to a stop he is pushed off by tired attendants
vho don't give him the opportunity to even think before he is forced to
"behave." He walks into a barn area full of new sights and sounds he has never
een and is thrown into a strange stall with strange neighbors. If that isn't
nough, the next morning he is paraded back and forth for hours on end in front
f all kinds of people who want to punch him, poke at him, open his mouth, pick
p his legs, and look under his tail. He is led up to a sales ring, with glaring lights
nd screaming loudspeakers, and with the drop of the gavel he has entered a new
ra. He is led back to his stall where he is allowed to rest a short while before he is
oaded onto another one of those strange vans and hauled to a new farm to begin
n entirely new life. And people say that a horse isn't adaptable!

When the training process will actually begin will be based on why the yearling
s being broken. If he is going to race for an owner who prefers early two-year-old
acing the process may start in August or September. For many big stables, year-
ings are broken in early fall and then turned out for the winter. This is particular-
y common in the northern climates. It is generally accepted in the horse business
hat many yearlings will get a "second growth" if they are broken early and
urned out. Some horsemen question whether the ultimate size of the three-year-
ld horse was really helped by this practice. The disadvantage of this method is
ost. When the yearling becomes a two-year-old and reenters training, at least
alf of his early education is lost, not because he has forgotten it but because he
as lost the condition, the muscling that he built up during the 60 to 75 days of
riginal schooling and galloping.

For economic reasons, more yearlings are being broken later than was the case
ears ago. Early two-year-old racing is less prevalent because it has proven so
hysically damaging. Later breaking, which means later training, in turn means
ater racing, which ultimately has to benefit the young horse by preventing
remature stress on immature bodies and bones.

For those yearlings entered in two-year-olds in training sales, the date of the
ale and the training requirements for that sale obviously dictate that the breaking
rocess be started in early fall.

Training Centers

While the training centers in the Carolinas, Florida, and Southern California
ave been in existence for many years, there has been a new surge in training
enter construction and use in the past five years throughout the country. The
versupply of horses has led to a scarcity of stalls at the race tracks on one hand,
while the extended racing dates in all localities have put greater demands on the
vailable horses. This seeming contradiction of oversupply and shortage is being
artially met by more extensive use of training centers, not only for young horses
ut for older horses, too. Many trainers with large stables currently maintain a
ivision at a neighboring training center to supplement their racing stock at the
rack.

There are several arguments in favor of training centers over race tracks for the purpose of training horses. At an operating race track, the hours available for training are obviously limited by racing hours. At a training center, the training surface may be available full time, except for the minimal time required for actual maintenance. This means that training can proceed at a more leisurely pace (leisurely meaning patient), and more can be done to and for each individual. The well-designed training centers are spacious, more serene, and more attractive than most race tracks. They are away from the hustle and bustle of the afternoon racing activity, crowd, and noise, all distractions also for the help. TLC, time, and attention are all contributing factors to making a horse happy and giving him a feeling of well-being, which will ultimately turn him into a better athlete. At training centers, several forms of exercise may be available that are not normally available at a race track, such as swimming, turn-out paddocks, treadmills, and uphill exercise.

The negatives to training at a training center (none of which apply to yearling breaking, which should definitely be done at home or at a training center, not at race track) include: 1) the cost and trouble of always shipping to the race track for racing; 2) the difficulty of maintaining a training track surface equal to the quality of that at the track itself; and 3) the cost of stall rental.

The training centers that have been started the last few years are far different from the old ones that were open mainly during the winter for yearling breaking and early two-year-old preparation. Training centers such as Fair Hill in Maryland, Rancho Santa Fe in California, and Delray in Florida have extensive facilities that permit emphasis on every aspect of a horse's racing career. Many are centrally located, within vanning distance of several race tracks.

In England and France horses are not stabled at race tracks at all. Trainers each have their own private "yard" or "stable" where their horses are kept. These private yards are grouped in one area to make use of common "condominium"-type gallops (training tracks). On race day, the horses are shipped to the track for their engagement and shipped home that same day. Since European racing is on grass, the same course cannot be used day in and day out as is done in this country. Race meetings rotate from course to course on a daily or weekly schedule. Europeans have long been utilizing the training center concept that we are now adopting.

Interval Training

Many of the new training centers and trainers using them are adopting modern techniques, including interval training and the concepts of equine sportsmedicine. You will undoubtedly be hearing the term "interval training" more and more in the future, but beware! Because of its newness, interval training is experimental and some of the people using the term are using it loosely, and incorrectly. Interval training, above all things, is not a substitute for good horsemanship. In fact it requires better horsemanship than conventional training. Combined with poor horsemanship, it can prove to be a total disaster both to the horse and its owner

In broad terms, interval training means conditioning a horse during the final stages of his training with many short-distance, high-speed works with rest periods—or intervals—in between. Tom Ivers has written a very comprehensive book on the subject entitled *The Fit Race Horse*. This book is listed in our bibliography.

There is a great deal more involved in interval training than can be described in summary form. The basic purpose of interval training is to help the horse recondition his cardiovascular, muscular, and oxygen-delivering systems to allow him to perform at his maximum athletic ability without injury. This is done by demanding considerably more physical activity of the horse than is required of the average racehorse ·in training today. Along with exercise, modern scientific analysis of performance is utilized, including use of heart rate monitors, infrared thermography, synovial joint fluid analysis, specialized nutrition, videotaped motion analysis, and detailed blood analysis. Interval training has been introduced to the thoroughbred industry in recent years as a spillover from the success trainers and coaches have had in improving performance of human athletes with these same methods over the past few decades. While the magic number for the human one-mile run years ago was four minutes, high school students today surpass the four-minute mark with regularity, and the record for the mile is now approaching 3:45. During the same time span, horses which are "selectively bred for superior race performance" have not improved the mile record at all. The thoroughbred record for a mile is 1:32⅕, and it was set by Dr. Fager in 1968. As a matter of fact, no horse has run a mile on dirt in less than 1:33 since 1968, although Royal Heroine (Ire) did run a mile on grass in 1:32⅗ in winning the Breeders' Cup Mile Stakes.

The thoroughbred industry has always been resistant to change and such has been the case with interval training, but possibilities for improvement of the racehorse with interval training are becoming more evident, with some practitioners who are using it showing excellent, sometimes spectacular, results.

A few words of caution, particularly to those of you who are new in the horse business. Do not be taken in by a prospective trainer for your horses just because he can glibly use interval training terms that you cannot understand. Interval training is no substitute for quality care or horsemanship, and there unquestionably will be many charlatans in this new field. Interval training, properly done, takes longer than conventional training and is more expensive, so if you are looking for a way to cut costs, this is not it. However, if you are looking for a way to cut injuries and produce sounder, fitter racehorses that will give you more potential return on your investment in the long run, this may be the way.

Naming a Yearling

One of the fun exercises you get to do as a new thoroughbred owner before your horse goes to the races is pick out a name for your potential Kentucky Derby winner. This is not as easy as it sounds, because any name used for a thoroughbred during the past 17 years is not available, and more than a half-million names are already taken. Which reminds us of a little anecdote:

A friend of ours, Howard Baker in California, sent in three names for his yearling just prior to the November 1 deadline. In January, he received a letter from The Jockey Club stating that the three names submitted were "not available." In February, he submitted three more names and again received the same reply. In March, he submitted three more names but, alas, got the same reply, "not available." Since his two-year-old was about ready to make his first start, Dr. Baker, with a deep sense of frustration, submitted the name Not Available. And got it! So when you see a horse running named Not Available, you will know where she got her name.

To help you name your yearling, The Jockey Club annually publishes a book called *Registered Thoroughbred Names.* This includes not only the names of all horses of the past 17 years but the names of famous horses, such as Man o' War, Secretariat, Seabiscuit, etc., that no longer can be taken. Remember, though, this book does not include the names being applied for this year so there are 40,000 or so more names not available that are not listed.

There are some restrictions on the names that you can use. If you use the name of a living person, you must secure his or her permission in writing. Names may not have advertising implications or political overtones. There can be a maximum of 18 characters including spaces. Numbers cannot be used unless spelled out. Obscenities are not allowed (whatever language you might try to pass them off in). The Jockey Club tries to prevent phonetically similar names, but it is a tough job.

There is a deadline for naming your yearling without penalty, and that is November 1 of his yearling year. Most yearlings sold through auctions are not named, but even if yours is, you can change his name for $100 if you want to (before he makes his first start; after that it's too late).

The Jockey Club issues the name on a small form that has the horse's registration number and the approved name. This form must remain permanently attached to the Registration Certificate.

Work hard at naming your yearling and give him one you will be proud of when it hits the headlines!

One further suggestion: The Jockey Club is a big, impersonal place. Things do get lost there and the best way to establish your communications record with them is by using certified mail, return receipt requested, on all correspondence that has a deadline involved. For some reason this type of correspondence does not get lost as often.

Now that we have digressed into training centers, interval training, and naming your yearling, we will get back to the business at hand, getting your horse to the races.

Getting to the Races

After your yearling has been at the training center four to six months and the breaking process has been satisfactorily completed, then, and only then, will your horse be ready to seek his ultimate goal—winning races. By then he will have learned to accept a rider on his back, he will have learned to be guided, and he will gallop in company with other horses. He will have learned to respond to his rider's commands and will have had his basic instructions at the gate. Depending on the facilities and the length of time he stays at the training center where he has been broken, he may have been asked to show some of his ability in the form of short, controlled sprints.

When he gets to the race track he will probably be as traumatized as he was when he went to the yearling sale. He is faced with a totally new environment, a new set of rules and regulations, a new way of life. Is it any wonder that many youngsters get the "snots," run a fever, and go off feed? Is it any wonder that they all don't go through these maladies? Depending upon the size of the training center where your horse was broken, he may go to the race track the first morning and see ten times as many horses as he has ever seen in his life, zooming by in different directions. With so many distractions, it is not surprising that they sometimes forget their manners and their lessons for a few days. But they all seem to survive and settle in and, if they were properly broken, in a few days will be going about their gallops in a businesslike manner.

How soon your youngster starts his speed work will depend upon how much basic leg work (long-distance gallops) he has behind him when he goes to the track. The trainer will evaluate the stage of his training and determine when he will be asked for his first serious speed work. Trainers like to have a horse under their shedrow for at least a couple of weeks to determine his habits, conditions, and precocity before asking him to display his ability.

From that point on, it is a matter of developing his ability and condition until he is fully ready to perform. If he gets ready to race without the onset of ailments and injuries which befall young horses, such as bucked shins, osselets, hot knees, coughs, runny noses, etc., he will soon get his final okay from the gate crew, and be tattooed by the identifier prior to running. Every horse starts out as a maiden—meaning he has never won a race. This puts him in the same category as 38,000 other foals born in 1982. This means there may be a lot of other horses ready, willing, and able to run in the same maiden race, and one of the difficulties facing an owner, today, is limited racing opportunity for maidens. A racing secretary would describe that not as limited racing opportunity but as "too many maidens." The racing secretary, of course, has a different point of view than the owner of a prospective Kentucky Derby winner who still happens to be a maiden.

The Racing Secretary

Every race track has a racing secretary. He is employed by the track and it is his job to design the racing program for and from the horses he has available for racing at his track. In order to design his program he takes into consideration both the horses he has available and the primary function of his job, which is to provide entertainment for racing customers—the people who come and bet their money. Without an attractive, competitive racing program, people will not come to the track, they will not bet, and there will be no purses. Ultimately, then, there will be no racing. So when you have difficulty running your maiden when and where you want, understand the racing secretary's problem, too.

A racing secretary designs his racing program in two ways. Before a race meet starts, he will design a stakes program for the entire meeting. This program is established on a fairly permanent basis, normally with only minor changes from year to year for realignment or expansion.

By way of example, at the right, we have used Latonia's 1984 winter-spring meeting, since Arnold Kirkpatrick is president of that track. On the stakes schedule there is a stakes every Saturday of the meeting for various categories of horses. The purpose of these stakes is to give the best horses at the track an opportunity to race for an attractive purse and to earn black type. It is not unusual for a racing secretary to schedule his best stakes during the latter part of the race meeting, so that the climax comes with the closing of the meeting. In the case of Latonia, it is the Jim Beam Stakes which towers over all the other races of the meeting with its $300,000-guaranteed purse for three-year-olds.

The second and more difficult part of the racing secretary's job is to design a daily racing program. While every owner wishes they could run a horse in one of the big stakes races, from a practical standpoint, it is the nine supporting races on Saturday and the ten races daily during the week that keep racing going. That is true for all tracks, be it New York, California, or New Mexico. It is in these races that most of the horses compete. And it is the betting on these races that provides the money for the big races. But make no mistake, big purses and good horses bring out the fans!

The racing secretary designs his racing program on a periodic basis in the form of a condition book. At most tracks the condition books are issued by the secretary in ten- or 12-racing day segments, providing the racing secretary with flexibility as the meeting progresses and conditions change. Before each race meeting starts the horsemen applying for their stalls need to know the quality of racing offered, what type of racing (emphasis on younger horses or emphasis on older horses, distance racing, turf racing, etc.), the purses being offered, minimum claiming price, etc., so he can determine whether or not his stable fits and if there will be opportunities for his horses to pay their way.

The condition book is the bible containing all this information. This is the book that tells the horsemen what kind of purses will be offered and what type of racing will be emphasized. The purse size is dictated by the mutuel handle, but the emphasis can be at least partially the preference of the racing secretary, tempered by his knowledge and experience about what kind of horses he has had available for racing at this particular meeting in the past. Normally the first condition book is written before the racing secretary has allocated stalls, so this condition book is a statement of purpose of the racing secretary, based on his experience. Once the race meeting has started, subsequent condition books should reflect a realistic appraisal by the racing secretary of the horses he has available and an effort to give all the horsemen who have been granted stalls an opportunity to race their horses, and earn purse money.

1984 WINTER-SPRING STAKES SCHEDULE

Saturday, January 21
THE MY CHARMER — $10,000 Added
Fillies and Mares, Four Years Old and Upward   Six Furlongs

Saturday, January 28
THE DUST COMMANDER — $10,000 Added
Four-Year-Olds and Upward   Six Furlongs

Saturday, February 4
THE WISHING WELL — $10,000 Added
Fillies and Mares, Four Years Old and Upward   Six and One-Half Furlongs

Saturday, February 11
THE FOREGO HANDICAP — $10,000 Added
Three-Year-Olds and Upward   Six and One-Half Furlongs

Saturday, February 18
THE WINTERGREEN — $10,000 Added
Fillies and Mares, Four Years Old and Upward   One Mile

Saturday, February 25
THE CINCINNATI TROPHY — $10,000 Added
Fillies, Three Years Old   Six Furlongs

Saturday, March 3
THE PRESIDENTS — $10,000 Added
Three-Year-Olds   Six and One-Half Furlongs

Saturday, March 10
THE VALDALE — $10,000 Added
Fillies, Three Years Old   Six and One-Half Furlongs

Saturday, March 17
THE JOHN BATTAGLIA MEMORIAL — $10,000 Added
Plus $5,000 Breeders' Cup Prize Award
Three-Year-Olds   One Mile

Saturday, March 24
THE PIONEER — $10,000 Added
Three-Year-Olds and Upward   One Mile

Saturday, March 31
THE FAIRWAY FUN — $20,000 Added
Plus $5,000 Breeders' Cup Prize Award
Fillies and Mares, Three Years Old & Upward   One Mile and One-Sixteenth

Sunday, April 1
THE BOURBONETTE — $10,000 Added
Plus $5,000 Breeders' Cup Prize Award
Fillies, Three Years Old   One Mile

Sunday, April 1
THE JIM BEAM STAKES — $300,000 Guaranteed
Three-Year-Olds   Grade III   One Mile and One-Sixteenth

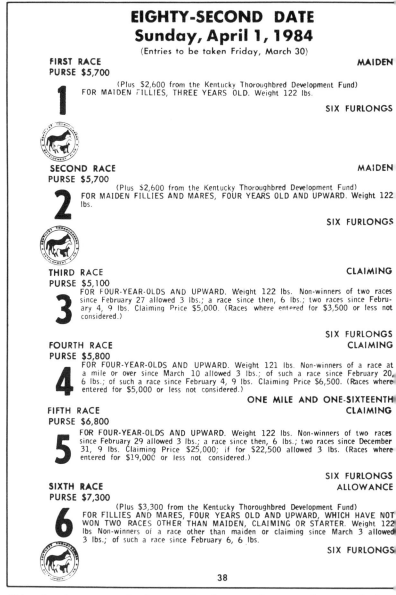

EIGHTY-SECOND DATE
Sunday, April 1, 1984
(Entries to be taken Friday, March 30)

FIRST RACE
PURSE $5,700
MAIDEN

(Plus $2,600 from the Kentucky Thoroughbred Development Fund)
FOR MAIDEN FILLIES, THREE YEARS OLD. Weight 122 lbs.

SIX FURLONGS

SECOND RACE
PURSE $5,700
MAIDEN

(Plus $2,600 from the Kentucky Thoroughbred Development Fund)
FOR MAIDEN FILLIES AND MARES, FOUR YEARS OLD AND UPWARD. Weight 122 lbs.

SIX FURLONGS

THIRD RACE
PURSE $5,100
CLAIMING

FOR FOUR-YEAR-OLDS AND UPWARD. Weight 122 lbs. Non-winners of two races since February 27 allowed 3 lbs.; a race since then, 6 lbs.; two races since February 4, 9 lbs. Claiming Price $5,000. (Races where entered for $3,500 or less not considered.)

SIX FURLONGS

FOURTH RACE
PURSE $5,800
CLAIMING

FOR FOUR-YEAR-OLDS AND UPWARD. Weight 121 lbs. Non-winners of a race at a mile or over since March 10 allowed 3 lbs.; of such a race since February 20, 6 lbs.; of such a race since February 4, 9 lbs. Claiming Price $6,500. (Races where entered for $5,000 or less not considered.)

ONE MILE AND ONE-SIXTEENTH

FIFTH RACE
PURSE $6,800
CLAIMING

FOR FOUR-YEAR-OLDS AND UPWARD. Weight 122 lbs. Non-winners of two races since February 29 allowed 3 lbs.; a race since then, 6 lbs.; two races since December 31, 9 lbs. Claiming Price $25,000; if for $22,500 allowed 3 lbs. (Races where entered for $19,000 or less not considered.)

SIX FURLONGS

SIXTH RACE
PURSE $7,300
ALLOWANCE

(Plus $3,300 from the Kentucky Thoroughbred Development Fund)
FOR FILLIES AND MARES, FOUR YEARS OLD AND UPWARD, WHICH HAVE NOT WON TWO RACES OTHER THAN MAIDEN, CLAIMING OR STARTER. Weight 122 lbs Non-winners of a race other than maiden or claiming since March 3 allowed 3 lbs.; of such a race since February 6, 6 lbs.

SIX FURLONGS

38

The condition book can vary in form and substance from track to track, but the basic ingredients are the same. The condition book will include the stakes schedule; local rules of racing that apply, including entry time and scratch time; post time; stakes nomination blanks; entry preference rules and regulations; stable area regulations; eligibility rules; and a variety of other pertinent facts. The meat of the condition book is the pages devoted to describing the races proposed for each racing day. We have included, for discussion purposes, pages 38 and 39 of the sixth condition book from Latonia for the 1984 winter-spring meet.

SEVENTH RACE   ALLOWANCE
PURSE $8,400

7

(Plus $3,800 from the Kentucky Thoroughbred Development Fund)
FOR FILLIES AND MARES, FOUR YEARS OLD AND UPWARD, WHICH HAVE NOT
WON $6,250 THREE TIMES SINCE NOVEMBER 25 OTHER THAN MAIDEN, CLAIM-
ING OR STARTER. Weight 122 lbs. Non-winners of $7,100 since February 29
allowed 3 lbs.; of $6,100 twice since December 2, 6 lbs.; of $4,875 twice since
November 25, 9 lbs. (Races where entered for $20,000 or less not considered.)

SIX FURLONGS

EIGHTH RACE   ALLOWANCE
PURSE $8,400

8

(Plus $3,800 from the Kentucky Thoroughbred Development Fund)
FOR FOUR-YEAR-OLDS AND UPWARD WHICH HAVE NOT WON $5,875 THREE
TIMES SINCE JUNE 30 OTHER THAN MAIDEN, CLAIMING OR STARTER. Weight
122 lbs. Non-winners of $6,800 since March 1 allowed 3 lbs.; of two races other
than maiden or claiming since December 31, 6 lbs.; of such a race since then, 9 lbs.

SIX FURLONGS

NINTH RACE   STAKE
PURSE $300,000 GUARANTEED

THE JIM BEAM STAKES
(Third Running)
GRADE III

9

FOR THREE-YEAR-OLDS. Colts and Geldings, 121 lbs.; Fillies, 116 lbs. By subscription of $100, $1,500 additional to enter, and starters to pay $1,500 additional with
$300,000 guaranteed. The added money and all fees to be divided 65% to the
winner; 20% to second; 10% to third and 5% to fourth. Starters to be named
through the entry box on Friday, March 30, 1984, by 11:00 A.M. EST. This race
will be limited to twelve (12) horses, with as many as four (4) horses on an also-
eligible list. Preference to start will be given to those horses having accumulated
the highest career earnings at the closing of entries on Friday, March 30, 1984 at
11:00 A.M. EST. Highest career earnings shall be determined at the time of closing
based upon information published and/or provided to the Kentucky Jockey Club,
Inc., by the Daily Racing Form. In addition, no same owner entry may be entered
regardless of earnings to the exclusion of a single entry. Scratch time and naming
of riders shall be Saturday, March 31, 1984 at 12:30 P.M. EST.
      Closed Friday, February 24, 1984, with 197 nominations.
      The Kentucky Jockey Club, Inc., and Daily Racing Form will exert reasonable
effort to verify the accuracy of the earnings of each nominee for this race, the
determination of preferred starters by the Kentucky Jockey Club, Inc., shall be final
and incontestable; neither the Kentucky Jockey Club, Inc., nor Daily Racing Form
shall be liable for damages, consequential or otherwise, by reason of any error in
compilation of such earnings.
      Subscription fees may be paid with the subscription or paid at a later date when
invoiced, however, starters must have paid all fees including subscription fee prior
to running of race.
      NO SUPPLEMENTARY NOMINATIONS.
      NOTICE—In addition to the conditions on the back of this blank, which it is under-
stood and agreed are a part of this contract, it is also understood and agreed that
the above entry or entries are accepted, with the understanding that the horse or
horses so entered will only be allowed to start if in good standing at the time of the
actual running of this event.

ONE MILE AND ONE-SIXTEENTH

EIGHTY-SECOND DATE
Sunday, April 1, 1984 (Continued) ⇨

39

This is the day the Jim Beam Stakes was run for a purse of $300,000
guaranteed, and there were nine other races on the card. Most racing days will include a maiden race and, depending on the track, some days two or three maiden
races. It will also contain several claiming races and, when the horses are
available, an allowance (nonclaiming race) or two to support the feature. The
more quality races the secretary is able to conduct the bigger the crowd will be
and the higher the mutuel handle will be.
      On the 82nd day of racing, which was conducted on April 1, 1984, at Latonia,

there were two maiden races scheduled, one for three-year-old fillies which was a nonclaiming maiden race, also known as a maiden special weight race. This race was scheduled to be run at six furlongs for a purse of $5,700, with all starters carrying 122 pounds. Maiden special weight races are the type of race in which most horses make their first start. Should you own a three-year-old filly who is ready to run and make her first start, this would be her spot.

FIRST RACE   **MAIDEN**
PURSE $5,700
(Plus $2,600 from the Kentucky Thoroughbred Development Fund)
FOR MAIDEN FILLIES, THREE YEARS OLD. Weight 122 lbs.

SIX FURLONGS

The symbol indicates the race has a $2,600 purse supplement from the Kentucky Thoroughbred Development Fund. If the filly you have ready to run in this race is Kentucky-sired, she is eligible for this supplement. The purses for maiden races are normally among the lowest offered at any track, because the horses have not yet demonstrated their ability and the level of competition is usually weakest.

There is no entry fee for this race. Many people think there are entry fees for all thoroughbred races. Except for stakes races, however, that is not the case. The purses for these races come from a percentage of the mutuel handle taken from each betting dollar. The size of each individual purse is determined by the racing secretary, based on his assessment of the quality of competition in the race—better horses run for better purses. The overall amount of purses awarded at a race track during the course of the meeting is determined in some states by law and in some states by contract with the horsemen's association. Normally, though, it amounts to about half of the race track's share of the mutuel commission.

The operating funds for race tracks come from mutuel commissions, parking fees, program sales, and concession income. The major portion comes from the mutuel commission. Although the details vary from state to state, a commission of approximately 15% to 21% is deducted from each dollar bet, before the payoff to the bettors is determined. This commission is determined by law and the split of that commission is also determined by law, again varying widely from state to state, between taxes for the state, operating funds for the track, and purses.

Fees, Etc.

Although you pay no entry fee to run your horse except in stakes races, you must pay a jockey fee. Jockey fees are normally established and regulated by agreement between the horsemen's association and the jockeys' association, although in some states they are established by the racing commission. Louisiana is fairly typical in fee charges.

JOCKEY'S RIDING FEES (LOUISIANA)			
10% on Winning Mounts			
	Second	**Third**	**Unplaced**
$5,000 to $9,900	$ 65	$ 50	$ 40
$10,000 to $14,900	$ 75	$ 60	$ 45
$15,000 to $24,900	$100	$ 75	$ 50
$25,000 to $49,900	$150	$100	$ 60
$50,000 to $99,000	$225	$150	$ 75
$100,000 and Up	$400	$250	$100

The riding fees paid to jockeys in Louisiana are typical of most states.

You must put these fees on deposit with the horsemen's bookkeeper before you race. The horsemen's bookkeeper handles collection of fees and disbursement to the jockeys. Should you use a pony to help get your horse to the gate, in most states you will be assessed an additional fee by the horsemen's bookkeeper as a contribution to the horsemen's association. This is not the fee you actually pay the pony person, who will be paid by your trainer and billed to you, but is an additional fee.

The horsemen's bookkeeper, as his name implies, keeps the financial accounts of all owners. His office is normally adjacent to the racing secretary's office. It is his job to credit purse money to winning owners; make appropriate charges to each owner's account for jockey fees, pony fees, stakes engagements, etc.; and to disburse funds when requested. As an owner, you are entitled to your purse earnings as soon as the postrace test clears the state lab, but not before.

Weights and Weight Allowances

FOURTH RACE   CLAIMING
PURSE $5,800

4 FOR FOUR-YEAR-OLDS AND UPWARD. Weight 121 lbs. Non-winners of a race at a mile or over since March 10 allowed 3 lbs.; of such a race since February 20, 6 lbs.; of such a race since February 4, 9 lbs. Claiming Price $6,500. (Races where entered for $5,000 or less not considered.)

ONE MILE AND ONE-SIXTEENTH

If you have invested in a claiming horse you might be interested in the fourth race, which is scheduled to be run at $1\frac{1}{16}$ miles for horses who are entered to be claimed for $6,500. This particular race is available to any horse, male or female, four years old and upward whose owner is willing to sell his horse for $6,500. The weight conditions in this race call for all male horses to carry 121 pounds. Fillies and mares get a sex allowance. The sex allowance varies. In spring (breeding season), fillies are considered to be at a bigger disadvantage than during fall and winter, so they get a five-pound sex allowance. In fall and winter they get only a three-pound sex allowance. Since this race is during the spring, a filly or mare will get a five-pound weight allowance.

Regardless of the sex of the starter, if he has not won a race at a mile or over since March 10 he will get a three-pound allowance, meaning he will carry 118 pounds (or five pounds less than that for a filly or mare). If he has not won a race at a mile or over since February 20, he will get a bigger allowance—six pounds. If he hasn't won a race at a mile or over since February 4, he will get a nine-pound allowance. One provision—no race with a claiming price of $5,000 or less counts in calculating the weight allowances. For example, if your horse won three races at a mile or over since February 4, he would still get the nine-pound allowance if the races were for claiming prices of $5,000 or less. The theory is that the competition in those races was considerably less than in this race, and the racing secretary is trying to coax trainers to move their horses up into this category by offering them a weight allowance, in spite of their previous wins.

This weight allowance is important and can be critical in longer races. Over the years, Jimmy Kilroe, one of the nation's most prominent racing officials, has developed the following rule of thumb for adding weight to make a one-length difference at varying distances: mile—three pounds; 1⅛ miles—two pounds; 1¼ miles—1½ pounds; 1½ miles—one pound.

For example, if one horse beats another by two lengths at 1⅛ miles with each carrying 121 pounds, rematching them with the winner carrying 121 pounds and his rival carrying 117 pounds should produce a dead heat. It won't, of course, because there are too many other variables, but that is the basis for weight allowances.

There is one other weight allowance available, and that is the apprentice allowance. When a jockey first starts riding he is known as an apprentice jockey. To make up for the lack of experience and to give trainers an incentive to use an apprentice, such jockeys are given weight concessions. This allowance is in addition to any other weight allowance a horse is eligible for. Although the apprentice allowance has some variations (for special circumstances, it can vary from three to seven pounds), in most cases it is five pounds. In the race described above, you could run a filly carrying 102 pounds!

Weight for four-year-olds		121
Sex allowance	5 pounds	-5
Nonwinner since February 4	9 pounds	-9
Apprentice allowance	5 pounds	-5
		102

This means your apprentice fully clothed, helmet, boots, saddle and all, should weigh 102 pounds—mighty light. Theoretically, since your filly gets a weight allowance of 19 pounds, she would have an advantage over the horse carrying 121 pounds, at 1$\frac{1}{16}$ miles, of about 7$\frac{1}{2}$ lengths.

There is a catch in all this—the youngsters coming into the jockey ranks today are bigger boned, better nourished, and larger than their counterparts of 20 years ago. That is one reason you see so many foreign riders. Overweight is a common condition in racing today. Riders can't reduce enough to stay thin enough to make the weight. In most states, a maximum of five pounds (seven in Louisiana) overweight is allowed.

The jockey, with his saddle, is weighed before he leaves the jockeys' quarters—this is called weighing out. If the horse's assigned weight is more than the jockey's normal weight he either uses a heavier saddle (most jockeys have two or three different weight saddles), or has lead weight pads added to his tack. After the race, jockeys finishing first through fifth weigh in on a scale located at the finish line to determine if they carried the correct weight. It is the trainer's responsibility to calculate the proper weight allowances and claim them at time of entry.

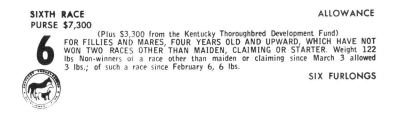

SIXTH RACE   ALLOWANCE
PURSE $7,300
(Plus $3,300 from the Kentucky Thoroughbred Development Fund)
FOR FILLIES AND MARES, FOUR YEARS OLD AND UPWARD, WHICH HAVE NOT WON TWO RACES OTHER THAN MAIDEN, CLAIMING OR STARTER. Weight 122 lbs Non-winners of a race other than maiden or claiming since March 3 allowed 3 lbs.; of such a race since February 6, 6 lbs.

SIX FURLONGS

The sixth race is restricted to fillies and mares, four-year-olds and upward, who have not won two races other than maiden, claiming, or starter. A lot of horses will not be eligible for this race, even though it is an allowance race (non-claiming), also known as a conditioned race. Most allowance races are conditioned, and they are for horses that are just a notch below stakes quality (or are on their way up to stakes class), or horses whose owners don't want to sell them. The purse in this race, $7,300, is higher than the maiden race and claiming race, and will, therefore, be tougher to win. Such a race would normally be used in the latter part of a racing program. Since this race is restricted to fillies and mares, there is no sex allowance, but there are weight allowances for those horses who have not won a race since prescribed dates. This could turn out to be very competitive. A casual reading of the conditions says nonwinners of two races other than maiden, claiming, or starter. The condition ''other than'' is the hooker. Your filly has won a maiden race and an allowance race, and could be tough, until you pick up the *Racing Form* and find entered in the race a five-year-old mare who's been running in $50,000 claiming races in New York and has won $120,000 already. Conditions can be tricky!

TENTH RACE   STAKE
PURSE $10,000 ADDED

10

THE BOURBONETTE STAKES
(Second Running)
(Plus $2,500 from the Kentucky Thoroughbred Development Fund)
(Plus $5,000 BREEDERS' CUP PRIZE AWARD)

FOR FILLIES, THREE YEARS OLD. By subscription of $25. $50 to enter and $100 additional to start. $10,000 Added. The added money and all fees to be divided: 65% to the winner; 20% to second; 10% to third and 5% to fourth. Weight 121 lbs. Non-winners of a sweepstakes allowed 3 lbs.; of $7,800 twice since October 7 allowed 6 lbs.; of two races other than maiden or claiming since November 25, 9 lbs.; of such a race since then, 11 lbs.

Starters to be named through the entry box on Friday March 30, 1984, by the usual time of closing. In the event this race is not divided this race will be limited to twelve (12) starters, with as many as four horses placed on the also eligible list. Preference to start will be given to those horses having accumulated the highest career earnings at the closing of entries on Friday, March 30, 1984. Highest career earnings shall be determined at the closing of entries based upon information published and/or provided to the Kentucky Jockey Club, Inc., by the Daily Racing Form. In addition, no same owner entry may be entered regardless of earnings to the exclusion of a single entry.

The Kentucky Jockey Club, Inc., and Daily Racing Form will exert reasonable effort to verify the accuracy of the earnings of each nominee for this race, the determination of preferred starters by the Kentucky Jockey Club, Inc., shall be final and incontestable; neither the Kentucky Jockey Club, Inc., nor Daily Racing Form shall be liable for damages consequential or otherwise, by reason of any error in compilation of such earnings.

ONE MILE

The conditions for stakes races are somewhat more complicated than conditions for other races. Money for the purse comes from the track in the form of added money and from the owners whose nominations, entry and starting fees are added to the purse.

Take the Bourbonette Stakes for example:
$10,000 Added by Latonia
$5,000 Breeders' Cup premium award
$2,500 Kentucky Thoroughbred Development Fund
26 Nominations at $25 each
13 Entries at $50 each
12 Starters at $100 each
$20,000 Total purse

The purse was divided:

Winner	$12,450	(65% + Breeders' Cup money)
2nd	$ 3,000	(20%)
3rd	$ 1,500	(10%)
4th	$ 750	(5%)

$2,300 Reverted to Breeders' Cup in unclaimed premiums

Since the Bourbonette had a $5,000 Breeders' Cup premium added to the purse, the winner actually benefited even more than normal.

Here's the breakdown of fees for the 1984 Kentucky Derby:
$250,000 Added by Churchill Downs
312 Nominations at $200 each
20 Entries at $10,000 each
20 Starters at $10,000 each
$712,400 Total purse

Many stakes races today are restricted to the number of starters the track can safely handle. This restriction is being handled in one of three ways: 1) some racks, like Churchill Downs for the Kentucky Derby or Latonia for the Jim Beam Stakes, are restricting the number of starters based on previous earnings of he horse—the horses with the highest previous purse earnings are given preference over those with lower purse earnings; 2) high weights are preferred—in handicaps and stakes races with allowance conditions, the horses assigned the highest weight by the handicapper or the allowance conditions are assumed to be the most qualified and are given preference; or 3) prep races one or two weeks before the main race—the winners and/or runners-up in the trial races are given preference to enter the main race. This is an adaptation from quarter horse racing and is found mainly in the Southwest in races that have big sustaining payments that result in a large purse. An example is the Jean Lafitte Futurity at Delta Downs in Vinton, Louisiana, where normally purses range from 2,000 to $10,000. In the 1984 Jean Lafitte Futurity, there were so many entries that even with trials the race had to be split into two divisions! The purse for each division was $187,500, a total $375,000, with only $25,000 of that actually put up by the race track. There were 12 trials involving 120 horses for this big purse, with 350,000, 93%, being put up by the owners.

Nominations for a stakes race may close a week or two before the race, as the Bourbonette, or three months before the race, as the Kentucky Derby, or as much as two years before the race, as is the case with some futurities where the foal is nominated in utero.

The Jim Beam Stakes is somewhat atypical of stakes. It has a large guaranteed purse rather than added money. Very few stakes are offered under such circumstances. For the Jim Beam Stakes the track guarantees the size of the purse, with the assistance of the sponsoring company, Jim Beam. In this case, the nomination fees, entry fees, and starting fees go toward the guaranteed purse with the difference added by the track and Jim Beam. In 1984, for instance, nomination fees, entry fees, and starting fees totaled $55,700. Thus the difference, $244,300, was added by Latonia and the sponsor.

The majority of racing cards will be primarily made up of claiming races. While the racing secretary makes an attempt in his condition book to offer several high-class allowance races, in many cases these races do not fill (they do not receive sufficient entries to justify inclusion on the racing card). Most race tracks do not like to include on their program races with less than eight separate betting entries. The public likes to bet on horses with reasonable odds, and short fields with a small number of entries do not provide the kind of odds that would entice people to wager. Most race tracks avoid races with small fields as much as possible.

The racing secretary will normally offer three or four substitute races each day to be used in case the originally prescribed number of races does not fill. At Latonia these races are not in the condition book but are published on a daily basis. At many other race tracks, substitute races are included in the condition book, although the inclusion of substitute races in the condition book does not prevent the racing secretary from offering even more substitute races (or, as they are called, "extras"), should it become necessary to provide races with full fields.

In the condition book for the Fair Grounds in New Orleans, for example, substitute races are included with each day's card, but are set off by an "S". You will find that they usually are of lower quality and have lower purses than the races in the rest of the racing program. The Fair Grounds condition book also contains two items the Latonia book does not, and are included also as reference material: 1) purse distribution and 2) scale of jockey fees. Although purse distribution is different in every state, the purse distribution in Louisiana is not uncommon. We have included it as a matter of reference, showing that the horses finishing first through fifth are paid declining percentages of the purse, from 60% to 4%.

DIVISION OF PURSES

Purse	First 60%	Second 20%	Third 11%	Fourth 6%	Fifth 3%
$20,000	$12,000	$4,000	$2,200	$1,200	$600
15,000	9,000	3,000	1,650	900	450
12,500	7,500	2,500	1,375	750	375
10,000	6,000	2,000	1,100	600	300
7,500	4,500	1,500	825	450	225
6,000	3,600	1,200	660	360	180
5,500	3,300	1,100	605	330	165
5,200	3,120	1,040	572	312	156
5,000	3,000	1,000	550	300	150
4,800	2,880	960	528	288	144
4,600	2,760	920	506	276	138
4,500	2,700	900	495	270	135
4,400	2,640	880	484	264	132
4,300	2,580	860	473	258	129
4,200	2,520	840	462	252	126
4,100	2,460	820	451	246	123
4,000	2,400	800	440	240	120

The division of purses listed above is for the state of Louisiana. Some states, like Kentucky, give a higher percentage to first, while others, like California, give less. The distribution for Louisiana is the more typical allocation.

Preference Systems

The previously mentioned examples of restricting the number of starters in stakes races when there is an overflow field brings us to the question of what happens in an overnight event in the condition book that requires no entry fee, such as a maiden special weight race, which draws an overflow number of entries. At some race tracks the number of maidens entered in one race may go as high as 30, so this becomes a very important question.

There are two methods that are widely used in the United States today. The oldest and most widely used is known as the "star" system. Under this system, when he is entered to run but is excluded (not allowed to run because others drew into the starting field instead of him), this horse receives a star by his name and is included on what is known as the preferred list. The preferred list is a list of horses who are given preference over other horses who have not been excluded from a similar race the next time they enter a similar race. If a horse is excluded a second time, he receives a second preference star. "Two star" horses receive preference over "one star" horses and horses with no stars. Should he be excluded a third time, he becomes a "three star" horse and, as a "three star" horse, he receives preference over "two star" horses, etc.

There is one catch to this, however. The "star" refers only to one particular type of race from which he has been excluded. It applies only to the same condition and the same distance. For instance, if a maiden enters a maiden claiming race at six furlongs and is excluded, this preference star does not apply to maiden special weight races, or maiden races at a different distance. Preference stars which are granted to fillies entered in a race exclusively for fillies and mares do not apply to races where this sex restriction is not included. The star program can be cumbersome, difficult to manage, and sometimes works to the disadvantage of a horse who may have been excluded several times from different types of races but does not have the necessary number of stars for the upcoming race that fits him.

In recent years some tracks have gone to a date preference system, in which every horse is assigned a date the first time he is entered, and horses with the earliest dates of entry are given preference over those with later entry dates. Once a horse starts in a race, the date of that race becomes his preference date, so horses who have waited the longest for an opportunity to run have the most preference. This works well because it allows a trainer to train for a particular race. By watching the overnight entries, he can determine the approximate time his date will become valid for entry for his particular type of race. The date system has the advantage of eliminating the crossover from one type of race to another and simply gives horses who have had the longest lapse of time since their last start the most preference.

At the Secretary's Office

The racing secretary's office is the nerve center of the race track and when your horse is ready to run this is where the trainer will go to enter him. The condition book contains information concerning entry time and scratch time and behooves you to read them. From 7:30 a.m. until 11:00 a.m. on entry day, th office is a beehive of activity. It is the nuts and bolts of the racing card. It is world unto itself. Spend some time there and watch what goes on.

Almost all race tracks in America today operate under the 48-hour rule (som opt for 72 hours) under which entries are taken two days before the actual rur ning of the race. In the old days entries were made the day before the race, but i order to assist the newspapers and race track publicity departments, the entrie are now made two days before the race in order to allow time for promotion an publicity. Closing time for entries at most race tracks is 10:00 or 10:30 a.m. and while some tracks adhere closely to this rule, the majority of race tracks hold thei entries open until the racing secretary is satisfied that he has developed the be; card possible and has sufficient entries in his feature races to make an attractiv race card.

One of the racing secretary's most difficult jobs is convincing trainers that thei horses have a chance in one of the feature races with a short field in order to hel him fill the race.

Like any other business, there has to be cooperation and help from both side; A trainer who helps a racing secretary fill a race may find it easier later to reques a race with particular conditions written to fit one of his horses. A trainer who i ready and willing to help a secretary is going to get help in return.

In the racing secretary's office there are private entry booths manned by entr clerks ready to take entries for the day's races. Each trainer or his agent enter

---

ENTRY BLANK

Every person subscribing to a sweepstakes, or entering a horse to be run at this track, accepts the decision of the Stewards to be final on any question relating to a race or racing.

At the discretion of the Stewards, and without notice, the entries of any person or the transfer of any entry may be refused.

LATONIA RACE COURSE

If this race fails to fill, enter in :—

PREFERRED

Race_____ Distance_____

Weight_____ Jockey_____

Cl. Price $_____ All_____ Penalty_____

RACE ....

DISTANCE ....

Owner	Trainer
Colors	

Number	Horse	Jockey
		Weight

Color	Sex	Age	Sire	Dam	Claiming Price

OFF TRACK STABLING ☐ LOCATION_____

Trainer..................

By ....

Equipment Change	Allowance
	Penalty

68

The theoretical purpose of handicaps is to bring all the horses together at the finish. This was done with brilliance by handicapper John B. Campbell in the 1944 running of the Carter Handicap, which resulted in a triple dead heat for win, the only such finish ever in a stakes race. Brownie (on the inside) carried 115 pounds, Bossuet (middle) carried 127 pounds, while Wait a Bit carried 118 pounds.

this booth so that the other trainers cannot determine who is being entered in each race. There, he makes his entries for the upcoming racing card. In so doing, he specifies the particular race in the condition book, the weight that the horse is to carry under the conditions of the race, and, if it is already determined, who the jockey will be. We have included a sample entry blank from Latonia showing these items (opposite page).

At tracks where the star system is in use there is a place for the number of stars being claimed. The trainer is responsible for the correctness of the entry form, even if he delegates this responsibility to an agent. A trainer who enters an ineligible horse or miscalculates the proper weight the horse is to carry may be subject to a fine and/or disqualification of his horse.

The racing secretary has a large filing box with slots for each race for which entries are being taken. There could be as many as 14 or 15 slots in cases where the entries are being taken for substitute races. As the entries begin to come in, around 9:30 a.m., the racing secretary begins to have an idea of which races have sufficient entries, which are borderline, and which ones are obviously not going to fill for the day. He then announces a "rundown" to the trainers and agents who are assembled in the office. This rundown will allow trainers of horses who are in races being called off to make alternate plans where possible. If there is more than one race with similar conditions, the rundown will allow the racing secretary to start hustling the trainers of horses that are eligible for the races. A little later, as entries continue to come in, the racing secretary will call off more of the races with fewer entries in an effort to encourage entries in the remaining races. At that time the racing secretary will attempt to solicit horses for the borderline races. When he is finally satisfied that he has done all he can—that he has developed the best possible racing card for the day—he will close the entries.

During the morning hours, when entries are being taken, there are assistants in the racing secretary's office who will verify the eligibility of horses for the particular races, and checking the entries for possible errors, checking the preference claims and the entry dates where the date preference system is used. All these assistants are making an effort to verify what the trainer has stated on the entry blank. Keep in mind, though, your trainer is ultimately responsible for what is on the entry blank, not the racing secretary or his assistants.

Drawing for Position

Once the entries are closed and a final check is made to determine the eligibility of the horses, it is time to draw for post positions. In order to eliminate any possible collusion in the drawing of post positions, two people are involved. There is always a crowd of horsemen around the drawing eager to find out if their horses are "in." All the entry blanks for a particular race are placed in a box facing away from the outside of the counter so that the only thing the horsemen who do the drawing can see is the back of an entry form. At the same time these entry blanks are placed in the box, balls or pills with numbers on them representing post positions one through 12 (or fewer if fewer than 12 horses are entered) are placed in a Kelly bottle, just like the one described earlier.

A second horseman, or a representative of the track, then takes the Kelly bottle and draws out one of the pills. At the same time the pill is drawn, an entry blank is pulled from the box by the designated horseman. The two are matched, so that a post position is not known until the horse's name is drawn from the box. In the event there are more than 12 entries (or whatever number constitutes a maximum field at a particular race track) the first 12 entries drawn comprise the field for the race.

In addition, four or six more entry blanks are drawn and these horses are called "also eligibles." This means that should one of the original entrants in the race scratch (that is drop out of the race for any number of reasons by the designated time), one of the horses on the also-eligible list may "draw in" to the race. In the case of the star system, the drawing in is determined by pill—just as the post position is determined, except that the horse that draws in will automatically be assigned the outside available post position. At tracks where the date system is used, the horse with the earliest preference date will draw in, but will also be assigned the outside available post position.

Should more than one horse scratch from the race, then more than one horse will be drawn in from the also-eligible list. The horses that were not selected for either the field or also-eligible list are the ones known as excluded, which we discussed earlier, and will be given a preference based either on the star system or the date system for future races.

After the post positions are drawn and the assistant racing secretaries check once more for errors and corrections, they make up what is known as the "overnight sheet." The overnight is so named because, when entries were taken the day before the race, it was the sheet that came out overnight for the next day's races. It has retained its original name even though it now comes out two days before the race and there are two overnights in existence at the same time. Since the racing secretary is attempting to develop some continuity in his racing program, which will develop fan interest and create the largest attendance and betting handle possible, the number of the race in the condition book will not normally correspond to its position on the racing program. The overnight is the same information sent to the *Daily Racing Form* for its production.

Scratches

Scratch time at the race tracks is found in the condition books, but it is now normally the day before the race. In the old days it was the morning of the race, but, again, to assist the publicity departments, the race tracks have moved scratch time up to allow more time to print the program, have the proper entries with the scratches included in the morning newspapers, and to help the publicity department in promoting the day's program.

Trainers of horses who have gotten sick since entry time, or whose trainers do not want to run them because of a change in track conditions or because they don't like the competition, turn in scratch cards prior to the prescribed scratch time. These scratch cards are reviewed by the stewards, who act upon them. If the size of the racing field is such that the scratch will not cause the field to fall below a certain minimum size, there is no problem. This is normally the case in races that have also eligibles and races with full fields. In these cases a horse can be scratched without reason. However, if the scratch of a horse causes the field to fall below a certain minimum (which at most race tracks is eight horses), the trainer must have a legitimate reason, such as sickness or injury, for his horse to be scratched.

In the cases where the field is reduced below the acceptable minimum, the stewards will usually order the state veterinarian to examine the horse and determine the legitimacy of the trainer's complaint. In cases where this occurs, the horse is placed on the veterinarian's list and cannot be reentered until he has been removed from that list, normally a minimum of seven days. Late scratches that occur because of emergencies after scratch time, such as cases of sickness or injury, again must be verified by the state veterinarian and approved by the stewards. The veterinarian's list restriction applies in these cases also. The only exception to this restriction on scratches is in a stakes race. Since the owner must pay to start his horse, he is entitled to scratch in most states right up to the afternoon of the race.

Track Condition

Since we've brought up the subject of track conditions, this is probably as good a place as any to describe and explain them.

The normal condition is "fast." This is when the track is in good shape and does not contain an abnormal amount of moisture.

When heavy rains fall, the track goes from fast to "sloppy," which means the track has a great deal of water standing on the surface, but it can still be firm underneath. A sloppy race track gives the appearance of a pond. Race times on a sloppy race track will be very close to those on a fast track. A sloppy race track is normally the result of a quick, hard rain.

As the rain persists or, if the rain comes more slowly over a longer period of time, the water soaks into the whole cushion of the race track, and the track becomes "muddy." A muddy race track, as its name would indicate, has the consistency of mud and is very difficult for horses to run through, except for some who seem to have a preference for mud, either because of infirmities which don't hurt them as much when they run in the mud, or a way of going which favors a holding type of surface.

The worst track of all is described as "heavy." This is merely the culmination of a soaking rain which results in a very tiring surface for a horse to run on as the mud sticks to his hooves . . . and everything.

As the track begins to dry out after a rain, it becomes "slow," which is essentially equivalent to muddy, except that it is in the drying stage, not yet really good but nevertheless better than heavy.

As the track continues to dry and is getting close to its optimum condition, it is described as "good."

There is one other track condition that perhaps should be mentioned, now that there is so much winter racing around the country, and that is "frozen," and it occurs, as one might suspect, when rain is followed by a drastic drop in temperature and the water in the track freezes. It is a very dangerous condition, not so much because it is slippery, but because the frozen moisture forms rock-like clods which can injure your horse, as well as the rider.

Turf tracks have five descriptions of condition. The normal turf condition is "firm," which means the track is in good shape and horses should run at their optimum.

The next condition, like dirt tracks, is "good," which means there has been some rain recently and the course is either drying out or on its way to a softer condition. On "good" courses, horses usually run to form, without being unduly hampered by the condition.

After rain, many races are taken off the turf, but when the turf is not firm but nevertheless good enough to race over, it is termed "yielding," which, as the name implies, means soft and tiring and more difficult to run over.

The worst condition of a turf course is "soft," which means the horses will sink into the turf, throwing up big clods of grass and dirt, as they run. Very few race tracks will keep races on the turf under such conditions, with the exception of stakes races.

The other condition, which occurs in periods of drought, is called "hard," and this is an adverse condition particularly when a horse has some infirmity with the foot or lower limb, because it causes his legs to sting when he runs on a very firm surface.

Before we get on to the race day, itself, there are two other items which should be discussed—getting licensed and designing your silks.

Getting Your License

Racing is the best policed sport in the world. Everybody from the lowliest hot-walker to the president of the track must be licensed by the state racing commission. This includes you, and it will probably require a trip to the track where you will fill out a form, get fingerprinted and photographed. The license fee ranges from $10 in some states to $200 in California. You will get your owner's license after your application is approved by the stewards and/or the state racing commission, and you will be issued a badge with your picture on it, much like your driver's license. This will allow you free access to the backstretch so you can watch your horses going through their morning exercise.

If you're going to race in more than one state, you'll have to go through this procedure everywhere you race your horses. It will probably seem ridiculous to you because you are presumably a logical person, but the various state racing commissions are so jealous of their authority that, despite years of effort, they have not been able to come up with a universal license *application,* much less a uniform license. It's just one of the frustrating antiquities of racing that you'll have to learn to put up with.

Selecting Your Colors

Another of the fun things you get to do as an owner is design your own colors (or silks). If you do not race in New York, you can design just about anything you want, from solid white to a multicolor rainbow, and register it with your state racing commission.

If you race in New York, however, you will have to register your colors with The Jockey Club. The Jockey Club registers colors on a ten-year basis or a lifetime basis and, once colors are registered in an owner's name, no other owner can have the same color combination. In addition The Jockey Club has some restrictions on what is acceptable in the way of specialized markings on colors. Even if you don't plan on racing in New York initially, it would be advisable to get your colors approved and registered there for the day when you ship to the Big Apple for the Belmont Stakes. The Jockey Club will be happy to send you the necessary forms and instructions if you request them.

A few suggestions: use bright colors; they are easier to see. Stay away from the basic colors as much as you can; everyone else is using them. Use one color for the jacket and a different color for the sleeves, or special markings on sleeves—such as hoops or chevrons—that are easy to see. Even though you may like your initials or the logo of your company, any symbol on the front or back of the jacket is not visible when the jockey is hunched down, whipping and driving so it will not help you pick out your horse. The place for your initials or symbol is on blinkers; you can spot them there.

Allow yourself some lead time; don't wait until your horse is ready to run to order your silks. It takes four to eight weeks to have silks made after they are registered.

DEFINITIONS AND MEASUREMENTS

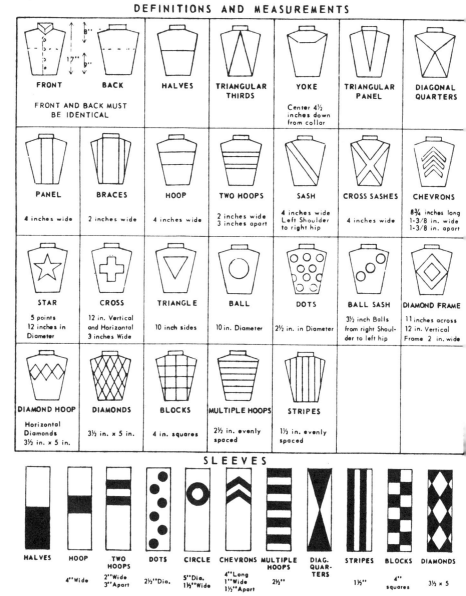

There are many decisions to be made when designing colors to be registered with The Jockey Club.

Race Day

Finally, the big day arrives, and your excitement is almost uncontrollable. You, yourself, can barely eat breakfast in your hurry to get to the barn to be sure everything is okay.

Your young horse knows something is up, too! He didn't go to the track this morning and perhaps his hay was taken away (this is known as "drawing" a horse, and it is something some trainers do before a race). He gets a little extra attention and loving encouragement from his groom.

Later, the call comes through the backstretch on the loudspeakers—"Get your horses ready for the fourth race." This is it! The groom gives your youngster a final brushing, checks the mane and tail for any unwanted straw or snags, cleans out his feet one more time, and slips the bridle on. A few minutes go by and the big call comes—"Bring your horses to the paddock for the fourth race."

In the paddock your prancing youngster is all eyes—what's this all about? Who are all these people? Why are they here staring at me? What a shock the paddock must be to a green two-year-old the first time he sees it! As a matter of fact, it's all so strange and new that most youngsters are too curious to be upset the first time they are there. They spend their time wondering what it is all about.

If they are going to be fractious and nervous, the second trip to the paddock is often the worst, especially if they had a bad experience in their first race. Keep that in mind. For a lot of horses the second start is likely to be the most traumatic—and may give the most disappointment. In the second start your youngster knows enough to worry but is still, in many cases, too green to perform well. Very few horses win their first start and many run poorly in their second start.

Your youngster gets saddled, behaves well though, and you are relieved. Here comes the jockey in *your* new silks. How splendid he looks!

Your trainer gives the jockey his instructions: "Break sharply. This colt is good from the gate. Lay third or fourth down the backstretch. Don't go four horses wide and lose a lot of ground on the turn. Tap him turning for home and let him go to the front. Don't abuse him; just let him win by a couple."

Of course, seven other trainers are giving their jockeys the exact same instructions! Remember, the best jockey in the world can't get off your horse and carry him home. There's an old story:

> A trainer gave his rider instructions to be fifth leaving the gate, fourth down the backstretch, third going into the far turn, second turning for home, and first at the eighth pole. As the race developed, the horse was first leaving the gate, second down the backstretch, third going into the far turn, fourth turning for home, fifth at the eighth pole—and nowhere to be found at the finish.
>
> The enraged trainer dashed down to the unsaddling area to meet his errant rider, where he screamed loud enough for everyone to hear, "You didn't follow my instructions—I told you to lay back early and go to the front at the eighth pole." The jockey sardonically replied, "I would have, but I thought I'd stay with your horse."

An old saying has it that there are a million ways to lose a race and only one way to win—get to the finish line first! It's true. In team sports there is one winner and one loser—in racing there is one winner and as many as 11 losers, so you will have more downs than ups no matter how successful you are—but what *ups*!

It would take a whole book to write about what can happen, and does happen, in a horse race. Take what you hear and see and analyze it for yourself. The race track is the greatest rumor mill and gossip center in the world. Don't accept what you hear as fact unless you can verify it yourself—learn from your experiences!

Good horses make good jockeys and good trainers. A good jockey and a good trainer get the most out of a horse but can do no more. A bad trainer or a bad jockey can ruin your chances.

Jockeys

Jockeys are an important part of the horse business. It will be the trainer's decision to select the rider who fits your horse. Most trainers have preferences and will use a few jockeys on most of their horses. It is preferable if the jockey has been on your horse before the race, in a morning workout, so that the jockey feels comfortable and has some knowledge about your horse.

Remember, the selection of a jockey is your trainer's responsibility and where and when your horse races is his responsibility. You have hired a professional, and if you have paid any attention to our advice at all, you must let him do his job to the best of his ability.

The purpose of this book is to help you understand the business you are in, and to understand your trainer's problems better, not to encourage you to go around with a condition book in your pocket, looking over his shoulder. If you are going to do that, you are doomed to failure and our advice has gone for naught. Training horses is his business and he is a professional. When you hire a plant manager for your business, you give him the authority to do a job. Consider your horse business as another plant, your trainer as a plant manager, and give him the authority and support to do his job.

The saddling ring at Saratoga in New York.

Chapter 4

At The Sales

While the title of this chapter is "At The Sales"—and it will, indeed, contain a great deal of information about what an investor in the horse business should look for and do at the sales—it is also about the things that you should do before you even go to the sales. Those things are, we think, more important than most of the things you'll actually do at the sales.

In this section of the book, we'll attempt to tell you a little bit about what to expect at the sales, what to look for and what to avoid. We'll explain the different types of sales, and discuss the advantages and disadvantages of each. We'll try to teach you how to work over a sales catalog, and include a little bit about conformation, your responsibilities and those of the sales company, how to bid and what to do after you've purchased your horse.

There's one further thing you must do, though, even before you begin your presales preparation. In Chapter 2, "Choosing Your Advisor," we recommended that you set out a game plan, a written program, for your participation in the thoroughbred business. As part of that plan, you, along with your advisor and accountant, will have decided what kind of horse or horses you want to buy and how much you want to spend. If you haven't taken that step, it doesn't make any sense to spend the time to work over a sales catalog. As you'll see in the section on sales catalogs, when we say "work over" a sales catalog, we do mean work. For instance, if you have $100,000 to spend in the business, you can look over a catalog for the Keeneland July yearling sale and drool a little, but it doesn't make much sense to put in a lot of work on it, or for that matter, even to go to the sale when you know the average price is going to be around $550,000.

So, now that you've decided on whether you want to get into racing or breeding, decided on your price range, and decided to get in through the auction route, rather than through private sales, here are your choices.

Types of Sales

The best place to start is with the yearling sales, since they are the best known, most prevalent, and most visible. In 1983, there were 76 major yearling sales conducted in North America, and a few others which were considered minor. In all, a total of 8,705 yearlings (which represented about 23% of the entire foal crop) were auctioned for a total of $359,148,103, an average of $41,258. They ranged in price from a couple of hundred dollars to $10.2-million, for a Northern Dancer colt sold at Keeneland (see pedigree on page 89). It's interesting to note that the $10.2-million colt increased the average price of all the yearlings sold in 1983 by $1,167. And, to show how times have changed, you could have purchased the entire crop of yearlings sold at public auction in 1960 for $10-million.

At any rate, if you're going to the yearling sales you'll have one more choice to make—whether to go to a select sale or an open sale. The select sales—headed by the Keeneland July sale, the Saratoga sale, and the Fasig-Tipton Kentucky July sale—are the premier yearling sales in the world. They are the most desirable for consignors, because they attract the leading buyers in the world, and they are the most desirable for buyers because the yearlings which make it into the sales have been selected from thousands of entries by some of the finest experts in the business.

When a horse is nominated to a select sale, a team goes over his pedigree and assigns it a rating, generally from A+ to C. A+ yearlings have the best, most commercial pedigrees available, and they'll probably make it into the sale, even if they have a few conformational defects. C yearlings have pedigrees which are below the normal range of acceptability for the select sale and they'll have to be exceptional physical specimens, and, in most cases, have a top salesman making a case for them, before they'll be admitted to the sale. As is implied by the foregoing, the next step is a physical examination by another team, this one conformation experts, for all the yearlings whose pedigrees seem to warrant consideration. Then the two teams get together and decide which yearlings will be accepted for the sale. At that time, a few of the ones with excellent pedigrees are thrown out for conformational reasons, while others, with less attractive pedigrees, are let in because of exceptional conformation. The benefit of select sales, most people believe, is that two teams of experts have already completed part of the selection process for them, and they don't have to pore over thousands of pedigrees and look at hundreds of horses to find the ones in which they might be interested. The reverse side of the coin is that buyers are obviously going to have to pay more for yearlings in select sales.

"Open" sales are for yearlings who do not necessarily qualify for select sales or whose owners did not even enter them in a select sale for one reason or another. In either case, the only qualifications for an open auction are that the yearling be a thoroughbred and that his breeder has paid the cataloging fee (price of entry).

While the board reads $200,000, the bid is actually $10,200,000, since eight figures would not register. This record-priced yearling was a colt by Northern Dancer out of My Bupers.

In the last few years, several companies conducting "open" sales have attempted to become more selective and reduce the size of their sales by increasing the entry fees to the point where it would not make sound economic sense to enter low-class yearlings in them. For example, in 1982 the entry fee for the Keeneland September sale, which is "open," was raised to $1,000 and the 5% commission was dropped on sales below $20,000. This was done on the theory that it wouldn't make sense to enter a yearling unless it was worth at least $20,000. It hasn't seemed to work particularly well, however, in reducing the number of horses entered.

There will be a lot of excellent racehorses sold at open sales every year, but then there are a lot of horses sold at open sales. For example, there were 3,487 yearlings cataloged for the Keeneland (2,322) and Fasig-Tipton Kentucky (1,165) September sales, held from September 7-17, 1984.

The advantages of purchasing yearlings are mainly in the area of selection. With 23% of the foal crop going through the ring, you can just about find anything you want. The disadvantage, if you're looking for excitement, is that you're normally about six to nine months away from seeing your horse under silks, and that can be a fairly expensive period, as you'll learn in Chapter 6, because yearling breaking and training up to a race are among the most expensive propositions in the business.

If you're not as patient as some (and you don't want to incur the expense of yearling breaking), you might want to try one of the sales of two-year-olds in training which are usually held during the first few months of the year in southern climes. At these sales, the horses are usually 60 to 90 days away from a race, so your lead time will be less, but you'll also normally pay for the training that the young horses have received—that is a two-year-old in training will usually bring more than a comparable yearling. As a matter of fact, there are a number of people who make a pretty good living by "pinhooking" (buying yearlings and then reselling them at the two-year-old in training sales). Since such a large percentage of the two-year-olds sold at auction are a result of pinhooking, you have the additional advantage of being able to find out what they brought as a yearling and acting accordingly.

There are other advantages and disadvantages, of course. The sales companies require that the two-year-olds at these sales at least be able to breeze, so one advantage is your trainer can get a better idea of the young horse's way of going watching him on the track breezing or galloping. You can also generally avoid some of the attrition that occurs during yearling breaking and early training. However, some people also feel that owners who are selling at a two-year-old in training sale have already had a look at what the horse can do, and they are selling because they didn't like what they saw (or can at least place reserves at appropriate levels).

There are two lessons to be learned here. First, know (or find out about) the person who is selling a horse at auction, any auction. This can tell you quite a lot. For example, if a person has a history of making a living by pinhooking yearlings for the two-year-old sales and he doesn't race, you can feel pretty safe about buying from him. However, if the consignor is someone who generally races homebreds and he's selling one two-year-old, it might be something to be wary of. The second lesson is that nobody, *nobody,* can tell you what a horse is actually going to do on the race track until the gate has opened on him in an actual race, and generally they can't tell until it's opened a couple of times. They can get a clue as to ability, but there are so many indefinable qualities about a horse, that there's absolutely no way to tell how well a horse is going to turn out. And anybody who says he can is a liar.

At any rate, the two-year-old sales have been a very successful entry point to the business for quite a number of people. For instance, one of the first horses that the Kirkpatrick half of your team ever syndicated at Spendthrift was SKS Stable's Lord Avie, who was among the first horses ever purchased by his owners. They bought the colt for $37,000 at the Hialeah sale of two-year-olds in training in March of 1980, then watched him win the Eclipse Award as champion two-year-old, earn nearly $440,000, and be syndicated for $10-million before he ever started at three. Despite suffering an injury at three, Lord Avie ranked at the top of his division again, winning the Florida Derby and retiring with purse earnings of $705,977. That's a pretty good start in anybody's league.

There are also regular sales for older horses in training at major racing centers around the country. In contrast to the sales for two-year-olds, these do often contain culls—horses which can't stand the competition where their owners race and don't particularly have the pedigree to make them saleable as breeding prospects. It's important to remember, though, that one man's ceiling is another man's floor, and a horse who's a cull in New York or California can be a very useful racehorse in some of the other racing centers around the country.

The jubilant owners of Lord Avie gathered in the winner's circle following the colt's triumph in the 1981 Florida Derby. Lord Avie was purchased at the Hialeah Sale of two-year-olds in training by the partnership of SKS Stable.

The final type of sales you might want to attend is a breeding stock or a "mixed" sale. At these sales, you'll find yearlings, weanlings, broodmares, broodmare prospects, stallions, stallion prospects, and about any kind of horse you want to see. Obviously, if you're going into breeding, you'll attend this type of sale.

In 1983, broodmares ranked second only to yearling in numbers sold and volume of sales, as 7,023 were sold for gross receipts of $240,244,133, an average of $34,208. While we're on the subject of the size of the breeding stock market, it might be appropriate to mention here that some of the sales companies are now offering "select" or, as they are more commonly called, "preferred," sessions at the breeding stock sales, just as they have select yearling sales. Even at Keeneland, where they don't admit to having preferred sessions, they make the consignors divide up their sales offerings, putting the better quality horses in the first couple of days of the sales, and the lesser quality animals later in the sales.

When you buy a broodmare in foal, you're usually about two years away from seeing any return on your investment. However, you can look forward to a very exciting and beautiful event, the birth of her foal, normally within five to eight months, if you buy her in November when the majority of the mares are sold. There are also large breeding stock sales held in January, in which case you won't have to wait so long for your foal to arrive. As a matter of fact, occasionally

81

mares have been known to foal right there at the sale.

The mixed and breeding stock sales also contain a large number of weanlings which are normally a little cheaper than a comparable yearling, once again because the owner doesn't have as much money into raising the weanling. (You'll find very few select sales quality horses being sold as weanlings.) There are, of course, other reasons why weanlings are cheaper than comparable yearlings, but then, again, most of them also relate to cost. Sales preparation, for instance, is much less complicated and costly for weanlings than for yearlings, when you consider all you have to do with a weanling is to teach him to lead, whereas yearlings have 60 to 90 days of specialized care and training. Also, there's a lot of attrition between weaning time and yearling sales time, because horses are just like children—they love to play and often get hurt in the process of that play.

It is very important at breeding stock sales—probably more important there than at any other type of sales—to attempt to ascertain *why* the animals are being offered for sale, as well as the other things we'll discuss shortly about the catalog.

Normally, a breeder who is in the business for the long term will be very reluctant to sell a decent broodmare, unless he's in a tremendous cash flow bind (broke). So, if that's not the case, he might be selling her because she's got some problems, because he's had her for a while and doesn't believe she's going to turn out well as a producer, or because he's seen some of her foals and they're as crooked as a West Virginia highway. For that reason, it's important to try to get a look at some of her foals, too. Good broodmares are almost irreplaceable at any sort of cost-effective price, so, at the risk of being redundant, let us say once again that, if an established outfit is selling a broodmare, especially one who looks pretty good on paper, it would behoove you to find out why she's being sold.

The same goes for weanlings. While there are a few people who specialize in the sale of weanlings, most of the ones you'll find in the November sales are there for some other reason. Often it's a cash flow problem, but occasionally a breeder who usually sells his stock as yearlings might believe that the pedigree of the weanling is particularly hot (fashionable) at that time and doesn't have faith that the fashionability will last. It's also pretty tough to tell how a weanling is going to turn out. You'd be amazed at the amount a young horse can change, for the better or the worse, between the time he's a weanling and the time he's a yearling (more often than not, though, it's for the worse). There are a few, a very few, real good pinhookers who seem to be able to pick out a weanling who'll develop into a yearling that will turn a profit for them, but those people are few and far between, and they'll tell you it doesn't always work out as planned for them either.

Before the Sales

Once you've decided what you want to do and which sales you want to attend there are a few other things you'll have to take care of before you actually attend the auctions.

The first is to establish some sort of identity with the sales company. You'll need to write or call them to receive the catalogs for the sales you wish to attend

You should have to do this only once, because once you get on the list of the sales company, you'll normally find you get just about all their catalogs. In the front of the catalog you'll find a credit application, which you should fill out, take to your bank for verification, have notarized, and send to the sales company. You should do this well in advance, so you won't get lost in the rush.

A week or so after you've done that, you might want to call the sales director and see if the credit application is in order. This is an introductory call, really, and it'll give you an opportunity to ask any other questions you might have about the sale and the area where it's being held, for instance motels, restaurants, etc. Also, if you've ignored our repeated advice about choice of advisors, the sales director can possibly point you toward some trainers or veterinarians who can assist you at the sales. Of course, he won't give you any specific recommendations, but he'll give you a list of people from whom you can choose. You can also inquire about state sales taxes at this time and, if it's appropriate, you can send in the sales tax exemption form which is included with almost every sales catalog which is mailed today.

The bottom line of what you'll be doing, though, is getting acquainted with someone at the sales company. While he won't have much time for socializing at the sales, if you get into a problem, it's nice to know someone who can possibly help you out, someone whose name you know and who knows your name.

If you're planning to attend the sale in person, you probably should check on seating. While many sales companies will just let you sit anywhere if you're a buyer, others have reserved seating and they are at a premium at the more important sales. If you're sending an agent, you'll need to fill out (and have notarized) the Agent Authorization form which is also located in the front of the catalog.

There's one more thing we'd like to urge you to do before you begin to work over the sales catalog—you should read the conditions of sale.

Conditions of Sale

While this section of the catalog is written primarily for the protection of the sales company, it can also afford some protection for the buyers and, at the very least, it sets forth the rules and regulations under which you'll be operating. The conditions of sale are printed in the front of the catalogs by some sales companies, while they are printed at the front of each session by others—that's how important they are.

There are, as you'll see when you look at them, quite a few conditions of sale, but there are three which are of primary importance to buyers.

> **Soundness.** The conditions of sale state, in boldface capitals, **"UNLESS OTHERWISE EXPRESSLY ANNOUNCED AT TIME OF SALE THERE IS NO GUARANTEE OF ANY KIND AS TO THE SOUNDNESS, OR CONDITION OR OTHER QUALITY OF ANY ANIMAL SOLD IN THIS SALE."** If, however, a sales horse is unsound of eye, is a "cribber," or is unsound of wind, an announcement must be made to that effect at the time of the sales. However, there is no guarantee as to soundness of wind for yearlings or two-year-olds. Also, any horse which

is sold as a colt and turns out to be a ridgeling or gelding—or vice versa—is subject to return. Normally, horses which are not as announced at the time of the sales may be returned, along with a veterinary certificate stating what's wrong, within seven days after the sales. However, **in the case of yearlings and two-year-olds, the buyer normally has only 48 hours for filing notice of rejection.** Also, in the case of horses of racing age, if the new owner works or starts the horse, he no longer has any right of rejection.

Breeding Status. At breeding stock sales, one of the most important things for a buyer to know is the pregnancy status of the mares he's trying to buy. Through 1983, broodmares were offered in one of three categories: "In Foal," which means the mare has been bred and is believed to be in foal by a veterinary examination within ten days of the sale; "Barren," which means the mare was bred but did not conceive, although she is believed to be breeding sound, according to a veterinary examination within ten days prior to the sale; and "Not Bred," which means that, for whatever the reason (a very late foal or a difficult foaling), she was not bred, but she, too, is supposed to be breeding sound, according to a veterinary examination within ten days prior to sale. This is a really important place to find out, if possible, why a mare was not bred, and indeed, why she is being sold.

Beginning in 1984, because of some lawsuits, most sales companies have added an additional status of "Slipped," which means the mare was bred and conceived, but she either resorbed or aborted the foal prior to the sale. The latter condition is also supposed to carry the implication of breeding soundness. This is, in some instances, combined with "barren" on the sales board as "not in foal."

Further, this, more than any other condition of sale, might illustrate the necessity of listening to the announcements of the auctioneer. They take precedence over the pregnancy status as published in the catalog. (Going from "in foal" to "slipped" will probably be the most frequent change of breeding status you'll hear at the sales.) If the catalog says the mare is in foal, and you don't listen to the announcements which say she's barren or has slipped, you're responsible for the price you paid, thinking she was in foal. The sales are videotaped, today, and the sales company will play the videotape of the announcement back to you, and say, "Sorry about that."

It is important to know that **buyers must have mares checked by their own veterinarian within 24 hours after the sale and before the mares have been removed from the sales grounds for any notice of rejection to be valid.**

It is also very important for buyers to know that stallion service fees become payable by the seller at any time a mare is sold, and the contract does not follow the sale of the mare. What that means is if a mare has been bred on a "live foal" contract or a "return" contract, those rights do not follow the mare and, if she slips or fails to produce a live foal, there'll normally be no refund or return from the stallion or share owner.

Title. When the auctioneer bangs the gavel and says "sold," title passes to the new owner, along with all risks and responsibility of ownership of the horse in question. As a matter of fact, if the auctioneer pronounced a horse as sold to you and then someone were to shoot it in the ring, the loss would be yours. Most insurance companies, today, offer "fall of the hammer" insurance, to protect you from the instant the horse is sold and, that, too, is something you should arrange prior to the sale (you don't have to tell them what horses you'll be bidding on in order to be protected, incidentally). Also, as a practical matter, even though the horse becomes your responsibility at the moment it's sold, most sales companies require that consignors provide care for it until the next day.

There's one other very important point with respect to title. Title to a thoroughbred is carried by The Jockey Club Registration Certificate—**nothing else.** When you buy a horse at the sale, you'll get a release certificate, which permits you to take the horse off the grounds, but you will not receive the Registration Certificate until the horse has been paid for and the check has cleared. Unlike other forms of business, in the thoroughbred business, possession is not nine points of the law.

There are other conditions of sale, primarily having to do with the fact that the auctioneer is the final authority in the adjudication of any disputes arising with respect to the sale, what the sales company will do upon default of the buyer, and what the sales company will do in case you're late with your payment (charge you 1½% a month, generally), but the aforementioned ones are the most important.

While there has been an effort among the major sales companies to standardize conditions of sale over the past five years, there are still variations from sales company to sales company, and if you take 20 minutes or so to read the conditions of the sale, it will someday wind up saving you a lot of time, trouble, embarrassment, and, most importantly, money.

Working over the Sales Catalog

Now you are ready to tackle the pedigree pages, the meat of the sales catalog.

The single most important thing to remember about a sales catalog is that each one of those pedigree pages is an advertisement. Each catalog page is prepared by a trained expert, often with years of experience, to emphasize the most attractive portion of the horse's pedigree and minimize the least attractive parts of the pedigree. As a consequence, *what doesn't appear on the catalog page is often more important than what does appear.*

There have been several lawsuits in the past few years, which have resulted in sales companies being more specific in certain parts of their catalogs, especially the produce records of broodmares who are being sold, but it is still important that you check up further on the information that is on the catalog page.

The first thing you do with respect to study of the pedigrees in your sales catalog is to scan the entire catalog and eliminate anything that doesn't fit in with your plans and/or is obviously out of your price range. At the same time, you can mark the ones you're interested in. Once you've done this a couple of times and you've got a sort of idea of price ranges, this shouldn't take too long. Then you really get down to work.

Reproduced on the facing page is a catalog page which was marked up by Cary Robertson Jr. for an article on pedigrees which appeared in *The Thoroughbred Record,* October 18, 1975. While it is a bit of an extreme example (neither of us has ever seen a catalog page marked up quite that much), it does illustrate the extent to which you can go in supplementing a fairly normal catalog page.

There are a number of sources to which you can refer for the sort of information which is needed to produce a good catalog update, and most of them are listed in the Bibliography under "Reference Sources." Many, if not most, of them can be found at the offices of your local breeders' association, so you won't have to go to the expense of purchasing a breeding library. However, if your time is at a premium, you can get most of the material you want from the time sharing computer of Bloodstock Research Information Services. This service is available at a very nominal cost if you have your own terminal, or at a slightly higher cost from the terminal which most breeders' associations now provide for members.

For the purposes of this section, we're going to run a catalog page, identifying some of the essential elements of the page, then follow that up by tearing apart some catalog pages and printing the elements of them, both good and bad, accompanied by some reproductions of the computer printouts from which they were derived, and/or explanations of why we feel they are good or bad. Also, we'll show you how a pedigree can change very rapidly, due to the exploits of a close relative of a horse, and how that can increase its value. Throughout, we'll try to give you some hints on what makes a pedigree good, what makes one bad, and what we think you should look for in a pedigree.

About Black Type

First, though, there are some other things you should know about pedigrees in catalogs. In 1957, Fasig-Tipton Company, the world's second-largest sales company, adopted a system of highlighting the better horses in a pedigree by setting them out in what is called in the industry today "black type." The names of stakes winners on a catalog page are printed in boldface type and all capital letters, while the names of stakes-placed horses appear in boldface type, with capital and lower-case letters. While this practice has remained in effect until the present and is likely to remain in force in perpetuity, there have been some rumblings and mutterings through the years that some stakes races, especially cheap stakes at small tracks, weren't a true indicator of class. In the early '70s racing authorities in England, Ireland, and France got together and came up with a system of identifying their leading stakes as "pattern races," and later changed them to group races. They are further subdivided into Group I, Group II, and Group III, according to importance, with the Group I being the most important. The U.S. followed the next year with the same system, except that the stakes were called graded stakes, instead of group stakes.

Today, knowledgeable pedigree people realize, as they always did, that there are some stakes in this world that are not as good in terms of the quality of horses entered in them as the second half of the daily double on an off Tuesday in New York or California. As a matter of fact, there have been some pretty high-toned

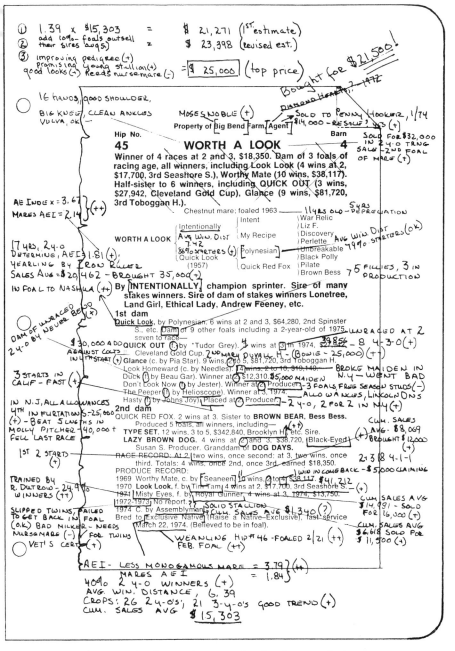

An example of a catalog page that has been worked over.

claiming races out in California recently and there was one run on November 10, 1984, in which the claiming price was to be $1-million (see Appendix 1). In some countries, there are *group* races which fall into exactly the same category, i.e. they aren't much of a race, so the worldwide system of cataloging is currently undergoing a tremendous change—for the better, we believe.

At The Jockey Club Round Table Conference, held in August, 1984, a whole new system of cataloging standards was proposed. What the system would provide, effective in 1985, is essentially:

- Stakes with less than $15,000 in added money would not qualify horses for black type in sales catalogs, but the names of the stakes would be identified in the catalog.

- Stakes with $15,000 or more in added money would be divided into three categories—graded stakes (as explained above), listed stakes (nongraded stakes with $50,000 or more in added money), and stakes ($15,000 to $49,999 in added money). They would qualify for black type.

- North American allowance or handicap races with purses of $30,000 and up would qualify for black type and an "A" or an "H," respectively, would follow the name of the horse who won or placed in it.

None of these changes are scheduled to take place until after January 1, 1985, and it's probably a good thing, because we'd hate to be given the assignment of figuring out how to handle the $1-million claiming race. There will be no ex post facto changes, that is no horse will lose the black type it earned in any race prior to January 1, 1985, so you're still going to have to look up stakes, until you get familiar with the business, to find out if they really have any meaning or not.

Elements of a Pedigree Page

Now, on to the pedigrees. The first catalog page we'll present for the purpose of explaining the elements of a pedigree is a yearling **Pedigree!** (in boldface type, with a capital "P" and an exclamation point). It is the pedigree of the yearling which brought $10.2-million at the 1983 Keeneland July Sale (see opposite page).

It differs from a pedigree for a breeding stock sale in terms of the emphasis on the immediate pedigree, rather than the produce record, which would be considered more important in a breeding stock sale. Also, in a sale of horses of racing age, there would be a race record for the horse being sold and that would be backed up by an insert featuring the latest past performances of the horse in question. We'll discuss those elements further on.

> **A) Ownership/Consignor Line.** As mentioned previously, this can be very important, more so in breeding stock sales than in yearling sales. This line will either read "Property of," which means it is being sold by its owners, or "Consigned by," which means it is not being sold by its owners, but by

A

B

Property of Crescent Farm

C

Barn **16**   **DARK BAY OR BROWN COLT**   Hip No. **308**

D
Half-brother to 7 winners, including MY JULIET (24 wins, $548,859, champion sprinter, Michigan Mile and One Eighth H.-G2, etc.), LYPHARD'S SPECIAL (at 2, 1982, in England, Champagne S., etc.), Embarrassed (3rd Prix du Calvados-G3), Double Revival ($141,249).

E
─────────────────── Foaled February 25, 1982

			Nearco
DARK BAY OR BROWN COLT	Northern Dancer	Nearctic........................	*Lady Angela
		Natalma........................	Native Dancer
			Almahmoud
	My Bupers	Bupers...........................	Double Jay
	(1967)		Busanda
		Princess Revoked	Revoked
			Miss Muffet

G
By NORTHERN DANCER (1961). Canadian horse of the year. Leading sire twice in England and U. S., sire of more than 90 stakes winners, 17 champions, including Nijinsky II (European horse of the year), The Minstrel (horse of the year in England, Epsom Derby-G1, etc.), Try My Best (in England and Ireland), Northernette ($404,914, Top Flight H.-G1, etc.), Giboulee ($358,578), Fanfreluche ($238,688), Storm Bird (William Hill Dewhurst S.-G1, etc.), Danzatore (to 3, 1983), Minsky, Woodstream (in Ireland).

1st dam
MY BUPERS, by Bupers. Placed at 3. This is her 11th foal. Her tenth foal is a 2-year-old of 1983. Dam of 8 foals to race, 7 winners, incl.—

H
MY JULIET (f. by Gallant Romeo). 24 wins in 36 starts, 2 to 5, $548,-859, champion sprinter, Michigan Mile and One Eighth H.-G2, Vosburgh H.-G2 twice, Cotillion S.-G2, Black-Eyed Susan S.-G3, Vagrancy H.-G3, Test S.-G3, Next Move H., Las Flores H., Anne Arundel H., Fair Haven H., Doylestown H., Ta Wee H., Endine H., Neshaminy H., Pocahontas S., Ak-Sar-Ben Princess S., etc. Producer.
LYPHARD'S SPECIAL (c. by Lyphard). 3 wins in 5 starts at 2, 1982, in England, Champagne S., 2nd Royal Lodge S.-G2, Lanson Champagne S., 3rd William Hill Futurity S.-G1.
Embarrassed (f. by Blushing Groom (FR)). Winner at 2 in France, 3rd Prix du Calvados-G3.
Double Revival (g. by Grand Revival). 20 wins, 2 to 9, 1982, $141,249.

2nd dam
Princess Revoked, by Revoked. 8 wins, 2 to 4, $33,629, 3rd Hurricane H. Set ntr. Dam of 8 other foals, 7 to race, 5 winners, including—
READYFOURSHOES (f. by Gallant Romeo). 14 wins, 3 to 6, $53,995, Imp S., 2nd Independence Day H., 3rd Delta Queen H., etc. Dam of—

I
SHOE'S FIRST SHOE (c. by Hempen). 9 wins, 3 to 5, $80,874, Forest City H., Ohio Harvest H., Summit Silver Cup H., Eagle S. Romeo's Coquette. 2 wins at 3, $11,486. Dam of 3 foals, including—
BILLY SUE'S RIB (f. by Al Hattab). 8 wins in 10 starts at 2 and 3, 1983, $151,128, Ruffian H.-L, Governor's Lady H.-L, Silent Beauty S., Peach Queen S., Forget Me Not S., Gold Digger S.

J ──────── Vaccinated for influenza.

K ──────── **Engagements: Breeders' Cup Series.**
 ──────── Foaled in Kentucky.
L ──────── Jockey Club Parentage Qualification.

M

someone who is acting as agent for the real owners. In the case of yearling sales which are conducted by Fasig-Tipton Company, you can usually find out who the true owner is by looking up who bred the yearling, which is listed in a breeders' index at the front of the catalog. At the Keeneland sales, in many cases you can figure out who the real owner is because the line will read, "Consigned by Veryimportant Farm, Agent for John Littleguy," or words to that effect. If it just says "Veryimportant Farm, Agent," though, you'll have to dig for the owner. Another innovation from Fasig-Tipton is that it is now dividing its sales index into a consignors' index and an agents' index.

B) Hip Number. This is an identification number assigned to every horse in a sale. It is cleverly named Hip Number, because it is pasted on the horse's hip before the horse is sold. The only thing you really need to know about Hip Numbers is that they are assigned in the order that the horses are to be sold, and that is determined alphabetically according to first dams at yearling sales (the letter of the alphabet is chosen by lot for each sale to prevent anyone from gaining any perceived advantage of position).

C) Barn Number. The barn is where the horse is stabled on the sales ground. The only comment, here, is that you can save yourself some time and effort by organizing the horses in which you're interested according to barn number when you get to the sales.

D) Summary/Blurb. This just highlights what is on the rest of the page and is relatively useless. As a matter of fact, many sales companies have abandoned it completely as it takes up space for more important information.

E) Foaling Date. This, believe it or not, is very important in yearling sales. Since young horses grow at a phenomenal rate (up to 3½ pounds a day in certain phases of growth), a few weeks—and especially a couple of months—can make a great deal of difference in the size and maturity of yearlings at the sales. You can't expect a May foal to be as big as a January or February foal, and this must be taken into account when you're looking at yearlings.

F) Schematic Pedigree. This is just a normal three-cross pedigree of the horse who is being sold, and it shows, in addition to much of the information that's carried further down the page, how the sire is bred. An important thing to note here is the age of the mare at the time the yearling was born. Also, we find it's a good place to make notes on the pedigree, such as the sire's yearling average, what the mare's previous foals have brought, etc.

G) Sire Summary/Blurb. This merely highlights the stallion's race record (if he's a young stallion) and record at stud (if he's older). This will be discussed in further detail later in this section.

H) First Dam. This is undoubtedly the most important part of the pedigree. It, like the stallion summary, highlights the mare's race record and production record. It will also be discussed in further detail later in this section.

I) **Second Dam.** The second dam is, obviously, less important than the first dam, and the summary is usually shorter—at least it should be. All yearling pedigrees have at least something about the second dam. A "decent" pedigree on a yearling will have something about the third dam, too; while some show the fourth dam and, on rare occasion, a pedigree will be forced to go all the way to the fifth dam. If you have to get to the fourth and fifth dams to fill up the catalog page, though, it's not much of a pedigree.

J) **Health/Inoculation Record.** While this is stuck down at the bottom of the page, it is very important in terms of transportation and herd health at the farm where your purchase may be headed. Occasional influenza outbreaks, for example, have been devastating at race tracks around the country, so most tracks won't allow a horse on the grounds without an influenza vaccination. Also, if your yearling hasn't been vaccinated, you really don't want him to be put in with a lot of others that have been. Health requirements differ from state to state and from farm to farm. You should probably ask the consignor, after you've made a purchase, if there are any vaccinations, tests, and/or health records he can give you with respect to your purchase.

K) **Engagements.** This is also very important, because it lists the stakes and futurities to which a yearling has been nominated. Today, it also tells you whether or not the horse is nominated for the lucrative Breeders' Cup Series. This is very important, because most of the events listed here will require you, as the new owner, to make the subsequent nomination payments or your horse will be dropped from eligibility to the stakes. If that happens and the horse turns out as well as you hope, you might find yourself making a substantial supplementary payment at the time of the race. Also, with the Breeders' Cup Series, there's an optional series payment, so you should find out if the horse is paid in full, or just partially paid. At some sales, the notation will be made whether the yearling is "Fully nominated to the Breeders' Cup," which means he is all paid up, or "Provisionally nominated," which means there are more payments to be made by the purchaser. Again, you can find out these things from the consignor after the sale.

L) **State Where Foaled.** This is important because of the many lucrative state breeding programs that offer more than $8-million a year in purse supplements and owners' awards for state-bred horses (see Chapter 9). This is usually stated in terms of state of foaling, or, in many cases, it is stated in terms of eligibility for a specific program.

M) **Parentage Qualification.** In 1978, The Jockey Club began a program of blood-typing foals to make sure there was no mixup in their parentage. If this notation appears on a pedigree, it means that the foal has been blood-typed, along with its parents, and The Jockey Club certifies that it is by the stallion which appears on the page and is out of the dam who appears on the page. It's an excellent program. The blood type of every stallion standing at stud is on file, as is the blood type of almost all broodmares now in production (a few old mares might have been exempted—or "grand-fathered"—at the time the program was started, but now all mares must be blood-typed before their first foals can be registered). At present, foals are blood-typed (cross matched against the blood types of their parents) only for parentage verification at the request of the breeder. It costs $75, foal only, and you'll normally see parentage verification only on the more expensive yearlings. You can, if you wish, request parentage verification on a yearling you purchase.

The Stallion Summary

The stallion summary is very important, of course, because it tells you a little bit about the sire of the horse you intend to purchase. While it will tell you some things you need to know, it won't tell you a lot of things you need to know. For instance, does he get sound horses (indicated by high percentages of runners from foals, a high number of average years raced, and/or a high number of average starts per year)? Are his foals of high quality (indicated by percentage of stakes horses and superior runners, or by average earnings per start), or are they too slow to break down? Are they good commercial prospects (indicated by average yearling price and research into his sons and daughters who have entered the breeding ranks)?

While we're on the subject, it should be noted that the sires of horses at a breeding stock sale are just as important as they are at a yearling sale, because statistics show that, while there is a definite sex bias among stallions (i.e. some sires are better producers of fillies than colts, and vice versa), in general good sires make good broodmare sires.

The sire you pick also depends, like everything else you do, on what your goals are. If you intend to race, you'll take one tack or, if you intend to breed, you'll take another. For example, if you're looking to race on a moderate scale, you want a horse with a high percentage of starters and a high percentage of winners, with moderate average earnings per runner and average per start.

The business has, of late, become something of a slave to fashion, which leaves a lot of good sires producing excellent runners which produce horses that can be bought at moderate prices.

You can learn such matters by going to your friendly computer and pulling up some sales and stallion performance reports, but you can also get some help from *The Thoroughbred Record* and *The Blood-Horse,* which publish stallion supplements prior to many of the major sales to update you on the recent race track and sales performance of the stallions featured in the sales.

Incidentally, at breeding stock sales, there will be similar stallion summaries at the bottom of the page to tell you about the sire to whom the mare was bred, if she's in foal. It will probably be a little more brief than the summary of the sire of the horse which is being sold, though. The other major difference you'll find is that the sire summary of a mare selling in a breeding stock sale will often mention stakes winners produced by his daughters. However, the same basic rules apply in both cases.

Here are some examples of good and bad stallion summaries, along with reasons why they are good or bad.

By NORTHERN DANCER (1961). Canadian horse of the year. Leading sire 5 times in England and U. S., sire of more than 100 stakes winners, 19 champions, including Nijinsky II (European horse of the year), The Minstrel (horse of the year in England, Epsom Derby-**G1**, etc.), El Gran Senor (to 3, 1984, General Accident Two Thousand Guineas S.-**G1**, etc.), Try My Best (in England and Ireland), Northernette ($404,914, Top Flight H.-**G1**, etc.), Giboulee ($358,578), Fanfreluche ($238,688), Shareef Dancer.

This is not a summary of a good stallion; it is one of the best in the world. Northern Dancer is the sire of more than 100 stakes winners, 19 of them champions, and a few are mentioned there. What it does not say, but you'll quickly learn, is that Northern Dancer is the most commercially successful stallion in the world. His yearlings have *averaged* more than $3-million in 1984 and they *averaged* over $1.75-million in 1983; of 115 yearlings who have brought prices in excess of $1-million to date, 59 were sired by Northern Dancer or by his sons Nijinsky II, The Minstrel, Lyphard, and Nureyev. The first yearling ever to bring more than $3-million was by Northern Dancer; the first yearling ever to bring more than $4-million was by his son Nijinsky II; the first two yearling fillies to bring more than $2-million were by Northern Dancer; and the only yearling to bring more than $10-million was a son of Northern Dancer, as was the only other one to go over $8-million. Also, the world-record price for a syndicated stallion, $40-million, was reported for Shareef Dancer, a son of Northern Dancer.

For most people, the problem is being able to afford one. However, if you're in the breeding business and you can afford to pay a stud fee of $800,000 or more, with no guarantee (on a 23-year-old horse), we can safely say that any Northern Dancer yearling with at least three legs is going to get into a select sale somewhere, and if the other leg is not on backwards he'll bring a pretty good price.

By MR. PROSPECTOR (1970). Stakes winner. Among the leading sires, sire of more than 40 stakes winners, including It's in the Air (champion 2-year-old filly, $892,339, Vanity H.-**G1** twice, etc.), Conquistador Cielo (horse of the year, champion 3-year-old colt, $474,328, Belmont S.-**G1**, etc.), Gold Beauty (champion sprinter, to 4, 1983, $251,901), Fast Gold (to 5, 1984, $547,532, Paterson H.-**G2**, etc.), Fappiano (10 wins, $370,-213, Metropolitan H.-**G1**, etc.), Gold Stage (5 wins, $292,917).

Here is a summary of another pretty fair sire. Mr. Prospector not only sports the credentials mentioned in the summary, but he is from an excellent sire line, the Raise a Native line, which has also produced the likes of leading sire Exclusive Native, the excellent young sire Alydar, Triple Crown winner and Horse of the Year Affirmed, and a number of other good ones. If you get a printout on Mr. Prospector, you'll discover that he has a fairly high percentage of starters, an excellent percentage of winners, average earnings per start of $3,256, which is also good, and 27% of his runners turn out to be stakes winners. He is also the sire of Conquistador Cielo, who was syndicated in 1982 for $36.4-million, so he can hit a home run if you happen to get lucky. Best of all, despite a number of high-priced yearlings, his yearling average is about $292,000.

Then, there is the other side of the coin.

By JUNGLE SAVAGE (1966). Stakes winner of $113,925. Half-brother to stakes winners Belle Noire, Warlance. Sire of 10 stakes winners, including Angel Savage (MEX) (horse of the year, champion 2-year-old filly in Mexico, Clasico Anahuac-**G1**, etc.; $81,131, in U. S., 2nd La Brea S.-**G3**, etc.), Amadevil (33 wins, $653,534, Count Fleet H., etc.), Palm Hut (5 wins, $157,518, Spinaway S.-**G1**, etc.), Chief Tamanaco (9 wins, $109,680, Bold Ruler H.-ntr, etc.), Sparkling Savage ($94,068, Denville S., etc.).

This was a pretty good racehorse and he's fairly well bred, but if you look at a printout on him you'll see in ten foal crops to race, he's had only one really decent runner—Palm Hut, who won two graded stakes in New York—and only 5% stakes winners from starters. Angel Savage (Mex) was Horse of the Year in Mexico, it's true, but, at the risk of offending our friends south of the border, that doesn't mean much, and she was several cuts below the top when she was brought up to the U.S. While Amadevil earned a lot of money and did, indeed, win three stakes in New York, it took him seven years and 33 wins, including 20 stakes (most of them in the $20,000 range in Nebraska), to reach his earnings of $653,534. Basically, Jungle Savage gets a lot of runners, but they're just hard-knocking old horses, and this is going to be a difficult place to hit a lick.

By JUST PLAIN TUFF (1970). Stakes winner of 17 races, 3 to 7, $125,053, Western Reserve S., Rubber City H. twice, Premier H., 2nd Forest City H., Autumn H., Rubber City H., Warrensville Heights H., 3rd Summit Silver Cup H. twice, Decathlon H., Buckeye H. Sire of winners Dust Angel (6 wins to 5, 1984, $61,807, 2nd Red Rose H., 3rd First Lady H.-L), Just Plain Kristy (12 wins, $49,661), Jim's Game (11 wins to 6, 1984, $28,749), Just as Tuff (to 6, 1984, $14,631), U Bolt (4 wins, $14,502), etc.

This horse was well named, but little else. He had to be tough, because it took him seven years to earn $125,000, racing on the Ohio circuit. His four stakes wins were all for $20,000 or less at Thistledown, and, at this writing, he's had only 30 registered foals in five crops to race. Only 57% of his foals ever reach the race track, and 53% of those win a race. He has no superior runners, and doesn't appear likely to have any. However, the same thing could have been said for Ole Bob Bowers before he sired John Henry, but you really shouldn't go against the percentages (Ole Bob Bowers still has only four superior runners).

Here are some things to look for in a sire summary:

• If a stallion is old enough to have several crops racing, the sire summary shouldn't have to mention his family in order to fill out the necessary lineage. He should be making it on his own, not because he's a son of a good sire or a half brother to a stakes winner.

• By the same token, if he's producing at stud, the summary shouldn't have to go into great detail about his race record, denoting that he was third in some minor stakes somewhere. That indicates that the person writing the sire summary is having trouble filling up the space, rather than cutting the performances to fit. The same applies to his offspring.

The Fasig-Tipton sales are taking a step toward making the sire summaries a little more comprehensible, in some cases, by including the number of crops a horse has sired, along with the number of foals, winners, stakes winners, and total earnings of the stallion's offspring. This enables the buyer to get a little better line on what's happening without going to the computer, but they're not doing it in all catalogs yet.

Mare Summaries

Just as on the top side of the pedigree there are certain things you should seek and others you should avoid, the same is true for the distaff side.

Since a mare produces one foal a year as opposed to 40 or 50 for a stallion, you should expect the mare summary to be more explicit, especially in the first and second dam, than a successful sire summary would be. Once again, remember this is an advertisement. If a mare is a consistent producer, the summary line will say, "Dam of 11 foals, all winners, including—" and then go on to list performances on the best of them. If the mare is the dam of 11 foals and two winners, her summary line will probably say, "Dam of—" or "Dam of two winners—." Also, if a horse is mentioned as a stakes winner and/or shows a lot of wins, and there's no mention of earnings, you can just about bet that the victories were in very cheap races.

There are several definitions which should be repeated here. The two most commonly misunderstood words on the pedigree page are "sire" and "producer." For the record, it should be noted that a horse is not a "sire" in a pedigree until one of his offspring has won a race—he can sire 2,866 horses that hit the race track and, if none of them ever wins a race, he will not be listed as a "sire" in a catalog. The same thing goes for "producer." A mare is not a producer until one of her offspring wins a race.

There are other things to remember about the distaff side of a pedigree, whether you're buying a yearling filly or a broodmare.

The first dam that appears on the pedigree page will be the second dam of any offspring you eventually sell, and the second dam will be the third dam, etc. As a consequence, any black type beyond the first dam will be virtually meaningless to buyers insofar as anything you sell out of her.

When you look at a pedigree of a filly or a broodmare, check on her female relatives and the stallions to whom they've been bred. If the filly or mare you're looking at has several sisters or half sisters who look like good potential broodmares themselves and they have been bred to good stallions, there is a very good likelihood that your mare's pedigree may improve through no effort of her own. It doesn't have to be a female half sibling, though. An extreme example might be the case of the Mr. Washington filly, Looigloo, whose first dam looked like this when she was sold as a yearling in 1979 for $25,000 at the Fasig-Tipton Kentucky Summer Sale.

1st dam
ONCE DOUBLE, by Double Jay. 2 wins at 3. Dam of 3 foals to race—
JOHN HENRY (c. by Ole Bob Bowers). 9 wins at 2 and 3, 1978, $172,899,
Round Table H.-G III, Lafayette Futurity, Chocolatetown. H., 2nd
Lexington H.-G II, Hill Prince H., 3rd Volante H.-G III, etc.
Double Mix (c. by *Ambiorix). 11 wins, 2 to 6, 1978, $29,258.
Ein Dust (f. by Dust Commander). Winner at 3, $5,743.

Several years later, her pedigree looked like this when she went through the
1983 Arkansas Breeders Mixed Sale, selling in foal to Secretariat.

1st dam
ONCE DOUBLE, by Double Jay. 2 wins at 3. Half-sister to **Istria, Once Irish.**
Dam of 8 foals, 7 to race, 6 winners, including—
JOHN HENRY (g. by Ole Bob Bowers). 32 wins, 2 to 8, 1983, $3,706,297,
horse of the year, champion grass horse twice, champion handicap
horse, world's leading money winner, Jockey Club Gold Cup-G1, Santa
Anita H.-G1 twice, Oak Tree Invitational H.-G1 three times, Hollywood
Invitational H.-G1 twice, San Juan Capistrano Invitational H.-G1, San
Luis Rey S.-G1 twice, Hialeah Turf Cup H.-G2, etc.
LOOIGLOO (f. by Mr. Washington). Stakes winner, see below.
Double Dial (f. by Tom Tulle). 5 wins at 3 and 4, $73,710, 2nd Old South S.,
3rd Delicada S.
Double Mix (c. by *Ambiorix). 12 wins, 2 to 7, $30,518.

The second time around, she brought $700,000!

If you're looking for colts, this doesn't matter quite as much because, to be
honest, if your colt can't run he's not going to bring much as a sire prospect, no
matter what his family does.

Here's another example of a good dam on a pedigree page.

1st dam
NOSEY NAN, by Nantallah. Unraced. Sister to **GEORGE SPELVIN.** This is her
11th foal. Her tenth foal is a 2-year-old of 1984. Dam of 6 winners—
REGAL RUMOR (f. by Damascus). 17 wins, 2 to 5, $266,321, Marion H.
Van Berg Memorial H., Pink Platinum H., Florence R. H., Gala Fete
H., Four Winds H., Mill Race H., Thelma S., Pan Zareta H., etc.
TABLE THE RUMOR (f. by Round Table). 11 wins, 2 to 5, $259,534, Gold-
en Harvest H., Fair Grounds Oaks, Fleur de Lis H., Furl Sail H.,
2nd Sooner H., Fair Grounds Oaks Prep, 3rd La Canada S.-G1, etc.
NO CABEZA (f. by Executioner). 3 wins, $48,025, Children's Hospital S.
Other winners: Start a Rumor (f. by Nijinsky II), at 3, 1983, $21,040;
Sarawilha (f. by Sir Ivor), $15,240; Delisle (c. by Round Table).

While this mare was unraced and she has some age on her—a couple of
minuses—you'll note that she has a very high number of fillies who were sired by
good sires, and a number of them could run (as a matter of fact, 77% of the runners in the family had a Standard Starts Index in the area of 2.0 or better—see
Chapter 10). Further investigation shows that, in addition to the five fillies shown
in the summary, there are three more (in addition to the one which was being
sold) in the family, and they must be in pretty good hands because those that are
old enough to be in the breeding ranks have been bred to some pretty good sires

While this is a pretty good family already, it still stands an excellent chance of moving up further, whether the filly being sold makes it as a runner or not. Here's a slightly different situation:

1st dam

QUEEN SAN, by Middle Brother. 3 wins at 3. Dam of 5 foals to race, 4 winners—
FIRST MARTINI (c. by Three Martinis). 8 wins, 2 to 4, $36,262. Techefuncta H.
Idiot Savant (f. by Circle). Winner at 2, placed at 3, 1984, 2nd A. M. Fisher S.
Middle Prince (g. by *Ridere II). Winner at 4 and 5, $11,871.
Magic Emperor (c. by Circle). Winner at 3, 4 and 5, $10,313.

While this looks pretty good at first blush, the computer shows that all this mare's winners are pretty cheap horses (even the stakes winner, First Martini, has SSI of less than 1.0), there are not many fillies going for the family, and none of them are sired by horses that would make anyone sit up and take notice.

```
                                           Hill Prince 47
                    Middle Brother 56      Alablue 45
Queen San, B, F 68                         Roman 37
                    Social Side 47         Tyche 28
```

```
Race Record
   3 Wins At 3   $3,984

Produce Record
  74 Middle Prince, Dkbbr, C, By *Ridere 2nd. 2 Wins At 4-5 $11,871 (.29):61
  76 Woodgrain, B, F, By *Bric-Brac. Unraced
  77 Original Copy, B, F, By Copy Chief. Unraced
  81 Bud's Joy, Dkbbr, F, By Wichita Oil. Unpl 2-3 $1,195 (.07):15
  78 Magic Emperor, Dkbbr, C, By Circle. 3 Wins At 3-5 $10,383 (.5):25
  79 First Martini, Dkbbr, G, By Three Martinis. 9 Wins At 2-5 $39,135 (.8):46
       1st  Techefuncha H. (Jnd)
  81 Idiot Savant, B, F, By Circle. 1 Wins At 2 $11,254 (.9):12
       2nd  A. M. Fisher S. (Elp)
  82 Queen O' Shine, B, F, By Pumpkin Moonshine. Unpl 2 $350 (.05):6
```

Here's another deceptive example:

1st dam

ROLLABOUT, by *My Babu. Winner in 1 start at 2. Dam of 5 winners, incl.—
LADY FACE (f. by Proud Clarion). 8 wins, 2 to 5, 1983, $163,548, Selene S., 2nd Cosmah S., Old South S., 3rd Canadian S., Duchess S., Ontario Colleen H., Portage S.
Gallant Sword (c. by *Gallant Man). 11 wins, $29,966.
Sable Princess (f. by Cornish Prince). 2 wins at 3, $25,468. Producer.

The printout shows that Rollabout is, indeed, "Dam of 5 winners," but it also shows that it was five winners from 11 foals, and even Lady Face, the stakes winner, was a step or two below a top horse.

```
Produce Record For Rollabout
  68 Rolling, B, F, By Fleet Nasrullah. 1 Wins At 2 $2,559 (.88):7
  72 Rolling Swaps, Dkbbr, C, By Swaps. 9 Wins At 3-10 $25,574 (.46):45
  73 Fleet Swaps, Ch, C, By Swaps. 1 Wins At 3 $4,650 (.8):9
  74 Flag Lily, B, F, By Raise A Native. Unraced
     78 Buzzy's Brew, B, C, By Princely Native. 2 Wins At 3 $11,208 (1.45):8
     79 Nearly A Native, B, F, By Sadair. 1 Wins At 3 $2,825 (.25):12
  75 Go To Judson, Gr, C, By Decidedly. 7 Wins At 2-7 $90,134 (1.34):84
  76 Kenwood Lady, B, F, By *Taj Rossi. 1 Wins At 2 $3,837 (.36):15
       Sent To Venezuela
  79 Savage Roll, Dkbbr, C, By Jungle Savage. 1 Wins At 4 $1,210 (.36):4
  81 Rollin List, Ch, C, By List. Pl 2 $364 (.08):4
  82 Roll On By, Ch, F, By Lot O' Gold. Unraced
```

(Continued)

```
69 Graustabout, Ch, C, By Graustark. Unpl 4 $135 (.04):8
70 Happy Roller, B, C, By Fleet Nasrullah. Unraced
72 Lovely Action, Ch, F, By Vitriolic. Unraced
   75 Dancing About, Ch, F, By Dancing Count. Pl 2 $468 (.18):4
   81 Teasabout, Ch, F, By Lord Treasurer. Pl 3 $2,383 (.3):8
   82 Dancing Secretary, Ch, F, By Alligator Reef. Unraced
78 Vader, B, C, By Sevastopol. 2 Wins At 3-4 $15,741 (.89):21
73 Gallant Sword, Ch, C, By *Gallant Man. 11 Wins At 5-9 $29,966 (.84):55
74 Sable Princess, Blk, F, By Cornish Prince. 2 Wins At 3 $25,468 (1.32):33
   80 Of Royalty, Ch, G, By Khyber King. 5 Wins At 3-4 $23,512 (.78):33
   81 Tartesh, Ro, C, By Khyber King. 1 Wins At 3 $12,691 (.89):14
75 Rural Miss, F, By Chieftain. Unraced
76 Saiko Hour, B, F, By Bold Hour. Pl 3 $2,270 (.44):7
   81 Rather Fly, Ch, F, By Sail To Rome. 3 Wins At 2-3 $20,487 (1.56):13
   82 Tovax, Ch, C, By Laomedonte. Unraced
78 Lady Face, Dkbbr, F, By Proud Clarion. 8 Wins At 2-5 $163,548 (2.87):62
      1st  Selene S. (Gr 3c) (Wo), 2nd  Cosmah S. (Lad), 2nd  Old South S.
      (Lad) (2 Div), 3rd  Duchess S. (Wo), 3rd  Canadian S. (Gr 3c) (Wo),
      3rd  Ontario Colleen H. (Gr 3c) (Wo) (2 Div), 3rd  Portage S. (Lad)
      (1 Div)
80 Rolling Prince, B, C, By Cornish Prince. 1 Wins At 3 $13,492 (.48):29
82 Cartographer, Ch, F, By Dactylographer. Unraced
```

As mentioned, in most instances, the better the horse in the pedigree, the mor specific the catalog page is going to be about it. If the catalog writer is no specific, find out what the specifics are.

Race and Produce Records

When you get to a breeding stock sale, the family of the horses you intend t buy becomes less important, while their own performance on the race track an their production record becomes more important. Once again, it simply takes little research to determine what is behind the scenes in the catalog.

It's important in a mare's race record, for example, to find out the quality o races she won, as well as the quality of the races her offspring are winning.

Here's the racing and produce record of a well-bred, stakes-winning mare wh sold in the 1983 Keeneland November sale:

RACE RECORD: At 2, two wins (Breeze-a-Lea S.) in 3 starts; at 3, four wins (Eastern Wings of Man S.), twice 2nd, twice 3rd (Lilac S.); at 4, one win in 2 starts. Totals: 7 wins, twice 2nd, twice 3rd. Earned $30,940.
PRODUCE RECORD:
1975 Peterloo, c. by *Le Fabuleux. 2 wins at 4, $12,561.
1976 Crimson Imp, f. by Crimson Satan. Unplaced.
1977 Fabulous Risk, c. by *Le Fabuleux. Placed at 4.
1978, 1979, 1980, 1981 no report.
1982 c. by Clem Pac; 1983 f. by Guillaume Tell.
Bred to Huguenot (*Forli--Captain's Mate), last service April 29, 1983.
(Believed to be in foal). Vaccinated for virus abortion.

If you were to go to the *Daily Racing Form Chart Books* (now published onl in microfiche form), you'd find that the Breeze-a-Lea Stakes was a $5,000 rac (small potatoes, even in 1972), which was run at River Downs, and the Easter Wings of Man Stakes was a $3,000 race (actually, it was the second division of race initially carded as $5,000 added), run at Florida Downs, the precursor o Tampa Bay Downs, where the competition is hardly top-notch.

Also, you'll note, this mare had trouble getting in foal from 1978-'81 We can tell you one thing for certain, in the thoroughbred business 99 44/100%

)f the time, "no report" means no foal. Furthermore, a little more investigation
vould have shown that Clem Pac was being used in 1981, at Spendthrift Farm, in
ı pasture breeding program with some mares who were considered absolutely
ıopeless. After Clem Pac and Mother Nature (who is better at this sort of thing
han any horseman, stallion manager, broodmare manager, and/or veterinarian
vho ever lived) got this mare back on schedule, she was bred twice again, the last
ime to Huguenot, who was as cold as Antarctica at the time, and put in the sales.

At the age of 13, with four blank years (six, really, if you count the unplaced
Crimson Imp and the Clem Pac foal), being sold by a top farm, you've got to
now this mare had absolutely no chance of being worth anything; as a matter of
act, the buyer should have been paid to take the mare.

Here's another beautifully bred stakes winner, this one a pretty legitimate
acemare, who had been bred to two top horses and was in foal to a third, being
old by a major farm:

Hip No.		Barns
438	**MASHTEEN**	**9 & 10**

Stakes winner of 5 races in 9 starts at 2 and 3, $81,985, Comely S.-
G3, etc. Half-sister to winners MARSHUA'S DANCER ($78,464, Royal
Poinciana H., etc.), Call Me Goddess ($23,938, stakes-placed), etc.
Out of MARSHUA (6 wins, $317,599, C.C.A. Oaks, Selima S., etc.).

Chestnut mare; foaled 1975

RACE RECORD: At 2, two wins in 4 starts; at 3, three wins (Comely S.-**G3**,
La Centinela S.), once 3rd (Santa Susana S.-**G2**) in 5 starts. Earned
$81,985.
PRODUCE RECORD: 1980 f. by *Vaguely Noble; 1981 f. by Caro (IRE).
Bred to Raja Baba (Bold Ruler--Missy Baba), last service February 24, 1981.
(Believed to be in foal). Vaccinated for virus abortion.

Why? Normally a young broodmare of that quality would be a pearl beyond
)rice. Undoubtedly she was being sold at the height of her value (she brought
)1-million), because her foals to that point had been nothing really special and
he consignor probably felt she wasn't going to improve.

There's another point to remember with respect to produce records—while the
awsuits previously mentioned are causing sales companies to attempt to account
or every year in a mare's production life, it has not prevented them from trying
ɔ hide open years as much as possible:

Produce Record: 1976 barren; 1977, 1980 no report.
1978 Miss Avum, f. by Grannys Boy. Winner at 3, $4,800.
1979 King Avie, c. by Jean-Pierre. Winner at 3, $5,953.
1981 Lady Avie, f. by Jean-Pierre. Unraced.
1982 **Royal Harmony**, c. by Majestic Prince. Placed at 2 in England, 2nd
Acomb S.
1983 c. by State Dinner; 1984 barren.
Bred May 21, 1984 and **BELIEVED IN FOAL** to—
EXCELLER (*Vaguely Noble—Too Bald)

While there are three nonproductive years listed right up where they'll be most apparent, there's another, 1984, placed in logical order, but it is also placed where it's least likely to attract the eye. This mare is well bred and, in fact, is in foal to a fashionable sire, but, if you count the filly who couldn't make it to the races, she's been a total blank 55% of the time. If you count her first two foals who weren't much better than blanks, she's been unsuccessful 77% of the time.

There's one other thing that ought to raise suspicion. After all these years, she's been bred to a stallion who is a lot more fashionable than anything to whom she's been bred before. That should be a possible warning sign that the owners are thinking of overbreeding her a little in anticipation of sales.

Now here's a produce record which shows some potential—a young mare who gets in foal on a regular basis, who has already produced a good horse in The Wedding Guest, and who is in foal to a fairly attractive sire:

Produce Record:
1980 Cordial Entente, f. by Hold Your Peace. Winner at 3 and 4, 1984, $20,720.
1981 **THE WEDDING GUEST**, c. by Hold Your Peace. 4 wins at 3, 1984, $163,066, Swift S-**G3**, 2nd Bay Shore S.-**G3**, 3rd Jim Beam S.-**G3**.
1982 Ms. Shecky, f. by Shecky Greene. Has not started.
1983 f. by Plum Bold; 1984 c. by Fappiano.
Bred April 7, 1984 and **BELIEVED IN FOAL** to—
VALDEZ (Exclusive Native—*Sally Stark), stakes winner of 8 races, $519,971, Swaps S.-G1, San Pasqual H.-G2, etc. His first foals are 2-year-olds of 1984. Sire of 29 foals, 3 starters, including Exclusive Dy (2 wins in 2 starts, $13,800).

Why is this mare being sold? She's being sold because the outfit which owned her was in the process of going belly up. Oddly enough, it was the same outfit on which we cited the strange risk factor under public companies in Chapter 8.

Another produce record which showed some potential when the mare was sold was this one:

Barn		**Hip No.**
457	**PRICELESS FAME**	**20**

Winner of 2 races at 3, $9,700. Dam of 2 foals of racing age, both winners, including DUNBEATH (in England, William Hill Futurity S.-G1, Royal Lodge S.-G2, etc.). Sister to BOLD FORBES ($546,536, in U. S. and Puerto Rico, champion at 3 in U. S., Kentucky Derby-G1, etc.).

Dark bay or brown mare; foaled 1975

PRODUCE RECORD:
1980 **DUNBEATH**, c. by *Grey Dawn II. 4 wins in 8 starts at 2, placed at 3, 1983, in England, William Hill Futurity S.-**G1**, Royal Lodge S.-**G2**, 2nd Heathorn. S., 3rd St. James's Palace S.-**G2**, Mecca-Dante S.-**G2**.
1981 Khwlah, f. by Best Turn. Winner in 1 start at 2, 1983, in England.
1982 c. by Alydar; 1983 foal died.
Bred to Alydar (Raise a Native—Sweet Tooth), last service May 18, 1983. (Believed to be in foal). Vaccinated for virus abortion.

This mare brought a potful of money ($3.2-million) when she was sold, because she was young, a proven producer, had a foal on the ground by a lot better sire han the ones to which she had been bred previously, and was carrying a foal by he same sire. She was a bargain even at that price, though.

A year later, after being bred to Seattle Slew, she was put back in the Fasig-'ipton Kentucky November Sale, and her produce record looked like this:

Produce Record:
1980 **DUNBEATH**, c. by *Grey Dawn II. 4 wins at 2 in England, William Hill Futurity-**G1**, Royal Lodge S.-**G2**, 2nd Heathorn S., 3rd Mecca Dante S.-**G2**, St. James's Palace S.-**G2**; placed at 4, 1984, $37,125 in U. S., 2nd El Monte S.-L.
1981 **Khwlah**, f. by Best Turn. Winner at 2 in England; placed at 3, 1984 in Germany and Italy, 2nd Premio Legnano-**G2**, Preis der Stadt Baden-Baden.
1982 **SARATOGA SIX**, c. by Alydar. 4 wins in 4 starts at 2, 1984, $304,940, Del Mar Futurity-**G1**, Hollywood Juvenile Championship-**G2**, Balboa S.-**G3**.
1983 f. by Majestic Light (died); 1984 f. by Alydar.
Bred May 26, 1984 and **BELIEVED IN FOAL** to—
SEATTLE SLEW (Bold Reasoning—My Charmer), horse of the year. Sire of 3 crops, 105 foals, 45 starters, 9 stakes winners, 27 winners, $5,303,516, including Slew O' Gold ($1,268,134, champion), Swale ($1,583,660), Slewpy ($710,248), Landaluce.

Priceless Fame sold for a world-record $6-million at this sale.

Priceless Fame probably ranks as the best illustration we can name of another)oint we'd like to make very strongly in this chapter. The arrival on the scene of

Priceless Fame lived up to her name when she brought a final bid of $6-million at the 1984 Fasig-Tipton Kentucky November Sale. She had been purchased at auction the previous year for $3.2-million.

the multi-million-dollar horse at public auction, combined with the large discrepancy between prices of horses sold at those auctions, has created a situation, today, where *average prices at sales where there are multi-million-dollar horses selling are virtually meaningless.* For example, when Priceless Fame sold at the preferred session of the Fasig-Tipton November Sale, the sales summary showed that 113 horses had been sold for $11,686,400 and the average, which many people regard as an indicator of the health of the industry, was $103,419. However, if you subtract the bid on Priceless Fame, the sales results would show 112 horses selling for $5,686,400, an average of $50,771, less than half the reported average. Another, less extreme, example is the effect that the $10.2-million colt had on the 1983 Keeneland July Sale. With that yearling counted in, the sales results looked like this: 301 horses sold for gross receipts of $150,950,000, an average of $501,495 (an increase of 48.5% over the previous year). Without the $10.2-million colt, the results would have been 300 horses sold for a total of $140,750,000, an average of $469,167 ($32,328 less than the average with him and an increase of 38.9% over the previous year). *We feel, today, that medians are a much more accurate indicator of industry health than averages,* and medians are not reflecting the growth indicated by averages. For instance, from 1980 to 1983, the average price of yearlings rose 40%, from $29,683 to $41,258. During the same period, the median price for all yearlings sold *declined* 15%, from $10,000 in 1980 to $8,500 in 1983.

The whole point of this section is that there are bargains to be had throughout the market—even at $3.2-million—but *be suspicious.* Find out why a mare is being sold; you don't want to buy a cull, *ever,* much less start out with one!

On the Grounds

Well, you've spent two weeks doing your homework and, as a result, you've been able to pare your sales prospects down from 1,500 in the catalog to perhaps 200 which interest you and are likely to fall in your price range. It is now four days prior to the sale, so you and your trainer or advisor pack your bags and head for the sale.

Most sales companies require the horses to be on the grounds for two to three days before they are to be sold, and the earlier you get there the better, because you're going to have to do a lot of footwork before the sale even begins. There's another reason to get to the sales early and that is the fewer horses you have to look at in a day the better off you are. When you start looking at 150 or 200 horses a day, it doesn't matter who you are, they all begin to look the same.

Conformation is almost as important at a breeding stock sale as it is at a yearling sale or a two-year-old sale. While broodmares, like people, tend to get out of condition with advancing age, you can still tell a lot about their basic conformation, especially the forelegs, which are the most important part of a horse because that's where they break down most often. And, you can take our word for it, conformational defects are inheritable. As a matter of fact, it seems, today, that it's a lot harder to breed a correct horse than it is to breed an incorrect one.

The next section is going to be on conformation, so all you need to bear in mind is that most of the statements with respect to yearlings and racehorses also apply to breeding stock in one way or another and that, secondly, we're only going to discuss some of the basic principles of conformation, because it's something that can't be learned from a book.

Conformation

The study of conformation is, more than anything else, an exercise in compromise. There are good-looking horses in this world, and there are *great*-looking horses in this world, but there are no perfect horses in this world.

If you go into the paddock before the Kentucky Derby or the Budweiser Million or any one of the races in the Breeders' Cup Series, you're going to see all kinds of horses. You'll see big horses and little ones, you'll see correct horses and incorrect ones, you'll see horses who'll knock your eyes out, and you'll see horses who'll make you scratch your head, trying to figure out how anyone ever paid $2 for them.

There is one indefinable difference between bad horses and good horses, and between good horses and great horses. That is courage, desire, and will to win. At the race track they call it "heart" and it's what makes some horses run well, in spite of injuries and bad conformation, while others who are physically superior won't do it. There's no way to measure that at the sales.

You can get an indication, though. Horses at the sales are in an unusual situation, a strange environment for them, and the way they react can be an indication of their mental outlook. Are they nervous and fractious? Are they curious about their surroundings, or dull and listless (possibly indicating that they've been tranquilized)? The way a horse reacts to the hustle and bustle of the sale may be an indication of the way he'll react to the life and competition of the race track.

When you look at conformation, what you're doing is hedging your bet, reducing your risk. Every conformational defect is a warning sign that a horse is likely to injure himself in a certain way. Evolutionarily speaking, the horse is running on the equivalent of the second finger, so when you consider that a thousand-pound animal who runs six furlongs in 1:10 is traveling at a speed of 38.56 miles an hour on its finger, you begin to wonder how any of them ever stay sound,

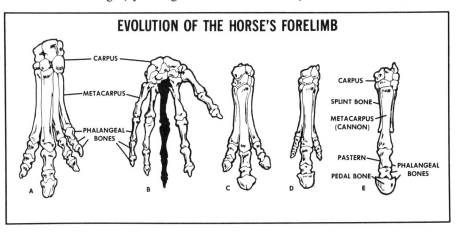

EVOLUTION OF THE HORSE'S FORELIMB

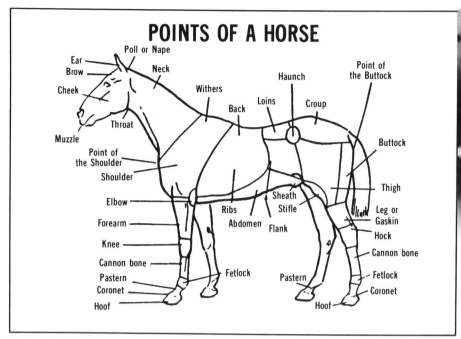

POINTS OF A HORSE

Poll or Nape
Ear
Brow
Neck
Haunch
Point of the Buttock
Cheek
Withers
Loins
Croup
Back
Throat
Muzzle
Buttock
Point of the Shoulder
Shoulder
Thigh
Elbow
Sheath
Forearm
Ribs
Stifle
Leg or Gaskin
Abdomen
Flank
Hock
Knee
Cannon bone
Cannon bone
Fetlock
Pastern
Pastern
Fetlock
Coronet
Coronet
Hoof
Hoof

rather than why they go lame. In fact, Dr. George Pratt has measured the force on a horse's cannon bone as its hoof hits the ground at approximately 9,000 pounds.

Every horseman has his "pet peeve," a defect that he finds particularly offensive. These are normally based on his personal experience, the defects with which he's had the worst time. On the other hand, he'll be inclined to overlook some faults which good horses he's had have been able to overcome.

For every conformational fault a horse has, it must compensate in some way, and often the compensation is as much a cause of lameness as the defect itself.

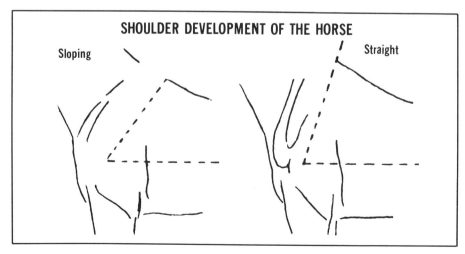

SHOULDER DEVELOPMENT OF THE HORSE

Sloping
Straight

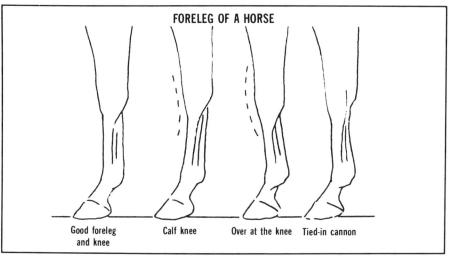

FORELEG OF A HORSE

Good foreleg and knee   Calf knee   Over at the knee   Tied-in cannon

That logically brings us to the most important quality of good conformation, the indefinable "balance." It's difficult to describe, and horsemen normally say, "The horse should be pleasing to the eye," which means very little to the layman. What he is trying to describe is that the horse should be in good proportion—the rear end shouldn't be too big for the front end, or vice versa; the head and neck should fit well with the rest of the horse. Most horsemen look at balance first, so when you see a horseman examining a horse he usually starts from a little distance away to see if the animal "looks like a racehorse." If he does not appear to be balanced overall, it will be difficult for him to produce an easy, ground-covering, coordinated stride.

Although a horse doesn't run with his head, an intelligent head with a good eye is an indication of good temperament, and the size of the head in proportion to the neck and body is important, too, because a horse does use his head for balance when he's running.

Look at his front legs. Look at the way they're set, the slope of the shoulder, the slope of the pastern. In looking at the front legs we like to see a well-

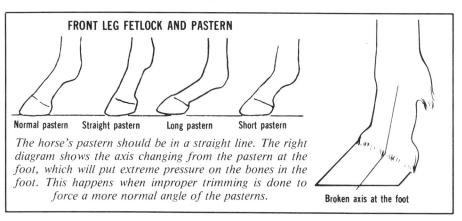

FRONT LEG FETLOCK AND PASTERN

Normal pastern   Straight pastern   Long pastern   Short pastern

The horse's pastern should be in a straight line. The right diagram shows the axis changing from the pastern at the foot, which will put extreme pressure on the bones in the foot. This happens when improper trimming is done to force a more normal angle of the pasterns.

Broken axis at the foot

developed and strong forearm. From the elbow to the knee, we like to see a smooth line that is neither "over" nor "back." A strong, medium-length cannon bone, a smooth fetlock, a medium-length pastern with a good angle to it, and a sound, well-made foot are also desirable. This all sounds simple but, of course, it's not.

A normal pastern, for instance, has about a 45-degree angle and medium length. Any deviation from this causes strain, or a lack of action in the fetlock, because the pastern is a very important part of the horse's shock-absorbing mechanism. The straight pastern passes the shock directly up the leg and the horse will be likely to suffer knee problems, whereas the long, low pastern does the opposite—it overstrains the tendons by letting the entire leg drop down in each stride.

Being over at the knee is unsightly but tends to be less of a problem than being calf-kneed. However, like many propositions in the horse business, it is often overdone in that many trainers will accept horses over at the knee, whereas they will absolutely reject horses that are back at the knee. A tied-in cannon is an indication that the tendons draw closer to the cannon at the knee than they do at the

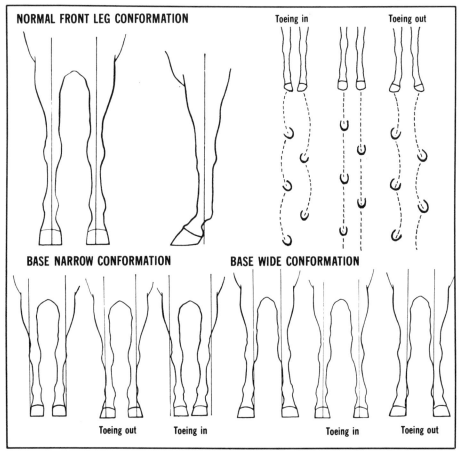

NORMAL FRONT LEG CONFORMATION   Toeing in   Toeing out

BASE NARROW CONFORMATION   BASE WIDE CONFORMATION

Toeing out   Toeing in   Toeing in   Toeing out

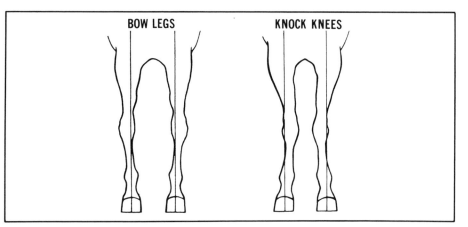

fetlock. This indicates a weakness and a fault at the point where the tendon joins the knee and can be an indication of future unsoundness.

While still looking at the horse from the side, you want to judge the strength of his withers, the length of his back, the overall relationship of his top line to his bottom line, the depth of his chest (which houses his heart and lungs), the strength of his gaskin.

Then go to the back legs. In judging the back legs from the side, we are looking for the set of the hocks, whether or not they are set straight underneath the tail.

Back leg conformation is more important to a horse than some trainers think—after all, this is the pushing power. A long, muscled gaskin with a well-set hock is extremely important, and the hock should appear directly in line with the back of the rump when the leg is set in a vertical manner. Sickle hocked horses, in particular, lose some of their motion because they cannot push out far enough in full stride. A curby hock may be a sign of excess strain being placed on the hock and could ultimately lead to trouble.

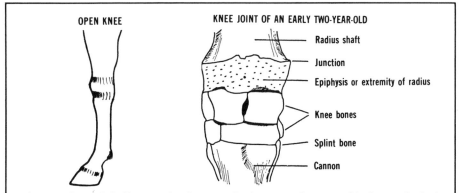

An open knee, left diagram, is often seen in the young horse, and is due to the lack of development. This will normally smooth out as the horse gets older. Observing the multi-bone structure of the knee of a two-year-old, right diagram, illustrates the importance of allowing him to mature before asking for any strenuous effort.

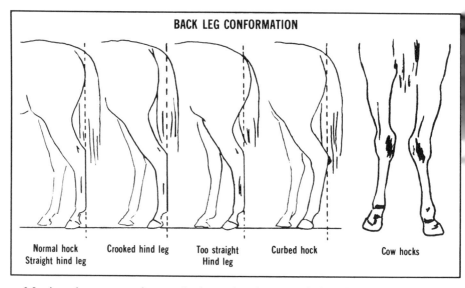

BACK LEG CONFORMATION

Normal hock
Straight hind leg

Crooked hind leg

Too straight
Hind leg

Curbed hock

Cow hocks

Moving closer, you observe the horse head-on, again looking at his general appearance, and the attractiveness and intelligence of his eyes and head. More importantly, you should look at the musculature of his chest and the way his front legs come out of his chest. A horse's legs should be well separated at the chest, and go straight to the ground. A plumb line dropped from the elbow to the ground should pass directly through the center line of the knee. Offset knees are just what they imply. They are offset from the plumb line which extends from the elbow to the ground. Horses can also be knock-kneed or bowlegged, which present serious problems because of the strain on the tendons and joints. Or they can be base narrow, which means that the legs start out wide, and he stands closer together at his feet than the legs start out at the elbows; or there is the opposite—base wide.

In the foot area, just as in humans, horses can be splayfooted, which means that he points out like a duck; or pigeon-toed, which means that his toes point toward each other. These are very common faults in horses, and may affect their walk. In addition, look for such things as splints (bony growths just below the knee), and ringbone in the ankle area.

Then, continue your trip around the horse, observing the other side, the off side, looking for blemishes which might be apparent from that side only. And then go to the rear of the horse, looking for curbs, which are bony enlargements in the hock, or thoroughpins, which are fluid involvements in the hock.

Next, ask the handler to walk the horse off while you stand directly behind. Observe the horse's manner of traveling as he walks away and the way he handles himself when the handler turns him to walk back. Look for any indication of incoordination, particularly in the back legs. Then observe him walking directly toward you for any toeing in or toeing out. Try to figure out whether this comes from the knee or from the fetlock. Also observe if he has a nice, long stride, which will be indicated by whether or not he places his back legs in front of where his front legs had been set down. This is called "overstepping" and it is considered very desirable as an indicator of future power.

One point which many observers tend to overlook is the feet. Without the feet there is no horse, and it is important that the feet be well made, sound, and free from severe corrective shoeing, which may have been done immediately before the sale. A badly formed foot is a fairly sure sign that there has been some lameness, or some fault in conformation, which may have been overlooked.

Never purchase a horse without first inspecting it.

Once again, you must remember that conformation is a process of compromise, and is a very subjective thing. You'll learn to like a certain type of horse, just as everyone else does. Just don't like that type to the exclusion of everything else.

Now, you and your advisor have spent two days looking at the horses in the sale (if it's a breeding stock sale, you might have traveled to some of the local farms to see what some of the foals of the mares look like); you've eliminated some horses outright for uncompromisable conformation defects, and you've adjusted some of your original estimates, either upward or down, to account for their physical appearance.

If you're smart and if you've had a little extra time, you also might have looked at a few horses which you considered to be just slightly above your head. Sales have a rhythm, a cyclical aspect, of their own, with soft spots and spots where everything seems to go out of sight. If something you formerly considered over your head happens to come in during a soft spot, you might be able to get it at a price you can afford.

In the Sales Arena

You and your advisor go in and find a couple of seats, or you take your assigned seats if it's that kind of sale. As you look around, everything is geared toward creating excitement, toward eliciting one more bid. There are bars every ten feet around many sales arenas, maybe to loosen up the buyers. Also, if you'll notice when you go into the arena, it's generally fairly chilly; they don't want anyone sleeping in there.

Some people recommend that you tell the bid spotters in your area what horses you'll be bidding on so that he'll be alert to your subtle signals—you don't want other buyers or, more especially a consignor, to know you're after a particular horse, so you try to conceal your bids as much as possible. We don't necessarily believe you need to tell the bid spotter what horses you want to bid on, just introduce yourself, tell him you'll be active, and he'll be sure to keep you in the corner of his eye, if he's any good. On that subject, most bid spotters are there for a reason—they're alert and they're sharp—and we feel, if you want to bid, you don't need to introduce yourself or anything else, just establish eye contact with him, then signal him and he'll take your bid.

Listen to the rhythm of the sale. Note in your mind the minimum jump in bids. Listen to the auctioneer and the bids he's asking. If he's got a horse at $5,000 and is asking for $6,000, you nod and the horse goes up to $6,000, or you can hold up five fingers and the bid will be $5,500. If he's got a horse for $1-million and you hold up five fingers, that's probably going to be interpreted as $1.5-million.

Also, there's one further admonition: don't be shy about correcting the bid spotter and/or the auctioneer. If the auctioneer has a horse, for instance at $20,000, asking for $25,000, and you hold up one finger meaning $21,000, but he jumps you to $25,000, you can tell the bid spotter you meant only $21,000; you can buy a lot of pride, not to mention hay and oats, for $4,000.

With three fingers up, the bid spotter here is asking for a bid of $2,300,000, as the board already registers $2,200,000.

The sales move very quickly—from 25 to 35 horses per hour at most sales—so there are bound to be occasional mix-ups. If the auctioneer knocks down a horse to someone else and you thought it was your bid, as happens sometimes, your bid spotter may be able to get him to reopen the bidding, but it'll be between only you and the other bidder; no new bidders are allowed to come in at that point. A clue to whether or not the final bid is yours is that the auctioneer always says the figure as he's about to bang the gavel. You can raise your eyebrows at the bid spotter and point to yourself, to ask if it's your bid.

Another thing which may sound stupid, but it's not—don't bid against yourself! In addition to the bid spotters, the auctioneer and the announcer often spot bids, and sometimes territories of two bid spotters may overlap so, believe it or not, a number of people have become excited and wound up bidding against themselves. The best way to avoid that, in our opinion, is to pick one bid spotter and stick with him. Further, you have to be careful to keep from being "run up" by a consignor or his shill. This is perfectly legal, according to the rules of sale, and some consignors are very good at it.

A final admonition with respect to bidding. Don't *ever* bid on a horse in the ring, if you haven't examined it previously, no matter how cheaply it seems to be going. If you think you're the only smart person in the arena, you're mistaken and there's undoubtedly a reason why the horse isn't going for what you think it's worth. The lighting in the ring is all overhead, which can make Woody Allen look like Mr. America, and it also can conceal many blemishes on the legs of a horse. If you get the impulse to bid on a horse in the ring, go out and have another drink. You'll thank us for it more often than not.

After you've purchased your horse, a member of the sales company staff will bring around an Acknowledgement of Purchase form for you to fill out. Be sure to check the Hip Number and the price before you sign it (at least one sales company has adopted the policy of taking pictures of buyers as they sign the Acknowledgement of Purchase). If you have any questions about the purchase, it's better to ask them at that time than later. Also, it is important to remember, if you haven't already established credit with the sales company, that *all purchasers are required to settle up for purchases within 30 minutes of the end of the session in which they purchase horses.* It's just another reason to take our advice about establishing credit early.

After the Sales

As we mentioned earlier, title will not pass until your check has cleared, but the sales company will give you a stable release form, which you can use to send your purchase to the farm of your choice.

If you haven't already arranged for insurance, do it now! There are all kinds of insurance agents hanging around the sales, in case you don't have your own. If you do have an insurance company with which you normally deal, call them and let them know what you've purchased, as soon as possible.

See if you can find the consignor at this point, and find out if there's any other special information you need to know about the horse, vaccinations, stakes not mentioned on the pedigree page, feeding programs, etc. This can save you a lot of time, and possibly money, later on.

Then go to the representatives of the van companies who are present at every sale and arrange for your horse to be shipped to the farm you've chosen to gentle your yearlings or to board your broodmare. If you're from out of state, it might be necessary—or at least cheaper—for you to find an intermediate place, locally, to board your purchases until the transportation company has a full load ready to go to your area. Most of the reputable van companies will be able to help you make these arrangements, if you have no local connections.

Finally, *let the farm know the horse is coming!* You would not believe how many times a horse van simply shows up at a farm to unload a horse without anyone at the farm knowing who the horse belongs to, or that the horse was even coming. This does not augur well for the future of your horse—or you—in the horse business.

Now, you are through at the sales and you can go back to the hotel, take a shower, and have dinner . . . or, go find a church and start to pray.

Chapter 5

On The Farm

The drama and thrills that are thoroughbred racing don't just happen. Those 12 prancing two-year-olds on their way to the post for the first time are the product of a multibillion-dollar industry, a huge agricultural enterprise that extends from Florida to Oregon, from New York to Southern California, and in most civilized countries of the world.

Not too long ago, a lady who had just made her first thoroughbred investment—purchasing an interest in three well-bred yearlings in a partnership—dropped by Clear Creek Stud in Louisiana to get the first look at her new investments. She was thrilled by their beauty, but amazed at the complexity of the operation of the farm and the breaking process. "My goodness," she exclaimed, "I had no idea so much was involved!" Neither do most racegoers, never really giving much thought to what must transpire before a race between 12 well-trained athletes can take place.

Horses, like people, come from varying backgrounds. Each one arrives at the track from different circumstances and methods of being raised. Many will be homebreds, racing for their breeders, having previously spent their first couple of years on one farm, from foaling through breaking, until readied to go to the track. On the other hand, since nearly 25% of all yearlings are offered at public auction, many of them will be racing for their second owners, while still others may have changed hands two or three times. Some will have been purchased privately. Some will have been broken by loving hands at "Mom and Pop" operations, while others will have been schooled at large training centers by professionals. Regardless of which background they come from, the major portion of each youngster's life took place amidst the beauty and serenity of a farm. And what takes place on the farm is what this chapter is about.

Breeding as an Investment

Over the years, the standard progression for newcomers entering the thoroughbred business was to start out as a racing fan and bettor. As the fascination of racing grew, many fans who could afford it bought a racehorse or two, either by claiming or privately. First thing he knew, a filly he owned broke down and, bingo—the race fan/owner found himself with a broodmare prospect. Not everyone followed this path, but a great many of today's breeders got where they are today that way. That was, in fact, the exact scenario on how actor Jack Klugman became a breeder. The cheap claiming mare he and John Dominguez owned who broke down was named The End All, and she eventually produced for the partners Jaklin Klugman, a graded stakes winner of $478,878, who finished third in the 1980 Kentucky Derby.

One of the most significant changes in the thoroughbred business in recent years is the number of newcomers that have become involved in the sport strictly from the standpoint of a business investment rather than as an outgrowth of being a racing fan. Several factors in the late 1970s established and encouraged this trend. First, while the costs of owning a racehorse rose, coupled with the inherently greater risks, purses failed to keep pace with the escalating cost of bloodstock and of training. Secondly, during a high inflationary period, there was an explosion in value of breeding stock. From 1978 to 1984, the record auction price of a broodmare went from $1-million to $6-million. The world-record syndication price on a stallion went from $14.4-million to $40-million. Top racehorses became so valuable as stallion and/or broodmare prospects that their owners could not afford to keep them on the race track. It made no economic sense to race a colt for a year to earn $1-million in purses, when it costs that much to keep him in training, and when he could be earning his owners $8-million to $10-million in the breeding shed. (And, if you don't see how it can cost $1-million to keep a horse in training for a year, consider this: if the horse is worth $10-million as a stud prospect, the insurance alone on that horse will run you around $750,000. Then add shipping, security, 10% of purse money to the trainer and the rider, stakes payments, and tips to everybody from the groom to the parking attendant when he wins, and you're probably actually losing money when your horse wins "only" $1-million a year.) Anyway, it was this explosion that attracted new investors in droves.

Breeding has been considered the safer segment of the thoroughbred business until the last couple of years, and still is by many. The laws of economics, which the thoroughbred business had seemed to ignore for many years, are at last exerting themselves to some extent in the business, and breeders, today, are forced to rely on the "home run" to break even or make money just like owners at the race track.

At the Farm

When you drive out to a well-managed thoroughbred farm on a sunny autumn afternoon, you are overwhelmed by its beauty and tranquility. The mares are fat and sleek as they graze peacefully in lush green pastures. Their foals romp about the pastures, pictures of health. The grass is mowed and the fences painted. The barns are neat and clean. Everything is beautiful and serene. It all looks so natural, but it takes a well-oiled, hard-working organization seven days a week, 52 weeks a year, to make it look that way. There are no holidays for horses—no Christmases, New Year's Eves, Sundays. Horses eat every day and need care every day. Contrary to what a lot of people may think, horse farming is not seasonal—the only thing that changes is which phase of the operation is paramount at the time, and this is determined by the season.

To familiarize you with the basics, we thought we'd run through the farm operation over the course of a year. No matter where we start, some of what happens is the result of what has gone on before, so we'll just start with January 1.

The Year Begins

This is a good place to start since it is the universal birthday of all thoroughbreds. No matter when he was born, even December 31, he becomes a year older on January 1. The January 1 birthday is a carryover from the early days of development of the thoroughbred in England. Since the racing season was over in late fall and did not resume until spring, the logical time to change the age of all horses was during the lull in racing. The changes in racing over the past 40 years have made this date less logical and convenient. Year-round racing in the United States (racing is still seasonal in Europe except for some minor race meetings in Southern Europe) has made January 1 merely an arbitrary day for change of age.

The primary problem with January 1 being the standard date for change of age is that it is out of tune with nature. A mare is a seasonal animal; she has her best heat cycles from April until August, so that the resulting foal after a 342-day gestation will be born in the spring or early summer, when the weather is right. Many mares actually go anestrous (do not come in heat) for a varying length of time during the winter months. However, because many people feel that an early foaling date is essential to the precocity of youngsters (this is not statistically based, however), this puts pressure on the breeders to have early foals, which, in turn, puts pressure on the breeding farms to develop methods which encourage early conception in the broodmare band. All of which goes against the laws of nature.

Colonel Phil Chinn, whom we have discussed earlier, was fond of saying that his biggest Christmas present came on New Year's Day, when he went to the tobacco barn (tobacco barns in many cases in Kentucky are used as a combination tobacco and horse barns) on the back of the farm and saw all of the big, good-looking foals that had been born the night before.

This story always brought giggles and nervous laughter—the obvious implica
tion being that the Colonel had foals born before the first of January. There is no
question that he is not the only breeder who has had foals born before the first of
January, either by design or by accident (a gestation period that is three weeks
short is unusual, but not rare). The truth of the matter, though, is that most
mares are difficult to get in foal in early and midwinter because it is not nature's
time.

Artificial Lighting

Modern science and research has proven a mare can be fooled into thinking it is
spring, thus ovulating earlier, by using artificial lighting. Original research in
chickens and more recent research in horses has established that the animal's conception of the time of year is a direct response to photoperiod—the length of the
day. For years, chickens have been kept under lights 24 hours a day to encourage
growth and egg production. Most well-managed commercial farms today put
their barren mares and their stallions "under lights" around December 1. Some
farms bring the mares into a stall, while other farms keep them in small pens
under strong uniform lighting. The hours vary but it is not uncommon to extend
the length of the day to 16 hours. It will usually give the farm a three- to four-
week jump on the normal spring cycle of the mare. This doesn't guarantee conception, but it does give the farm and the farm veterinarian a longer time to work
on getting her in foal. Similarly, a stallion's sperm is seasonal and the use of lights
with stallions produces similar results.

Fertility

On an annual basis, the number of foals registered with The Jockey Club
represents just over 50% of the mares reported bred the previous year. This is
staggering when you consider that good commercial farms need to maintain a
75% to 80% live foal rate in order to survive economically. This means that some
breeders are getting very few of their mares in foal. Horses, incidentally, have the
lowest reproduction rate of all domestic animals.

At least part of the fertility problem can be attributed to the unnatural breeding
season, although part of it can also be attributed to the previously mentioned ex
plosion in bloodstock values. The increase in values made it economically feasible
to keep mares in production that had extremely poor production records. Now
that yearling prices have at least temporarily reversed themselves, many breeders
will have to take a harder look at mares with poor production records and problems that require expensive veterinary treatment.

The standard breeding season used to extend from February 15 to June 15, 15
or 20 years ago. The February 15 opening date is established both by weather and
to avoid having December foals. With the use of artificial lights in recent years,
some breeding centers open a week or ten days earlier. June 15 was the practical
closing date because most breeders felt that if a mare was not in foal by that time,
her yearling with a resulting late foaling date would not sell well. Again, because

f the explosion in bloodstock prices, breeders in recent years have felt that a late oal from an expensive mare was better than no foal at all, and the breeding eason was extended to June 30. In some cases it has even been extended to July 5.

With the normal gestation being 342 days, it is difficult for a mare to produce a oal each year. Breeding a mare back on the foal heat period, called by many the ine-day period, has many advocates and detractors. At any rate, it brings the umber of days from conception to first possible breeding date to about 351. If or any reason the foal heat is not used for breeding, the next normal heat period s at 372 days, so even assuming that everything goes right each year—that the nare does not carry longer than the normal 342 days, she cycles promptly, and onceives the first time she is rebred—the foaling date gets a little later each year. 'ertainly things don't go right every year since we are not dealing with machines, nd, if the mare does not conceive on her first cover, she will foal as much as a 10onth or more later the next year. The use of prostoglandins to induce heat in 1ares in recent years has helped with the problem.

When all is said and done, the majority of thoroughbred foals are born be-ween April 15 and May 15, meaning that their dams conceived between early /lay and early June. The best heat period produced by mares (best meaning the 10st predictable, the shortest, the most obvious in terms of interest by the mare, nd the most breedable follicle) normally comes at that time of year, which is the atural time of year. By the time a horse is a three-year-old, if there was any ad-antage of a two- or three-month earlier foaling date, it has evaporated. Working /ith nature can be a lot more productive than working against nature.

Foaling Time

In the fall of the year, after weaning, mares are rechecked for their pregnancy status and normally divided into groups according to their anticipated foaling date. Every commercial farm has a foaling barn with a foaling crew that can range from one experienced night watchman on most farms to a four- or five-man crew in larger operations. The foaling barn will consist of one or more extra large stalls for the natural foaling process and a setup for emergency procedures, which may include medications, oxygen, heated stalls, etc.

Normally around the first of December, as the foaling date for the first group of mares approaches, these mares are moved to an area near the foaling barn. Each mare is checked to ensure her Caslick sutures have been removed. She will be properly opened when necessary just prior to foaling. (A Caslick suture is an operation named after its inventor in which a mare's vulva is sewn, either on the race track or after breeding, in order to prevent "wind sucking"—drawing air, along with attendant debris, into the vagina—which could cause infection and abortion.) The reasons for the Caslick operation are twofold. First, in breeding horses for speed, they have developed a rear end (anus and vulva) which is slanted forward more than was evident in the first thoroughbreds, and the placement of the anus above the vulva in this condition has tended to cause uterine infections.

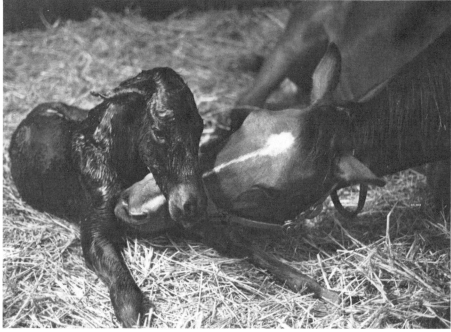

The foaling season brings some of the greatest joys, and work load.

Secondly, as a mare becomes older and has more foals, her anus tends to sink forward and her vulva loses its muscular tone, allowing wind sucking. A Caslick suture is required on most older mares, regardless of their original conformation.

Some farms have their mares foal outside, particularly those located in the southern climates. There are strong arguments in favor of foaling outside—this is where the mares would naturally foal and there tends to be less of a concentration of disease in open areas. Obviously in states like Kentucky, foaling outside during the winter months would not be a good idea.

We cannot emphasize enough that an experienced night watchman or night crew can easily be the difference between life and death of the foal and the mare in cases where difficult delivery occurs. In cases of abnormal presentation of a foal, many mares panic and will actually push their insides out trying to get rid of the pain of an abnormal presentation. Every farm has a veterinarian on call, but the time it takes a veterinarian to get to the foaling barn can be critical, and an experienced foaling crew can well make the difference between life and death for the mare and the foal.

Once the foal is born, he gets an enema and perhaps a tetanus and combiotic shot. Many farms are now using a new test to check his immunization system, too. The foal is up and nursing in a couple of hours—but the first three days are critical. Prenatal infections that may have been dormant can show themselves at this time, and the trauma of coming into the world will expose malfunctions or malformations of limbs and organs, plus any latent weakness which may be present.

After foaling the mare is resutured and is ready to be teased in preparation for being bred again.

Teasing

Teasing is the method used for determining when a mare is in heat (receptive to a stallion). Teasing is one of the most time-consuming and vital functions carried out at any breeding farm. Teasing can be done in many ways—in the open field or in the confinement of a stall—but it must be done thoroughly by a competent, experienced, interested member of the farm's staff, a person who takes pride in getting mares in foal.

Unlike humans, horses will normally accept mating only on or about the time conception is possible. Rather than expose the valuable stallion to the frustrations and the danger of determining which mares are ready, a "teaser" is used. This teaser can be a male horse, a male Shetland pony, a gelding full of male hormones, or it can be a stallion whose lack of popularity has made him available for other duties. In any case, the job is very frustrating for the teaser, because he is normally equipped with a shield or some other device to prevent him from breeding a mare by accident. As a matter of routine, 75% of the mares he teases are going to be anestrous and therefore eligible to kick him, bite him, or attack him in any way possible. A good teaser is worth his weight in gold. Many farms tease on an every-other-day schedule, which, when coupled with veterinary assistance, is normally adequate. There are exceptions, especially during the height of the breeding season when some farms opt for a daily teasing schedule, all season long.

Record keeping is the name of the game, just like it is in any other business. As the breeding season progresses mares will develop a pattern of behavior. This pattern, coupled with the teasing person's experience and observation, will be the overriding determinant in decisions on when to breed a mare. Although each mare is different, each one has traits and patterns of behavior that are peculiar to her and are relatively constant. Mares have a tendency to retain the same patterns year in and year out, so that old teasing charts from previous years can be an invaluable tool.

Booking Mares

The term "book" in the thoroughbred business applies to all the mares the stallion is contracted to serve during an individual breeding season. You will hear the phrase a stallion having a full book. Since most syndicates are made up of 40 shares, a full book usually means about 45 mares, but some farms, which believe in getting as many mares as possible to a stallion, will book 70 or 80 mares if they have a fertile, aggressive stallion. In the case of standardbreds and quarter horses, where the use of artificial insemination is allowed, a book may consist of 250 or 300 mares. A stallion referred to as having "a high-quality book" means that the mares that are contracted to be bred to him are of high quality in terms of pedigree and race record.

The stallion manager is responsible for filling the stallion's book. Depending upon the popularity of the stallion, the farm where he is located, and the stud fee, booking may consist of an extremely tight selection of mares in terms of quality, or the stallion manager having to go out and hustle as many mares as he can.

Syndicated stallions have an obvious advantage because the shareholders are inclined to use their seasons. This is particularly true if the outside demand is insufficient to allow them to sell their season or if the stallion is doing well. In either case, the syndicate manager starts out with a reasonable number of mares in the stallion's book, which makes the filling of the book much less difficult. Stallions standing as the property of a single owner are sometimes more demanding of a stallion manager since he has to find a great number of people to submit mares.

After having studied the various stallion registers, either from your home state or nationwide, if you have a mare of sufficient quality, you will select the stallion you want for your mare and then have to sign a contract, which is pretty much standard.

The stringency of a stallion contract in terms of payment is usually determined by the popularity of the stallion, i.e. how much abuse the mare owner is willing to endure to get to him. If he is very, very popular, such as Northern Dancer and Seattle Slew, you might be required to pay the entire stud fee "up front" with no guarantee (while the term "no guarantee" is freely used in the marketplace, it generally means there's no guarantee that your mare will get in foal, but it does carry the guarantee that the stallion will be breeding sound when your mare is ready to be bred. However, the emergence of some exchanges, such as the Matchmaker Breeders' Exchange, is changing that definition to be *exactly* what it says . . . you're not even guaranteed the stallion will be alive when your mare is due to be bred. Read the contract!). If the stallion is pretty popular, but not outrageously so, the stud fee might be due on a 50-50 basis, meaning that half the stud fee is due up front on a no-guarantee (the traditional kind) basis and the second half is due on a live foal basis. Still other stud fees are "live foal" fees but are due September 1 of the year the mare is bred. This is merely a method of the stallion manager or share owner using your money for six months. With the changing market these practices may not be as prevalent in the future as they have been in the past. For most stallions the fee is due when the foal stands and nurses.

In any case, in our opinion, you should never sign a contract without some percentage of live foal guarantee. There are just too many things that can go wrong and, unless you are breeding at the very top of the market and have a lot of money to spend, there can be no justification for a no-guarantee contract. You wouldn't pay for a car and not expect to get it, so there is no use to pay for a foal and not expect to get it.

If you sign a contract to breed to a stallion, honor that contract. It is very difficult for a stallion manager to plan the stallion's breeding season if people don't honor their commitments. There have been instances in recent years where people book a mare to a stallion and then just don't show. Obviously you have no financial commitment, but you certainly have a moral commitment to fulfill your contract, unless your mare is dead, unbreedable, or you have sold her. Should one of these occasions arise, you should notify the stallion manager promptly, just don't "no show," if you are going to stay in the business. (Some stallion contracts today contain a provision that half the stud fee is due, anyway, for "no shows.")

Breeding Your Mare

The term booking a mare is used interchangeably for signing a stallion service contract, discussed above, and for making the appointment when the mare is ready to be covered. Almost all large commercial breeding farms in Kentucky have too many stallions to allow all the mares being served by their stallions to board at their farm. As a matter of fact, the majority of mares bred at large commercial farms in Kentucky are boarded at smaller farms nearby.

When your mare comes in heat, the farm veterinarian will determine the approximate day and time she should be covered through a combination of ovarian

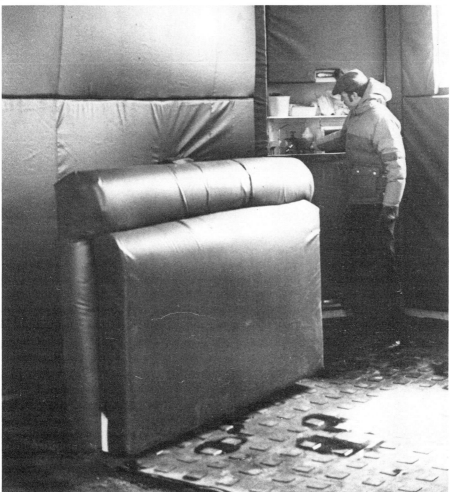

Safety and care in the breeding shed are of the utmost importance, and should be left to the professionals.

palpations and speculum examination. The manager of the farm where your mare is being boarded will call the farm manager where the stallion stands and book your mare to be covered.

Depending upon the popularity of the stallion, how well he is "stopping" his mares (getting them in foal), and the time of year, your mare may or may not get the exact day and time requested. This is a very tricky part of the business, since the optimum time to service a mare is 24 hours before ovulation. While sperm have been known to live several days under optimum conditions, the chances of your mare conceiving when covered more than 48 hours prior to actual ovulation are greatly diminished. On the other hand, if your mare is covered after she ovulates your chances are greatly diminished, also. Since heat periods and follicular development vary widely from mare to mare, you can see that familiarity with your mare and attention to detail are vital, if you are to exceed the national average of 55% live foal rate.

Depending upon the farm where you board, the mare will be either vanned by the farm itself or a local vanning service will be used. The mare will be delivered to the farm where the stallion stands and will be teased once again by the staff at that farm to be sure everything is in order. Her genital area will then be washed and she will be restrained, either with hobbles or a leg strap, to prevent her from kicking the stallion in a moment of fear or excitement. Then, she will be covered (serviced) by the stallion. The term "covered" comes from the fact that the stallion actually covers the top of the mare during service. The actual mating is not an amateur's business and requires a minimum of three, preferably as many as five, experienced people, as the stallion or mare can be seriously injured by an incompetent or careless crew.

The mare's foal, by the way, during this time, stays at the farm, squealing and complaining bitterly that he has been deserted in a dark stall. Believe it or not, by the time the mare is 15 minutes down the road, she has forgotten, at least temporarily, her foal and, except in rare instances, will be much better behaved in visiting the court of her stallion than she would be if the foal was there within hearing distance to remind her of his presence. Leaving the foal behind is much safer for everybody.

Most stallion managers will allow two covers per heat season. The second cover is in instances where the mare was bred early with the first cover, or the follicle did not mature and ovulate as rapidly as the veterinarian anticipated. "Doubles" are normally allowed 48 hours after the original cover but you can get a double only if you are not squeezing out another mare who has not been covered during her current heat period.

Pregnancy

Your mare has been covered and you hope she is in foal—what happens now? The normal cycle of a mare is 18 to 21 days. If your mare didn't conceive on her first cover, she should be back in heat 15 to 18 days after she went out of heat. Assuming she does not come back in heat, you have at least an 80% chance that

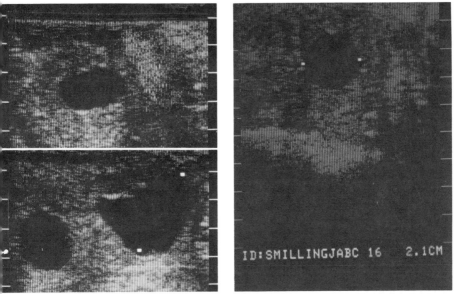

ID:SMILLINGJABC 16   2.1CM

A very unusual Polaroid picture of an ultrasound exam shows a mare with triplets (pictures on left). In the left horn (top) is a single fetus, while in the right horn (bottom) are twins. The picture on the right is a normal, single fetus.

she has conceived. On a speculum examination her cervix will be closed with no color and, on palpation, her ovaries will be inactive.

The introduction of ultrasound in the past two or three years as a method of examining mares for pregnancy at 15 to 22 days after service has some merit, particularly for early detection of pregnancy and immediate detection of twin pregnancies. It is an expensive procedure at this time but many consider it worthwhile—even essential—and many commercial breeding farms have instituted the ultrasound pregnancy exam as a standard operating procedure. Ultrasound consists of going into the mare rectally with a probe, which in turn takes a picture of her uterine horns and actually shows the forming fetus. It is not foolproof, however, and even an ultrasound picture with a single fetus is no guarantee that your mare is going to have a live foal next spring. Assuming that the ultrasound does show a single live fetus, the next step is a manual palpation by your veterinarian to confirm this presence and the "feel" of the uterus to determine both the health and the growth of the fetus. More than 5% of mares that conceive will lose their developing fetus between 30 and 90 days. This is known as early embryonic death, abortion, or resorption, but whatever you call it, it is a real loss and its presence requires continued observation of the mare, even after her original pregnancy announcement. You can't just have your mare shipped home after a 35-day pregnancy examination, turn her out in the field, and feel confident that she is going to foal when she is scheduled to next spring. Even after the breeding season your mare should be checked in September and December to determine her pregnancy status, so should an unpleasant surprise greet you, you have at least a jump on doing something about it for the next year.

Yearling Sale Selection

While all the foaling and breeding is taking place on the farm, the select and open yearling sales are drawing closer. As early as February, nominations are made for the select sales at Keeneland, Saratoga, Fasig-Tipton Kentucky, and Del Mar, and computers begin spitting out pedigrees to selection committees.

Sales are discussed in Chapter 4, from the buyer's point of view, but here we are the breeder hoping our yearling will be chosen for one of the select summer sales and bring a big price. After the computers are finished, the sales committees go to work reading and grading the pedigrees, and then fan out across the country for on-site field inspection. This on-site inspection is done by experts on conformation. During the spring of the year, yearlings are undergoing rapid changes in size, physique, and temperament, which makes judging what they are going to look like four months later an arduous, difficult, tricky procedure. After the physical inspection, the committee makes its final decisions and the breeders are notified. The yearlings that have not been selected will be sold in the fall in the larger, open yearling sales. Those that are going to the select summer sales are pampered and force fed so that they will grow rapidly.

Those that were rejected may be more fortunate because they are allowed to exercise longer, retain their freedom, and grow naturally. They will be picked up and put in stalls a little later, but not on the same arduous, crash program as those destined for the select summer sales. The homebreds are perhaps the most fortunate of all because they are allowed to grow naturally up until breaking time. They may well inherit an advantage later on because of the unrestrained, natural growth (assuming that they receive the same attention, nutrition, and health programs as the select sale yearlings).

While the select summer sales are wonderful, even top breeders do not get more than a small percentage of their yearlings in them. For the rest of us, select yearling sales are a hope and a dream for the future. Marketing is not a dream, though, and spring brings with it a necessary time of realistic reappraisal of your yearling crop and how the individuals have grown and changed over the winter. Some may have not done as well as hoped; others may have done better. Realistic appraisal at this time and selection of the right market for each yearling can well be critical to the price you achieve. Your advisor should play a strong part in what must be an objective decision. It is our feeling that being among the top 25% of any sale is much better than being in the bottom 25%. It's the old adage about it being better to be a big fish in a little pond than vice versa, but it's true.

June Is Fun

As the foaling season winds down, the final phase of the breeding season becomes more hectic. Your mares that "didn't do right" earlier are hopefully producing good, breedable follicles and getting covered—it's better late than never. The mares that foaled in May are being bred back for the first time. June is a desperately busy month on the farm. All the foals are born, and foals, like young children, are likely to get sick, very sick, very quickly. If there is trouble to be found, a way to get hurt, they'll find it. They need a lot of care and attention over and above routine mare management. The mares you're still working with that haven't conceived are the problem mares, which makes teasing more arduous and time consuming. Because all the other farms are having the same problems you are, booking mares to stallions at this time of year is sometimes more difficult than it was earlier in the season. Grass and weeds from spring rains are growing like crazy and trying to get ahead of you. On top of all that, it's time to start sales prep for the yearlings that will be in open yearling sales around Labor Day, and those yearlings in the select summer sales are being given constant attention.

Your herd health program requires a lot more attention now, too—your foals need worming and vaccinations, and all this is time consuming. A good commercial farm has an extensive herd health program, including worming every eight weeks, a variety of vaccinations, and monthly hoof trimming. The introduction of farm management software programs for home computers has made herd health more manageable. There are several programs available that will tell you when to vaccinate, when to worm, when to trim or shoe, along with keeping track of the breeding and billing. Before much longer, farms of any size will be using the computer as a management tool (see Chapter 10).

Yearling Sales Prep

As the breeding season comes to an end, around the first of July, the farm crew's attention is turned more and more toward preparation for the yearling sales. In recent years several innovations have been adopted in preparing yearlings for sales, including swimming, use of treadmills, and ponying yearlings, in place of the more established method of keeping yearlings in the barn during the day and turning them out at night. There are arguments for and against the various methods. Determinants include personal preference, costs, labor intensity, and potential value of the yearlings. Exercise, both treadmill and swimming, does help muscle up yearlings and make them more attractive for sale, but it also costs money.

Sales Day

Finally the big day arrives and your yearlings are shipped off to the sale. This is probably one of the only businesses in the world where your entire marketing effort is concentrated in one or two days a year. Three whole years of work can go down the drain if a yearling gets hurt or sick within a week or two of the sale. Or your profit for the year can be doubled if a close relative to one of your yearlings wins a Grade or Group I stakes just before the sale.

Think about it—the commercial breeder is marketing on one day what essentially is the product of three years of work. In year one, he purchased a broodmare because of her race record, pedigree, and conformation. He selected a stallion which he thought fitted well with his mare. In the second year, if everything went well, she produced a correct, attractive foal and the stallion continued as a successful sire. In the third year, assuming the foal didn't get sick or hurt himself or grow crooked, the breeder has a product to sell which he hopes will provide a satisfactory return on his money. And then, when the time to sell actually comes, he is given perhaps a minute or two to attract bids and attain the right price. Is it any wonder that commercial breeders have ulcers?

Foal Registration

August 31 is a very important date in the year. That is the deadline for registering your newborn suckling with The Jockey Club. The price for registration goes

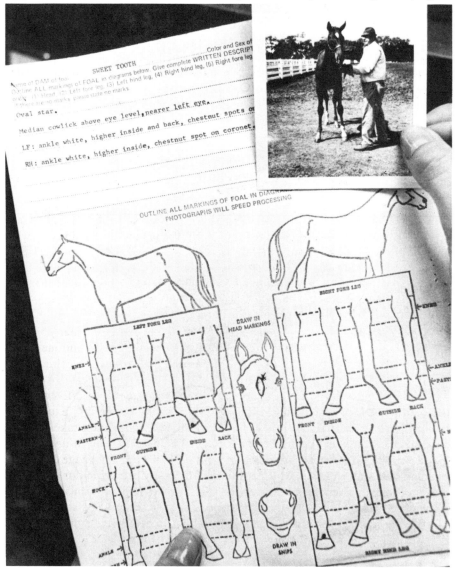

This example of a Jockey Club foal registration form was submitted for a 1975 colt out of Sweet Tooth. The awkward-looking youngster in the photo was later named Alydar.

up steeply after this date. It takes time and effort to complete the forms, so don't wait until the deadline is upon you to do something about it.

Some state breeders' organizations assist you with registration and some even do the job for you—for a fee. Independent operators in Kentucky and other areas specialize in registering foals for a fee. If you do the job yourself, do it meticulously. A properly filled out registration form flows through The Jockey Club relatively smoothly. An improperly filled out form with incorrect or incomplete information goes into a red flag department and may stay there indefinitely while seemingly endless correspondence and phone calls add up to a lot of needless frustration.

Get the proper forms early, fill them out carefully, and get *many clear* photographs. Don't be afraid to take extra close-ups of any unusual markings. The Jockey Club won't turn down your application for too many photographs, only for too few or unclear photographs. Remember that any mare having her first foal must be blood-typed before a foal can be registered. Get the blood typing done *before* she foals. Why? Suppose she dies foaling and you haven't done it—you have a real problem on your hands. If you buy a mare who has already had a foal, finish the paperwork and photographs for ownership transfer before foaling, for the same reason. Save yourself some grief.

Weaning

With fall coming on, your foals are four or five months old and it is time to separate them from their mothers. There are as many varying opinions on when and how to wean foals as there are breeders. Our preference at Clear Creek Stud is to interval wean in the field, after the weather cools off. In Louisiana we avoid the dog days of August and September as much as possible because of the stress on the foal and mare. The farm is large enough to allow us to move mares far enough from their foals that they are out of sight and hearing.

We normally wean starting with mares with the older foals, and mares who are not doing well as a result of the stress of nursing a foal. We pull out one or two mares at a time from a field of ten or 12 mares and foals, right at feeding time in the afternoon. The foals have been creep feeding since they were just two or three days old and most of them don't really notice their mother leaving. Even though they can't find her, they are convinced that she is there somewhere. Except for a few squeals the foals just go on about their business. The mares take it a little harder because they are aware that they have lost their foals, but it doesn't take long before they too accept their fate and settle down. The advantage of interval weaning over stall weaning, which is still used by many people, in our opinion, is that stall weaning is more stressful to the foal. It takes him out of his natural environment and may lead to accident and sickness. If two foals are weaned together, the two foals become attached and have to be weaned from each other at some later date. Many farms still use the "sign" of the zodiac to wean by, but we have never found any scientific basis for this procedure.

Weaning time is as good as any to reappraise your foals who have physical problems. You may want to separate some foals from others because of overeating, aggressiveness, ephysitis (enlargement of the joints), and such, which require dietary control. You may want to sell some of your weanlings early, particularly if they have growing faults. It is almost a sure bet that if they have conformation faults as weanlings the faults will grow worse and not better as they get older. By selling as weanlings you can minimize your expense both in upkeep and sales preparation. Although you can take a weanling to the sales with a rough hair coat and just a little grooming, if you are operating a first-class horse farm you must plan on 60 to 90 days of grooming and sales preparation to get yearlings ready to sell. The decision you have to make is whether or not the yearling value is going to justify this expense.

After weaning, the weanlings require daily attention and handling to keep them gentle and to allow close physical inspection. Some farms separate weanlings by sex at weaning time, while others wait until January or February, but in no case should weanlings of the opposite sex run together much after Christmas. Although puberty is not anticipated in horses until 15 months, there have been cases where it came a lot earlier, and accidents do occur. Even more important, colts do tend to play rougher than fillies.

Naming the Foal

Yearlings must be named by November 1 with The Jockey Club without paying a penalty. Since new owners like to name their own horses, we make a point of not naming any yearlings we plan to sell, either privately or at auction, even if it will be sold at a two-year-old in training sale. In the latter case, the way we avoid The Jockey Club penalty for us or the new owner (what could be more irritating than having to pay a $100 penalty to name your new horse?) is to submit a name already taken. This covers the requirement until the new owner is ready to name his racehorse.

Along about Thanksgiving a pregnancy check is made on all the mares, whether they were originally pronounced barren or in foal. On larger farms the foaling mares are then separated into groups according to their anticipated foaling dates and barren mares are put under lights. By December 1 the barren mares are being teased regularly with those coming in heat being cultured and those who need it being treated for uterine infection. In the meantime, barn repair, fence repair, road repair, and future construction, if any, are proceeding at a rapid clip. Before you know it Christmas arrives—the year is over and it is time to go back to day one and start again.

Board Bills

After you have been in the horse business a year or so you are going to get the feeling that your board bills are high. Twenty dollars a day! How can it possibly cost $20 per day to take care of a mare? Well, we hope the foregoing chapter has helped you to understand why it costs $20 a day. Running a horse farm is not just throwing a little feed over the fence. It is one thing if you have a mare in the back yard and you don't charge for your labor, or the time it takes you to go to the eed store, or your wife getting out and feeding on a cold, rainy morning, or having to arrange for someone to feed your horses when you go out of town.

In spite of all this there is still nobody around should the horse get sick, or injured. This never seems to happen except on Sundays or weekends or the middle of the night. If you think board bills are high, try paying interest on land at 13% on $10,000 per acre. Try nursing a mare colicking all weekend. Try replacing the night watchman who quit on April 3 without notice. Try mucking out all the stalls on the farm when half the farm crew doesn't show up on a Sunday morning.

After you've been in the horse business five years and you are totally devoted and more than adequately financed it is time enough to consider buying a farm. Perhaps by then you will be knowledgeable enough to know that the guy running a horse farm is earning every penny that you are paying him, and more.

Chapter 6

Costs Of Being
In The Horse Business

Unlike an investment in stocks, bonds or commodities, the cost of a thoroughbred investment doesn't end with the purchase price. Costs of care and maintenance can far exceed the original purchase price, particularly with a low-priced horse (many times they're more expensive in the long run). For instance, the cost of keeping a horse in training in New York with a top trainer can easily run as high as $25,000 a year. On the other hand, in some areas of the United States where racing is conducted on a more modest scale, costs can run as low as $8,000 or $10,000 per year. It is obvious, though, that your horse won't get the same care and attention for $8,000 as he would for $25,000, nor will the trainer have the same ability. In keeping with this disparity in costs, the earning opportunities for your horse will be substantially less at the smaller tracks. Training fees can vary widely, even at the same track, depending upon the reputation and success of the particular trainer and the quality of care he gives your horse. In either case, you normally get what you pay for, which reminds us of an old story:

Once there was a man named Smith who owned two broodmares. He wished to have these mares bred to good stallions in Kentucky, so he made a trip to Lexington and went out to Greenbush Farm, which he had heard of for many years and which had an excellent reputation. After finding the manager and discussing a breeding arrangement with him, he inquired as to the price of boarding a broodmare. "The price of boarding here is $18 per day per mare," the manager informed him, "and you get the manure." Now Mr. Smith thought the price was a little high and wondered what in the world he would do with the manure so far from home. He decided to go to another farm in the area just to check prices, and having heard of famous Footloose Farm, he decided to inquire there. The manager at Footloose told him, "The rate for boarding a broodmare is $20 per day and you get the manure." Well, this upset Mr. Smith because the price was even higher than at Greenbush Farm, and Mr. Smith still didn't have any use for the manure.

After long consideration about where to board the broodmares, Mr. Smith came to the conclusion that the manure must have some sort of special value for the board prices to be so high. However, being from a state distant from Kentucky, he really had no use for manure so he thought he'd check one more farm.

While drinking a cup of coffee in a local restaurant, Mr. Smith met a stranger who told him about Rinky Dink Acres, on the edge of the horse farm country. The stranger told him he would find the board rates much better there than at Greenbush or Footloose. He told Mr. Smith he could really save a lot of money by using Rinky Dink Acres, instead of "those fancy places." This appealed very much to Mr. Smith, so he headed out for Rinky Dink Acres. Getting to Rinky Dink wasn't as easy as getting to Greenbush or Footloose. The gravel road leading up to it was full of potholes and there was no sign out front except for the rusty mailbox. When he arrived, he was not as impressed as he had been with the well-kept facilities at Greenbush or Footloose, but then his mares were not used to such lush surroundings anyway. He finally located the manager of Rinky Dink, drinking coffee in one of the barns and inquired as to the board rates for broodmares. "The board rate at Rinky Dink Acres," the manager informed him, "is $12 per day per mare." Naturally this sounded much better to Mr. Smith than the $18 and $20 rates he had been quoted previously. However, the manure mentioned at the other farms stuck in his mind, and Mr. Smith thought perhaps he should inquire as to the ownership of the manure. Upon being queried as to who got the manure, the manager responded, "Mister, at $12 a day, there ain't no manure."

In Chapter 2 on Choosing an Advisor, we suggested spending a few days with your potential trainer, not only to determine your compatibility but to satisfy yourself that his training operation is being run in a way that will provide your horses with the best opportunity to fulfill their potential as athletes. The same thing would be true of the farm where you want to board your mares and foals. A recent article in the *Wall Street Journal*, discussing the pitfalls to be aware of when considering purchase of a retail establishment, suggested that the only way legitimately to determine the establishment's sales was not by looking over the records and ledgers, which could be altered, but rather by spending time standing at the checkout counter watching the operation firsthand—for a minimum of seven days, and preferably 30 days. If you are going to invest money in the horse business (in many cases the amount of the investment far exceeds the $100,000 or

AVERAGE PER DIEM COSTS
OF CARE AND MAINTENANCE
(Costs vary widely from area to area and from farm to farm)

	Kentucky [1]	California [2]	New York [3]	Florida [4]	Louisiana
Turned-out year-round boarders	$ 18	$ 11	$ 15	$ 15	$ 12
Breeding season boarders	$ 20	$ 15	$ 18	$ 17	$ 13
Additional for foal	$ 3	$ 2	$ 3	$ 3	$ 3
Foaling fees (for non-permanent boarders)	$150	$150	$150	$150	$100
Stallions (plus breeding rights)	$ 20	$ 20	$ 20	$ 20	$ 20
Sales preparation (plus 5% commission)	$ 25	$ 17	$ 25	$ 25	$ 18
Breaking yearlings/two-year-olds (per day)	$ 30	$ 26	$ 26	$ 15	$ 26
Training costs (plus 10% for first, second, and third)					
Large tracks	$ 40	$ 45	$ 50	$ 40	$ 35
Small tracks	$ 25	$ 32	$ 28	$ 25	$ 20
Layup costs (for stall care, blister, fire, swim, etc.)	$ 22	$ 20	$ 25	$ 22	$ 22
Private paddock turn-out (for racehorse layups)	$ 17	$ 15	$ 15	$ 15	$ 22
Insurance on breeding stock	3½-5%	3½-5%	3½-5%	3½-5%	3½-5%
Insurance on racing stock	5-8%	5-8%	5-8%	5-8%	5-8%
Vet, medication, and shoeing (breeding stock) (average annually)	$1,000	$ 750	$1,200	$ 700	$ 800
Vet, medication, and shoeing (racing stock) (average annually)	$2,000	$2,000	$4,000	$2,100	$1,500

[1] Courtesy of Thoroughbred Owners and Breeders of Kentucky.
[2] Courtesy of California Thoroughbred Breeders Association.
[3] Courtesy of New York Thoroughbred Breeders, Inc.
[4] Courtesy of Florida Thoroughbred Breeders Association.

so the purchaser of a small retail establishment may spend to buy a business), we urge you to spend the same minimum time and effort to determine that your investment is put in good hands!

Comparative Costs

In an effort to give you some cost guidelines, we have contacted trainers and breeders' associations in New York, Kentucky, Florida, and California for comparative cost information, and have included the costs at Clear Creek Stud in Louisiana (for possible comparison for rates for other smaller breeding states). Keep in mind that the basic board and training costs of care and maintenance do not include any allowances for blacksmith, veterinary, or vanning expenses, and do not include insurance, all of which you can expect to incur. Blacksmith charges can vary from area to area and farm to farm. Normal veterinary costs can vary even more widely, depending on the herd health program at a particular farm, including vaccination, worming, and frequency of pregnancy checks (including use of ultrasound).

In reviewing the table of costs for care and maintenance, there are a number of observations and explanations which may be helpful.

If you start out in the breeding business, your basic costs will be determined by the board rate for turned-out year-round boarders at the farm where you keep your mare. Keep in mind that this is the basic charge for care and maintenance of your mare, and that the rate charged will normally reflect the quality of care and feed your horse gets. Year-round boarders are the most desirable type of boarders for commercial breeding farms, both because they provide steady cash flow, which allows stability of the size of the farm's work force, and because they allow a farm more control of exposure to disease. In addition, a farm crew will be more familiar with an individual mare, and that can help her conception rate and her overall care. Believe it or not, horses are like people—they form a society within their group or herd. There will be a "boss" and a "pecking order," friends and enemies, likes and dislikes. They will establish who gets to eat first, who gets brought to the barn first, who gets to drink first—all within their own little group, and stability of the group tends to be reflected in the individual mare's happiness and outlook on life. There is less work with the mares during the summer and fall when the breeding season is over, and, with the grass lush, feeding requirements and care are reduced. For these reasons, year-round boarders get a lower board rate.

For breeding season boarders the rate will be higher for the same reasons that the rate on year-round boarders is lower. If you have to send your mare to another area for breeding because that is where the selected stallion stands, you will have to use a breeding farm that accepts seasonal boarders. Your rate may include an additional daily charge for a foal at side. It's not that the foal eats much, but the additional handling and health care at a first-class farm require much more time and attention to detail than is required for a mare without a foal at her side. If you send your mare to the boarding farm before she foals, you may also be billed for a foaling fee. The most critical time of year for your mare and her oal is just before, during and after the time of foaling. There are so many things that can go wrong at foaling that any fee you pay an experienced foaling crew ould be among the best money you ever could spend in the horse business. If you eep your mare "at home" and do not have a night watchman, by all means, end your mare off to foal. Checking every hour or two won't save your mare if he gets in trouble five minutes after you get back in bed.

There are many commercial boarding farms that load up on breeding season oarders, crowding their facilities during the peak season. Be careful of farms hat are overloaded with horses. This crowding can lead to less care and more exosure to disease than at less crowded farms. One of the primary causes of lisease in horses is crowding. Exposure to horses that are on different health programs and have different immunities and come from different areas of the country can introduce new and potentially dangerous diseases to a group of horses. 'or these and other reasons some of your better commercial farms will not accept easonal boarders. Mares sent to Kentucky to be bred, in the vast majority of ases, are not quartered at the same farm as the stallion to which they are to be red, but rather at one of the many commercial boarding farms to be found in the rea. It is very important that you make the proper arrangement for your mare at ne of these farms and are sure that you're satisfied with that farm prior to sending your mare there. Keep in mind that a good reputation takes time to build, and a farm with a good reputation may well be worth the higher rate it charges to take care of your prize mare.

Standing a stallion is a separate and distinct business from boarding mares. It requires specialized facilities, plus a qualified, experienced crew. Whether a farm stands one stallion or ten, a competent stallion man and breeding shed crew are vital. The physical breeding of thoroughbreds is an intricate operation that can be dangerous both to the horse and the handler if it's done incorrectly.

Standing a Stallion

Standing a stallion includes not only the physical breeding operation but requires personal contacts, advertising, and public relations on the part of the stallion manager and the farm. More organization and a larger staff on the farm are vital to handle the necessary paperwork and public relations required to "make" a stallion. Farms that specialize in standing stallions receive free breeding rights (normally four) to the stallion annually, in addition to the daily board rate which covers the basic cost of caring for the stallion. Taking the stallion to the breeding shed every day, showing the stallion, and the attendant promotional work are all extra work, and the reward is the breeding rights. These breeding rights are the profit to the farm, much the same as the 10% the trainers receive for winning races and 5% bloodstock agents get for buying and selling bloodstock. Without these breeding rights, the incentive to stand a stallion would be minimal. If a stallion turns out to be successful, these breeding rights can be very valuable!

A word of caution. Although we discuss making a stallion elsewhere in the book, *don't* try to make a stallion yourself. It takes at least four years to make a stallion, from retirement to "proof of the pudding." By that time you may have all your eggs in one basket, and the basket may turn out to have a hole in it. What happens if the stallion's first foals can't outrun a fat man? By then you'll have a crop of two-year-olds, a crop of yearlings, a crop of weanlings, and a bunch of pregnant mares coming behind the first unsuccessful crop.

Once you start trying to make a stallion, the tendency is to think of the seasons you are using to him as being "free," and most assuredly they aren't. You may pay dearly for them, especially if your mare does not match the stallion either physically or by pedigree, but you breed her to him anyway. After you've been in the horse business for a few years, and if you're lucky enough to have a racehorse good enough to retire to stud, keep an interest in him if you wish, but send him to a farm that specializes in standing stallions. Sell the major portion of him and hope for the best. You never go broke taking a profit, and, if the stallion is successful, you'll have a bunch of happy customers who may well be interested in your next offering.

Sales Costs

Sales preparation is another highly specialized area of the business. Prices vary widely, as do techniques. It is impossible to do justice to sales preparation at home "after work." Proper sales preparation not only includes having the horse in good flesh with a sleek hair coat, but includes teaching the individual to walk smartly and set up properly for showing. A horse which has been properly prepared for sale can bring considerably more than the same individual improperly prepared. There are as many different techniques used in sales preparation as there are sales agents. Once again we urge that you investigate your sales agent, his reputation, and his operation before you commit to him.

The length of time involved in sales preparation can vary from a couple of weeks to 30 days on broodmares, and 90 days or longer for sales yearlings. During that time they are kept in individual stalls, groomed daily, taught their manners, and exercised. In recent years some farms have introduced the use of swimming, treadmills, and/or ponying as techniques to develop more fully the physique of young horses being prepared for sale. Properly done, these techniques can add many dollars to the auction price of your horse.

Your agent at the sale will normally get 5% commission on the final bid, which is the real profit for him. (In addition, sales companies charge 5% commission to the consignor of horses sold.) His daily charge to you during the actual preparation doesn't much more than cover the costs of bringing that horse up to the sale.

Cost of Breaking and Training

Whether you race homebreds or buy yearlings at auction, one of the most critical decisions you'll make will be your choice of where your yearling is to be broken. The young horse being broken is like a child going to school. Breaking a young horse requires patience, knowledge, and experience, not necessarily in that order. An equal amount of all three is preferable, with perhaps the emphasis on patience. More than one potentially good horse has been ruined by lack of patience and judgment early in the breaking process. Bad habits once learned by a horse are almost impossible to break. Like children, young horses can become unruly and rebellious at the first opportunity to do so. Breaking young horses is properly done at a farm or training center and not at the race track. The race track is designed and built for racing fully trained athletes. Don't let anybody sell you on breaking at the race track. The only reason to break yearlings at the race track is that the trainer needs the per diem, in which case you don't need him.

Once your two-year-old is going well and is ready for racing, you enter into the most thrilling and expensive part of being in the horse business. Your horse has been educated to the point where he is ready for final training to reach his ultimate goal of winning races. At this point he requires more attention and more work, and, as a result, he costs more money, but you now have the potential to get a return on your investment.

Training costs vary widely depending upon region, size of track, etc. We cannot emphasize enough, however, that a low daily training rate must ultimately result in a lower quality of feed and care. A trainer who has one groom rubbing three horses and is paying top wages obviously must charge more per horse per day than a trainer who is using a glorified stall cleaner to give superficial attention to six or eight horses. The major portion of a trainer's daily fee goes into such direct costs as labor, workmen's compensation, social security, grain, hay and bedding, and tack and equipment. The profit for a trainer comes from his 10% share of first, second, and third monies rather than from the per diem.

Trainers can be roughly compared to coaches in the human athletic field. As you well know, coaches and managers come and go, depending upon the success or failure of their charges, and the same is true with trainers. Good horses make good trainers, just like good athletes make good coaches and managers. A good trainer is one that takes good care of his horses and gives them the opportunity to perform to their potential. If you find a trainer who does that, you will do well to hire him and stick with him through thick and through thin.

If you remain in the horse business any length of time, you will experience layups. Horses are athletes, and they do injure themselves in competition. The only ones that don't are the ones that don't try. When you consider the size of a horse's legs and the speed at which he runs, you have to be amazed that horses do not cripple themselves more than they do. Laying up a horse obviously costs less than actual training, but not a great deal less. During layup a horse may require blistering or firing and stall rest, plus swimming for rehabilitation. There is a lot of time, effort, and skill required in such care. After the initial stall care and attention, the horse may be turned out in a private paddock for some weeks or months at a lower rate before commencing his comeback. Normally, farms that do a good job of breaking horses will do a good job on layups.

Cost of Insurance

Insurance in the horse business has undergone a great change in the past four or five years. Up until the late '70s, Lloyd's of London was the primary underwriter of mortality insurance on horses. Because of the large sums that are involved with thoroughbreds, Lloyd's, with its syndicated underwriting abilities, was most able to cope with the large risk exposure. The rates were inflexible and, as happens in many industries where there is a monopoly or semimonopoly, enterprising companies saw a profit opportunity in the horse mortality insurance business and jumped in. The result is that now there are varying, competitive rates on mortality insurance offered by a number of companies, both domestic and international. In addition to the differing rates, there are quantity discounts, experience discounts, and experience refunds available to the larger owners. The latest innovation in horse insurance to come to our attention is a captive insurance company in Maryland. The idea behind this insurance company is that the people whose horses are insured are also the owners of the company, so that profits that accrue to the insurance company would actually revert to the insured as dividends. The secret to success of this company would appear to be selective risk-taking by restricting exposure to owners with well-run horse operations, where the mortality risk is reduced to the minimum.

The only caution we would offer in buying insurance is to investigate the company's track record in paying claims, and its financial soundness. As in other forms of insurance, the promise on the policy is easy to make but the payoff in time of disaster is not necessarily so easy to collect.

With year-round racing and the increasing advance in veterinary science, medication and veterinary charges have assumed an ever larger portion of the costs involved in the horse business. Some trainers rely on veterinarians more than others do, both for advice and routine treatments. Vitamin injections, routine fluid therapy, bleeder medication, bute, X rays, and "scoping" (optical examination of the horses' airways and lungs) have become high-priced, routine practices. Some farms are using the new and expensive ultrasound machines for early pregnancy examinations, and ultrasound is also believed to have potential for other uses. This makes it very difficult to average out veterinary and blacksmith charges, and the numbers we have used are subject to great variation.

Costs of Owning a Broodmare

If you decide on breeding as your avenue of investment in thoroughbreds, you probably will start out by buying a broodmare at one of the major breeding stock sales held during the fall or winter. With your advisor, you will pore over the catalog pages representing pedigrees of thousands of broodmares, looking for your diamond in the rough. The average price of in-foal broodmares in 1983 was just under $35,000, so we have used that price in our example for the cost of purchasing a mare. For comparison, we have used Kentucky and Clear Creek Stud in Louisiana. To interpolate for other areas of the country you should substitute daily costs where appropriate. Other costs which may vary widely are transportation, which would change depending on the distance the place of boarding is from the sale, and insurance, which could be of varying rates depending on company and type of coverage. Also, some states charge a sales tax on horses purchased at public auction.

INVESTMENT COSTS

$35,000	Purchase price
1,750	5% agent's fee
$36,750	Capital investment cost to be depreciated

Operating expenses for first year assuming purchase of mare was at a November breeding stock sale

Kentucky	Louisiana	
$ 1,575	$ 1,575	Insurance @ 4½% full mortality for one year
50	350	Transportation to farm
810	540	Board (45 days)
125	100	Vet/blacksmith (45 days)
2,560	2,565	Total operating expenses
$39,310	$39,315	Cash outlay first year

The operating expenses, plus the capital investment, will be your total cash outlay the first year. The taxable deduction for that year will be your operating expenses, plus your deduction for depreciation. Depreciation (discussed in Chapter 7) will vary depending on the age of the mare at the time of purchase. Even at the lowest possible deduction (15% the first year for young mares), the size of the deduction is significant. For a $35,000 mare under the age of 12, the depreciation comes to $5,512.50, whether you bought the mare on January 1 or December 31.

Your first year of ownership does not include a stud fee, since the normal stallion contract, even with a live foal guarantee, calls for payment of stud fee and cancellation of live foal guarantee when a mare is sold. When you buy your in-foal mare at auction, the stud fee is already paid and you get the stallion service certificate. But there is no live foal guarantee. (You can get insurance, at a fairly sizable premium, to guarantee a live foal.) The sales company delivers the stallion service certificate to you as the new owner, along with the mare's registration certificate.

OPERATING EXPENSES SECOND YEAR OF OWNERSHIP
(First year if you buy in January)

Kentucky	Louisiana	
$ 6,570	$ 4,380	Board (365 days)
1,000	800	Blacksmith and vet charges
1,575	1,575	Insurance
7,500	7,500	Stud fee (approximately 25% of mare cost)
$16,645	$14,255	
	Variable	Transportation
	Variable	Additional seasonal board charges

The second-year cash expense of keeping your mare *may* include a stud fee. This is because stud fees on many stallions are due September 1 of the year bred, even though there is a live foal guarantee.

For the purpose of this example we have used 25% of the mare's purchase price as the amount of the stud fee. As a rule of thumb, if you get outside a stud fee price range of 25% to 33⅓% of the purchase price of your broodmare, you are probably over- or under-breeding your mare, and may be disappointed in the resulting auction price you receive for the resulting foal.

If you send your mare away from her regular domicile to be covered you may have to add transportation, foaling fee, and some additional costs for the differential in seasonal boarder rates.

Costs of Getting Your Yearling to the Sales

In the fall, your first foal will be weaned from his dam and at that time will go on the payroll in earnest. Prior to weaning, the periodic worming, vaccinations, and trimming were the only items on the foal's bill, since the costs of keeping the mare include the board costs of her foal at most farms. From weaning to sale time, however, the youngster becomes a separate entity, with separate boarding and care costs. Broken out as separate entities, the costs look like this:

BROODMARE EXPENSES TO WEANING TIME

Kentucky	Louisiana	
$6,570	$4,380	One year board
1,000	800	One year blacksmith and vet
50	350	Vanning
1,575	1,575	Insurance
$9,195	$7,105	

OPERATING EXPENSE FOR WEANLING (Cash Outlay)

Kentucky	Louisiana	
$1,620	$1,080	Board (90 days)
75	50	Blacksmith and vet charges
$1,695	$1,130	

OPERATING EXPENSES FOR YEARLING (Cash Outlay)

Kentucky	Louisiana	
$3,240	$2,160	Board (180 days)
500	400	Blacksmith and vet charges
1,500	1,080	Sales prep (60 days)
50	100	Transportation to sale
200	200	Sales entry fee[1]
1,250	1,250	5% sales company commission[1]
1,250	1,250	5% agent fee[2]
$7,990	$6,440	

[1]In 1982, Keeneland raised the entry fee for all its sales, except the July sale, to $1,000 and eliminated its 5% commission on any sales below $20,000. Fasig-Tipton Kentucky maintained the $200 entry fee and 5% commission, but charges a minimum commission which ranges from $300 to $1,000, depending on the sale.

[2]A number of prominent sales agents have begun operating on the basis of a 5% commission on horses who are sold and 2½% on chargebacks. Still others reduce the commission percentage when a horse goes over $1-million, $2-million, etc.

When you put them all together, the operating expenses of bringing your first yearling to sale will look something like this:

TOTAL OPERATING EXPENSES GETTING YEARLING TO SALE

Kentucky	Louisiana	
$ 9,195	$ 7,105	Broodmare expenses to weaning time
1,695	1,130	Weanling expenses
7,990	6,440	Yearling expenses
18,880	14,675	Subtotal expenses
5,510	5,510	Broodmare depreciation first year
$24,390	$20,185	Capital outlay in getting a yearling to sales

In considering the variations in calculating costs of getting a yearling to the sales, several assumptions are made which can be altered to fit the situation. No insurance is carried on the weanling or yearling since the investment was made in the mare and she is, so to speak, the factory which produces the foals. Weanlings and yearlings, like children, will find a way to get hurt, but only in rare cases is the injury fatal. Since insurance is for mortality, not for fitness of purpose, it is difficult to justify the expense of insurance unless some mitigating circumstance, such as success of a close relative, has suddenly escalated the potential value of your sales candidate. Many breeders will insure their weanlings and yearlings for the amount of the stud fee to protect themselves at least for that direct cash outlay should something dire happen.

Although depreciation of your mare is a legitimate tax deduction, the normal course of events in the horse business would certainly suggest that your young mare is not going to depreciate in price nearly as rapidly as the tax code allows. With luck and good mare selection, as a matter of fact, you can anticipate appreciation of value rather than depreciation! This cost therefore is primarily a tax deduction and *not necessarily* a true cost of production.

Adding one year of broodmare expense to the cost of producing a yearling is not totally accurate because every fourth or fifth year your mare may go barren and her costs for that year will have to be prorated among her productive years or "eaten" the year she is barren. A homebred yearling has no depreciation deduction since all costs pertaining to raising him are deducted as operating expenses. Keep in mind, too, that there is no stud fee the first year, but this will be an added expense in future years. On the other hand, what you are anticipating is that your mare will be eminently successful and her future foals will be more and more valuable, based on success of her first foals.

John Finney, president of Fasig-Tipton Company, made the following observation recently: "The breeding business has changed in the last couple of years. Racing has always been the riskier part of thoroughbred investment. In a successful stable of six racehorses, three will lose money, two will break even and, *hopefully*, one will hit a home run, and make the stable a paying proposition.

"In the '70s and early '80s, the bloodstock market was so strong that almost every broodmare purchased resulted in a profit for its owners through selling her foals at yearling sales. Not so today, however, with a leveling off of demand and an oversupply of yearlings resulting in much more selectiveness by purchasers.

Today a breeder needs some home runs, too, to make up for the inevitable crooked yearling that ends up losing money for the breeder.''

We agree with John Finney's assessment of the market and wish to add our own words of caution. As we have stated elsewhere, the thoroughbred market is in the midst of a shakeout, which means a good advisor is all the more important since you need to purchase horses of quality.

When you review the costs of getting a yearling to market, keep in mind that most of them are fixed. Whether the mare and her foal are worth $10,000 or $1-million, the only varying factors are depreciation, insurance, and stud fee! It's much better to own part of a good horse than all of a bad one.

Costs of Raising a Homebred

Raising a homebred can be the most rewarding course of all for an investor who is financially and emotionally suited to that endeavor. Unquestionably the most suitable environment for a youngster is where a homebred is allowed his freedom to romp and play with his contemporaries in the field during the formative months of his yearling year. Putting a sales yearling in a stall and force-feeding him for three months during this important growth stage can be roughly equated to locking your son (whom you hope to see star as quarterback on his high school football team) in his room on a high carbohydrate diet for three months before fall practice starts. Neither method is particularly logical and, in fact, is counterproductive in the ultimate scheme of things.

COSTS OF RAISING A HOMEBRED YEARLING

Kentucky	Louisiana	
$5,400	$3,600	Board (300 days)
1,950	1,690	Breaking (65 days)
1,000	800	Blacksmith and vet charges
$8,350	$6,090	

Again some assumptions are made. At Clear Creek Stud, yearlings that have not gone through yearling sales are not broken until November and sometimes, depending on foaling date and physical maturity, even later. We do not advocate early two-year-old racing and, therefore, are in no hurry to remove a young horse from his natural environment in the field to put him in a stall. As a matter of fact, with many homebreds our early breaking is done while the yearling is still out in his paddock.

The operating costs of keeping the mare and weanling must be added to the costs of raising the homebred yearling to determine the total investment cost to the start of the two-year-old year.

INVESTMENT COSTS OF RAISING A HOMEBRED TWO-YEAR-OLD

Kentucky	Louisiana	
$ 9,195	$ 7,105	Broodmare expenses to weaning time
1,695	1,130	Weanling expenses
8,350	6,090	Yearling expenses
19,240	14,325	Operating expense
5,510	5,510	Depreciation of broodmare
$24,750	$19,835	Total expenses

To this figure we must add the expenses of continuing the breaking process and the final training. Those expenses can vary considerably depending on how much of his two-year-old year is spent at a training center and how much of it is spent at the track. Assuming six months at the farm and six months at a major track in the respective state, the following figures would apply:

OPERATING EXPENSES FOR A TWO-YEAR-OLD

Kentucky	Louisiana	
$ 5,400	$ 4,680	Farm (180 days)
7,400	6,475	Track (185 days)
2,000	1,500	Blacksmith and vet charges
250	250	Transportation
$15,050	$12,905	Total expenses

These costs do not include insurance, which you may want to add, particularly if your two-year-old is showing great promise. Insurance rates on racehorses are higher than on breeding stock because the mortality risk is higher. Remember, you can insure yourself into the poor house. The rule here applies as elsewhere—insure against any loss (or portion of loss) you can't comfortably absorb to continue your operation.

Other costs not included in the projection are nomination and sustaining fees for futurities and stakes, pony fees, jockey's fees, and the trainer's 10% share of winnings. You hope there will be a lot of the latter charges, because it means your horse is running and winning, but there is no way to project them.

Buying a Yearling and Racing Him

Our final cost projection involves buying a yearling to race. Again, as with a broodmare purchase, you and your advisor will pore over the pedigrees of thousands of yearlings offered at public auction, looking for the proverbial needle in the haystack. As we pointed out in Chapter 1, the needles are there—finding them is the challenge that makes this such an exciting game.

COST OF BUYING A YEARLING TO RACE
(1983 Yearling Average $40,000)

$40,000	Cost of yearling
2,000	5% agent's fee
$42,000	Total cost

OPERATING EXPENSES

Kentucky	Louisiana	
$1,500	$1,500	Insurance
50	350	Transportation
1,500	1,300	Breaking (50 days)
1,200	900	Turn-out (60 days)
400	300	Blacksmith and vet charges
$4,650	$4,350	Total expenses

TOTAL CASH OUTLAY BUYING A YEARLING TO RACE

Kentucky	Louisiana	
$42,000	$42,000	Capital investment
4,650	4,350	Operating expenses of yearling
15,050	12,905	Operating expenses of two-year-old (same as homebred)
$61,700	$59,255	Total outlay

DEPRECIATION ON YOUR YEARLING/TWO-YEAR-OLD

$ 6,300	15% First year (regardless of when purchased)
9,240	22% Second year
$15,540	Total depreciation

TAXABLE DEDUCTION—YEARLING YEAR

Kentucky	Louisiana	
$ 4,650	$ 4,350	Operating expense of yearling
6,300	6,300	First year depreciation
$10,950	$10,650	Total taxable deduction yearling year

TAXABLE DEDUCTION—TWO-YEAR-OLD YEAR

Kentucky	Louisiana	
$15,050	$12,905	Operating expense two-year-old (same as homebred)
9,240	9,240	Second year depreciation
$24,290	$22,145	Total taxable deduction two-year-old year

TOTAL TAXABLE DEDUCTION ON INVESTMENT

Kentucky	Louisiana	
$ 4,650	$ 4,350	Operating expense of yearling
15,050	12,905	Operating expense of two-year-old
15,540	15,540	Depreciation reduction both years
$35,240	$32,795	Total deduction

You can see that, of the $60,000 investment, over 55% is a taxable deduction during the first two years of operation. We have not included insurance during the second year because by the time insurance renewal time comes around in September, your youngster may well be worth a million dollars, or may not be worth insuring at all.

Whatever type of investment you choose, be it broodmare, yearling, or raising homebreds, be sure it fits your temperament and your pocketbook. At the risk of boring you, we repeat: quality is your best investment, in advisors, in bloodstock, and in facilities. It is far more prudent to own a small part of a good horse than all of a bad one.

Chapter 7

Taxation And Depreciation

As the gap between the price of bloodstock and the anticipation of return has widened, the matter of taxation has become an increasingly important consideration in the horse business.

While horses are considered to be a "tax shelter" by some people, there is one important admonition which was made in a 1979 equine tax case, *Engdahl vs. Commissioner*, following which a very perceptive judge noted, ". . . as long as tax rates are less than 100 percent, there is no 'benefit' in losing money."

The major tax benefit offered by the horse business is that it gives a taxpayer a chance to trade ordinary income, which is taxable to a maximum rate of 50%, for capital gains, which currently are taxable to a maximum rate of 20% for individuals (28% for corporations), and, at the same time, permits the taxpayer to write off his expenses of doing business.

Before continuing any further with this chapter, it is necessary to give one additional word to the wise for the reader. Neither of us is really qualified to give tax advice, and this section of the book is intended only to acquaint you informally with the tax advantages of horse ownership. We cannot emphasize too strongly that all tax decisions pertaining to your horse business, just as any other business, should be made in consultation with your accountant and/or attorney.

Furthermore, for a more complete overview of taxes than appears here, we urge you to buy a copy of *The Horse Owners and Breeders Tax Manual*, by Tad Davis, the tax counsel of the American Horse Council. Look it over yourself, then give it to your accountant or lawyer. With something in excess of 800 pages contained in 11 chapters, it is intended and written as a reference work to answer most of the tax questions which could possibly arise with respect to any equin operation, so it doesn't necessarily make very good fireside reading. At its curren cost of $90, however, it would be cheap at three or four times the price.

For someone who is only at the point of considering getting into the hors business, we'd suggest *Tax Tips for Horse Owners,* also published by th American Horse Council. It sells for $2, and is, essentially, a 16-page outline o the *Tax Manual,* but it contains most of the basics with respect to taxation of th horse business.

If you would like the bottom line, the substance of both of those publication condensed into one sentence, here it is:

"If you treat your horse operation as a business, then the IRS will treat your horse operation as a business."

Hobby Loss Provision

That brings us to the most important part of the tax law insofar as some hors operations are concerned, the so-called Hobby Loss Provision. Briefly, this pro vision states that if you're engaged in a certain endeavor and your motive is per sonal enjoyment, rather than making a profit, you cannot write off any of th expenses you incur in that endeavor. Conversely, if you can prove you wer engaged in that activity for a profit, it is a business and not a hobby, and you losses are fully deductible against other income.

Oddly enough, you do not necessarily have to *make* a profit to be declared business, but the facts and circumstances surrounding your activity must indicat that you're in the business to make a profit. In determining whether the profi motive exists, the IRS will, no doubt, take into consideration nine factors whic they have listed as important indicators of a profit motive.

Before we list them, though, you should bear in mind several things. First, th nine factors may not be the only ones used in determining whether or not you horse operation is a business or a hobby. Secondly, no one of these factors carrie more weight than any of the others. And, third, a determination will not be mad simply on the fact that you qualify under a majority of factors. That is, you jus can't expect to say, "I qualified on five counts and didn't qualify on four counts so it's a business," and be confident the IRS will agree.

So here are the criteria, along with some comments, where necessary:

1) *Whether or not the taxpayer carries on the horse operation in a businesslike manner.* This means you should carry on your horse business in a manner which is similar to other businesses of the same nature which you are conducting profitably; you should keep accurate books and records, and you should adopt new techniques or abandon unprofitable ones as necessary, etc.

2) *The expertise of the taxpayer or his advisors.* Refer again, please, to Chapter 2.

3) *The amount of time and effort expended by the taxpayer in carrying on his horse operation.* However, the fact that the taxpayer

spends only a limited amount of time on his horse business does not necessarily show the absence of a profit motive, as long as he has competent and qualified people to run the business for him.

4) *Expectation that the assets used in the activity, such as land and horses, will appreciate in value.*

5) *The taxpayer's success in other businesses, whether they're similar or not.*

6) *The taxpayer's history of profits and losses with respect to his horse activity.* This will be discussed further, immediately below, in the section concerning the "two-out-of-seven presumption."

7) *The amount of profits generated by the activity in relation to the amount of losses, the amount of investment, and the value of the assets used in the activity.* You can't, for example, lose $150,000 a year for five years, then make $10,000 for the next two years and expect the IRS to roll over and say, "OK, this guy's in the business for a profit."

8) *Substantial income from sources other than your horse business, especially if the losses from your horse activities create substantial tax benefits.*

9) *Elements of personal pleasure/recreation.* The fact that you happen to like racing and breeding does not, however, necessarily mean that you're not in them for a profit. The way you treat the "enjoyment" part of your business may have an effect on the IRS. If your travel and entertainment expenses are out of line or you deduct an inordinate amount for frills on your farm, you may create a problem for yourself.

Two-Out-Of-Seven Presumption

As mentioned above, there is a very useful provision in the Internal Revenue Code which creates a presumption that your horse operation is a business, under most circumstances, if you show a profit in two years out of any specified seven-year tax period. It seems, however, that anything having to do with the IRS gets pretty complicated and the "two out of seven presumption" is no exception.

Basically, there are two kinds of presumptions, a "general" presumption, which is automatic, and a "special" presumption. This special presumption applies only to the first seven-year period of a horse operation and requires the taxpayer to make an "election," in other words to choose the special presumption.

The general presumption comes into play automatically as soon as you have a second profit year in the horse operation in any seven-year period. It protects you for seven years from the first profit year in the period, but does not protect loss years, if any, between the first and second profit years. For example, assume your horse operation has profits (P) and losses (L) in the following years of a seven-year period:

1982	1983	1984	1985	1986	1987	1988
(P)	(L)	(L)	(P)	(L)	(L)	(L)

The second profit year is 1985, so, under the general presumption, you would be protected in the years 1985 (the second profit year) through 1988 (the seventh year inclusive from the first profit year). You would not be protected in 1983 and 1984, because they came before the second profit year. Therefore, in situations where the general presumption is in effect, it is best to have the profit years come back to back, for example:

1982	1983	1984	1985	1986	1987	1988
(P)	(P)	(L)	(L)	(L)	(L)	(L)

In the situation shown above, you would be safe from 1982 through 1988, because all years after the second year are protected.

Now, suppose you're just starting in the business. At the proper time, you can make an election to come under the special presumption and, if your horse operation shows a profit during any two years within the first seven years of its operation, you're safe for the entire seven years. So, at the risk of over-explaining, if you elected to take the special presumption in the first example, above, you would be safe for the entire period. In the second example, you wouldn't need to take a special presumption, because your first two years were both profit years.

A word of caution concerning use of the special presumption. Invoking this provision does two things—it waves a red flag at the local IRS office and it leaves your business open to audit beyond the normal three-year limit.

While the two-out-of-seven presumption provides you with insurance by placing the burden of proof on the IRS to convince the court that you are not engaged in your horse activities for a profit, rather than vice versa, there's no guarantee that your horse operation will be ruled as a business, if the facts and circumstances dictate otherwise, as mentioned in Number 7 on the list of considerations, above. However, *there is no negative presumption*, so, if you don't show a profit in two out of seven years, it does not automatically make your horses a hobby, rather than a business.

Finally, there's one other point to be made with respect to the two-out-of-seven presumption. There can be overlaps, because the seven-year period is a running period and can be any period of seven consecutive years which begins with a profit year and contains at least one other profit year, for example:

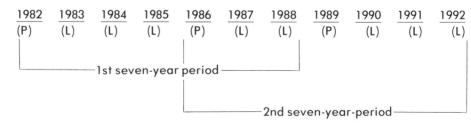

1982	1983	1984	1985	1986	1987	1988	1989	1990	1991	1992
(P)	(L)	(L)	(L)	(P)	(L)	(L)	(P)	(L)	(L)	(L)

1st seven-year period

2nd seven-year-period

As with all other businesses, you are entitled to deduct all ordinary and necessary expenses of breeding, raising, training, and racing your horses. This includes everything from stud fees to labor, veterinary and shoeing costs, and state and local property taxes, if you have a farm. Since the cash method of accounting is permitted for a horse operation, expenses are generally deductible in the year they are paid, although there are some restrictions on prepaid items, mainly if the prepayments are considered to be a deposit to be applied to future expenses or if they materially distort the operation's income picture.

Depreciation

A primary benefit of the horse business is that taxpayers are allowed to depreciate (recover the cost) of their horses as an ordinary business expense. Until 1981, horses were required to be depreciated under a fairly complicated "useful life" formula. Under the Economic Recovery Tax Act of 1981, depreciation was simplified, so that horse owners are now permitted to depreciate their horses over a three-year period or a five-year period, depending on their use.

The three-year cost recovery period applies to all racehorses more than two years old and other horses older than 12, while the five-year recovery applies to all the remainder of the equine population. For several years, there was some consternation and controversy over what was meant by "more than two years old" and "more than 12," especially in view of the January 1 universal birthdate for thoroughbreds and many other breeds. In February of 1984, the IRS finally got around to defining what it meant by those two phrases and, of course, it was the most complicated way of determining things. A horse is "more than two years old," according to the IRS definition, ". . . after 24 months after its actual birthdate" and it is "more than 12" if the horse was foaled more than 144 months and one day prior to being placed into service.

At any rate, the cost recovery schedule for horses which are eligible to be depreciated over a three-year period is:

AMOUNT OF COST RECOVERY DEDUCTION
Year Placed Into Service

Year 1_____	25%
Year 2_____	38%
Year 3_____	37%
	100%

This schedule also applies to cars, light-duty trucks, and certain other property.

The first year depreciation applies to individual horse owners, regardless of the date on which the horse is placed into service, so an individual taxpayer who, for example, bought a horse for $100,000 on December 31, 1984, could take a $25,000 depreciation deduction on it for 1984, despite the fact that he's owned the horse for only one day. *However, and this is very important, if the taxpayer is a partnership which was formed in the middle of the year, it must calculate the taxes according to a "short year" and prorate the amount of cost recovery according to the date on which the partnership began business.*

149

All horses which do not qualify for three-year depreciation must be depreciated according to the following schedule:

AMOUNT OF COST RECOVERY DEDUCTION
Year Placed Into Service

Year 1_____	15%
Year 2_____	22%
Year 3_____	21%
Year 4_____	21%
Year 5_____	21%
	100%

The five-year depreciation schedule also applies to all farm equipment, machinery, fencing, single-purpose agriculture structures (don't get your hopes up; horse barns, even though they may not be used for anything else, don't qualify here, according to the IRS), and everything else except general-purpose farm buildings.

There are several other points which should be made on the subject of depreciation.

- If a racehorse which is in the process of being depreciated over a three-year period is retired for breeding, the remainder of the cost recovery must be converted to a five-year schedule and prorated under a fairly complicated formula which is fully explained in *The Horse Owners and Breeders Tax Manual* and *Tax Tips for Horse Owners.*
- Salvage value is completely eliminated under the current schedules, so all horses and other depreciable assets can be written down to zero.
- The cost recovery schedules outlined above apply to all used property, as well as new property.
- Horses which have been raised by their owners cannot be depreciated if the cost of breeding and raising them has already been deducted as expense.

Capital Gains

We mentioned at the beginning of this chapter that one of the major benefits of being in the horse business is that a horse held for breeding or sporting purposes qualifies for capital gains treatment, provided it is held for at least 24 months. "Sporting purposes," insofar as the racing business is concerned, is defined as having raced at a public race track or having been trained to race at a public race track, which qualifies almost everything.

If a horse has never been placed into training, however, it doesn't qualify under the definition of "sporting purposes." Say, for example, you purchased a weanling filly for $1,000 in October of 1981, never put her in training and didn't breed her, but her full sister won the inaugural running of the Breeders' Cup Juvenile illies Stakes on November 10, 1984. The next day, there's a guy on your doorstep offering you $100,000 for your filly, but you'd have trouble taking capital gains on your profit, because she'd never been trained or bred.

If you have partially or totally depreciated a horse and then sell it, before you take capital gains you must "recapture" (pay back) the amount which was depreciated by declaring it as ordinary income. For instance, if you bought a broodmare for $100,000 and held on to her for two years, then sold her for $150,000, you'd have a gain of $87,000 ($50,000 actual gain, plus $37,000 of depreciation which you had taken on the horse). The $37,000 which you had depreciated must be treated as ordinary income, however, so you could take capital gains only on the $50,000 in appreciation of the mare.

Here are three examples to show the dramatic profit potential for taxpayers if they can convert ordinary income to capital gains.

$100,000	$100,000	$100,000	Purchase Price of Mare
		[15,000]	1st year depreciation
		[22,000]	2nd year depreciation
[37,000]	[37,000]	[37,000]	Total Depreciation
63,000	63,000	63,000	Book Value of Asset
200,000	100,000	150,000	Sale Price of Mare (after 24 months)
137,000	37,000	87,000	Net Profit
[37,000]	[37,000]	[37,000]	Depreciation Recapture (Taxed at ordinary income rate)
$100,000	[0]	$50,000	Capital Gains (Taxed at capital gains rate)

Yearlings, of course, do not qualify for capital gains, since it is impossible for them to meet the 24-month required holding period, and horses which are held primarily for sale do not qualify no matter how long they are held. This factor comes into play when your horses are considered inventory. For example, if you normally market young horses as two-year-olds in training, they are your inventory and are not eligible for capital gains regardless of time held. On the other hand, if you normally sell yearlings or race homebreds, an *occasional* two-year-old sale may well qualify as capital gains.

Investment Tax Credit

Finally, there is one less-than-happy note on which to end this discussion on taxation of the horse business. Horses do not qualify for the 10% Investment Tax Credit, even though most of the equipment you use in the horse business will. All other forms of livestock intended for breeding qualify for the ITC—cows qualify, sheep qualify, chickens qualify, goats qualify, llamas qualify, yaks and gnus qualify—but horses don't. Why? Because horses are specifically eliminated by name. The Tax Code comes right out and says there will be a 10% tax credit on all livestock intended for breeding "except horses."

All in all, though, you don't get too bad a shake on your horse business, if you treat it professionally.

Chapter 8

Alternative Sources Of Ownership And Financing

During the past 30 years, and especially the last ten, as the prices of thoroughbred racing and breeding stock have escalated in quantum jumps, there has been an increasing interest and emphasis placed by those with a long-term involvement in the business on the generation of additional capital.

This trend has been followed by a realization in the investment community that the horse business represents an untapped resource for investors who are interested in glamour issues with a high potential for return. Undoubtedly, this is a result of a good sales job on behalf of some of the industry's pioneers in the field, but whatever the reason, the industry is now deeply involved in the proposition of multiple ownership.

Multiple ownership is really nothing new to the horse business. While most people who are involved with thoroughbreds will tell you that the concept of syndication was developed in our business in the early '50s, *The Thoroughbred Record* reported the first $100,000 syndication in history in its issue of October 19, 1898, when the three-year-old standardbred Axtell was purchased by a syndicate for $105,000. And, if the whole truth were known, the ancient Romans formed syndicates to purchase their favorite teams for the chariot races held at the Coliseum.

So, the main thing that is new about the current emphasis on multiple ownership is the amount of sophistication and the size of the numbers which are contained in the deals.

The basic reason for multiple ownership is pretty much the same as it was in the Roman days, i.e.

It is Better to Own Part of a Good Horse
Than it is to Own All of a Bad One

There are variations and elaborations on that theme, which will be discussed in this chapter, but that's it in a nutshell.

Before proceeding with a full discussion of multiple ownership, it is time, once again, to put in another plug for the American Horse Council. They have published an excellent pamphlet, *Equine Syndications,* by Jay Hickey, a former lawyer for the Securities and Exchange Commission who is now with the law firm of Smathers, Symington & Herlong, general counsel to the AHC. It tells you a lot about partnerships, syndications, etc., and comes free with a membership. There's another excellent pamphlet on the subject, entitled *Choosing the Equine Business Form,* by John J. Kropp, John A. Flanagan, and Thomas W. Kahle, all of whom are partners in the Cincinnati law firm of Graydon, Head & Ritchie. It was published as part of the *Kentucky Law Journal* and may be obtained from the Michie Company, 405 Old Towne Road, Louisville, Kentucky, 40214; phone (502) 583-8874. Once again, we admonish you to consult with your lawyer and/or accountant before going into any sort of multiple ownership deal.

Pros and Cons of Multiple Ownership

As with everything else in this world, there are certain advantages and disadvantages to multiple ownership, but since it is a concept that has stood the test of time, one is forced to reach the conclusion that the advantages outweigh the disadvantages. Probably the best way to discuss them is to put them into historical perspective, beginning with the stallion syndications which became a factor in the business in the '50s. The syndication of a stallion, which gives each syndicate shareholder (a syndicate is usually made up of 40 shares) one breeding right to a stallion every year for the length of his stud career, is the most popular, and obvious, example of multiple ownership in the horse business.

When Leslie Combs II put together the first million-dollar syndicate in history to buy Nashua for $1,251,200 in 1957, stallion syndication was already an accepted form of operation in the horse business, and multiple benefits occurred for all participants—the horse's owner (in this case the owner was the estate of William Woodward, but the same advantages applied), the syndicator, the people who bought shares (undivided interests) in the horse, and the horse itself.

Even in those days, the owner benefited by sharing the risks and expenses of keeping the horse. It was a large risk back in 1957 to keep a million-dollar horse, and, since the syndicate manager planned to advertise the horse heavily, the expenses of standing him at stud were greater than they would be if he stood privately, so prorating the expenses among all the share owners really made sense. Further, the syndication raised the maximum amount of capital, because the horse was being sold at his peak as a racehorse, so he brought top dollar at the time. If the seller had not been an estate, the syndication would have allowed the stable which raced the horse to retain a percentage of ownership, rather than hav-

Nashua earned $1,288,565 during his racing career (he is pictured above with Eddie Arcaro up and owner William Woodward Jr.) and upon the death of Woodward was bought for $1,251,200 to stand at Spendthrift Farm (below, with groom Clem Brooks). The days of a one-to-one ratio between race track earnings and stallion value are long past.

ing to sell the horse outright. That way, they could have participated in the appreciation of the horse as a breeding animal, following his racing career.

To the syndicator (usually a farm) it offered an opportunity to obtain breeding rights to a stallion which he might not otherwise have been able to afford. The major benefit of standing a stallion is that the farm where he stands usually gets a number of annual breeding rights (free seasons) to any stallion which it stands. They can sell those rights or use them to breed their own mares. Whichever they decide to do, those breeding rights are a great incentive for the farm or syndicate manager to do his best to insure the stallion does as well as possible at stud. Standing a stallion helps to promote the farm where he stands, because every ad for the stallion carries the farm name, thus becoming an ad for the farm, also. Furthermore, the ad for the farm is paid by the syndicate members.

For the breeder who had some mares but not a really big operation, the syndication was a boon because it gave him an opportunity to insure access to a top horse no matter how difficult it became to get seasons nor how expensive those seasons became if the stallion became successful. Also, the mare owner didn't have to put all his eggs in one basket, that is, he didn't have to breed all his mares to one stallion as he might have done if he owned his own stallion. Finally, it gave the breeder who didn't own his stallion the opportunity to participate in the appreciation of a stallion if the horse were a success at stud.

All of this wound up working to the advantage of the horse. First, since his original owners (or anybody, for that matter) didn't have enough top-quality mares to fill his book—and, in our opinion, the success of a stallion is 80% or more dependent on the mares to whom he's bred—syndication worked to the benefit of the stallion by improving his book of mares and thereby improving his chances for success at stud. Also, it meant that rather than having one owner going around saying what a good horse he was, the stallion would have 30 or more owners promoting him, because each was promoting his or her own interest in the horse.

By 1973, the total yearling crop sold at auction averaged over $10,000 for the first time in history and the Keeneland summer sales average topped $50,000 for the first time, despite the fact that the average earnings per runner in North America that year would be but $4,263, hardly a sure way of recouping your investment. That year, Jim Scully, a Lexington, Kentucky, bloodstock agent, paid a world-record price of $600,000 for a bay colt by Bold Ruler—*Iskra, by Le Haar. After he'd signed the sale slip, Scully revealed that he'd purchased the yearling on behalf of a syndicate consisting of himself and six others, and that the syndicate bought two other yearlings to go into a racing stable along with the world-record one. It was the first really big yearling purchase by a syndicate, and it was, indeed, a precursor of things to come. Interestingly enough, the correspondent for *The Thoroughbred Record* noted in the sales coverage, "With prices the way they were, it was only natural that this was the year of the syndicated yearling. In addition to the syndicate that bought the highest-priced yearling, there were several others active and successful in the bidding, and as yearling

As a yearling (above) Wajima brought a record $600,000 in 1973, being from the last crop of the incomparable Bold Ruler. He developed into a champion, winning the 1975 Marlboro Cup over Forego (below), and when retired for stud duty was syndicated for a record $7.2-million.

prices continue to rise, there will undoubtedly be more and more syndicates active around the sales ring.''

That sale was significant in that it introduced two other reasons for forming syndicates—leverage, the use of other people's money for the purchase of horses, and diversification, the purchase of several horses in the hopes that one of them will be successful. As it turned out, that happened. The world-record colt, subsequently named Wajima, went on to be the champion three-year-old colt of 1975 and was syndicated (or resyndicated, actually) for another world-record price, $7.2-million, when he entered stud.

This was followed very closely by the emergence on the scene of a charming and innovative fellow, Cot Campbell, from Atlanta, Georgia. Under the nom de course Dogwood Stable, Cot began bringing new people into the business through small limited partnerships which would buy a horse (in some cases several horses), race it for two or three years and, if the horse turned out as they hoped, sell it for a profit. Since Campbell was originally in the advertising business, he knows how to treat his clients right, and they are kept well informed through calls from his office, "breezing parties" at his farm south of Atlanta, and a monthly newsletter. He has been very successful both with forming partnerships and buying horses. He now operates quite a number of partnerships and is, in our opinion, bringing people into the business in the proper fashion.

Today, with the Keeneland July sales average near $550,000, the overall yearling average above $40,000, broodmares averaging $35,000, and stallion shares—not stallions, shares—selling for sums in excess of $2-million, it's no wonder that you see syndicates getting together to purchase everything from racehorses to shares in other syndicates. People who are committed to the industry realize that the percentages for making a profit are better if you deal at or near the top of the market and, if they cannot afford to do that on an individual basis, they take in partners.

This brings us to the two most recent reasons for participation in multiple ownerships. First, the people who are in the industry need to generate new capital from outside the industry, so they are looking for investors who have not necessarily been involved in the business previously. At the same time, people who have venture capital and find the horse business attractive need the expertise of those within the industry to give them the best possible return on their investment. It sounds like a perfect marriage and, in the right cases it can be, but there are some pitfalls. Before discussing them, though, it is probably wise to discuss some of the types and elements of multiple ownership.

Types of Multiple Ownership

While there are almost as many types of multiple ownership as there are prospectuses floating around today, for the present purposes they can be divided into the five most common categories: partnerships (both general and limited), syndicates, joint ventures, Subchapter S corporations, and regular corporations. The financial size of each of them is more or less meaningless—two people could, for example, form a general partnership to purchase a mare for $10,000, while

William Haggin Perry had a partnership with Claiborne Farm for years, in which they divided up the entire Claiborne yearling crop. What is important are the goals that the participants want to achieve.

Partnerships. The Internal Revenue Code defines a partnership as ". . . a syndicate, group, pool, joint venture, or other unincorporated organization, through or by means of which any business, financial operation, or venture is carried on and is not . . . a trust, estate, or corporation." Whether your partnership is a general partnership, a limited partnership, a syndicate or a joint venture generally depends on the amount of control you want to have and the reasons it is established. In all forms, though, the income tax credits that accrue to the partnership "pass through" to the partners on a pro rata basis for their portion of the partnership. In other words, the partners pay taxes or take tax credits in proportion to their participation in the partnership. While the partnership files an income tax return, it is an information return only and the partnership itself doesn't have any tax responsibility.

In a general partnership, the partners have a relatively equal say in the operation of the partnership and, as a result, they are equally liable for the obligations of the partnership. This liability can extend past the partnership to the personal assets of each of the general partners. General partnerships can be formed for a specific purpose, such as racing or breeding, or for a combination of purposes, such as breeding, racing a few fillies, owning stallion shares, etc.

A limited partnership is similar to a general partnership, except there normally is only one general partner who is responsible for all the business decisions of the partnership and is also personally liable for the obligations of the partnership. The personal liability of the limited partners is held to a specific amount, normally the limited partner's capital contribution, which may be a lump sum or, more often, an initial payment and a promissory note, backed by a letter of credit from a bank or a performance bond. The thought behind the latter system is that income to the partnership might make some of the later payments of capital contribution unnecessary, or at least reduce them. By law, the limited partners have absolutely no say in the day-to-day operation of the partnership, but they do normally have the option of replacing the general partner in the case of fraud or other misfeasance. Quite often, there are restrictions on transferability in a limited partnership, so, if you get in a bind, you might not be able to sell your unit without the permission of the general partner. One of the major advantages of participation in a limited partnership is the acquisition of expert management you might not be able to obtain otherwise. Many of the top managers/advisors in the business today are looking towards the partnership avenue as a way of increasing their own equity in the business. Since limited partnerships rely on the expertise of the general partner for the success or failure of the partnership, limited partnerships are almost always regarded as securities under the federal securities laws. Consequently, they must be registered with the Securities and Exchange Commission, unless they meet one of four exemptions offered by the SEC to the registration requirement. Needless to say, most of the limited partnerships you encounter will fall under one of the four exemptions.

Syndicates. A syndicate can be either a co-ownership or partnership, depending on its purpose, and the purposes of a syndicate are usually more limited than that of a partnership, i.e. owning a stallion for racing or breeding, but not crossing over. If a syndicate doesn't engage in any business activities of its own, for example a stallion syndicate, it is usually regarded as a co-ownership, while, if it does engage in a business activity, for example selling excess seasons and distributing the proceeds, it is regarded as a partnership.

Joint ventures. A joint venture is a business structure similar to a partnership (and taxed as such), but typically narrower in purpose and scope, and often used simply for a single, specific business purpose. The benefit of a joint venture is that it can often be accomplished without a complicated written document.

Subchapter S Corporations. A corporation which has 35 or fewer stockholders (husbands and wives count as only one) can elect to be treated as a Subchapter S corporation for income tax purposes. Basically, a Subchapter S corporation is just like any other corporation, with limited liability to shareholders and easy transferability of stock (although there may be transfer restrictions placed on shares of any privately held corporation), except that it has one great advantage; profits and losses are passed through to shareholders, as in a partnership, so you avoid the double taxation which plagues most corporations. The drawback is that a Subchapter S corporation is more complicated than a partnership, and sometimes income and loss may pass through to a shareholder less favorably than a partnership. A Subchapter S corporation, however, might offer an attractive middle ground between not having any say as a limited partner in a limited partnership and worrying about the liability of participation in a general partnership.

Public Corporations. Since 1980, several major (and a couple of minor) thoroughbred operations have made the decision to become public corporations. While these offer the investor the option of participating in the thoroughbred business at a very nominal level (at the time this book was published, the average share in the four largest public offerings was selling for about $4.50), it seems to us that the only real benefit, generating capital, accrues to the company. In the meantime, the stockholders get all of the disadvantages of corporate investment (double taxation, etc.) and none of the advantages of the horse business (i.e. tax advantages, thrill of participation, etc.). This is not entirely a one way street, however. Certainly some of the top established organizations which have gone public recently have regretted it. You often need to move very quickly in the horse business to be successful, and the necessity of consulting an army of lawyers, accountants and assorted other advisors before taking a positive step has caused a considerable reduction in their effectiveness.

At any rate, there are a number of ways you can participate in multiple ownership of thoroughbreds, but there are also a number of very important considerations and things to do before you make the decision where to put your money.

Before You Invest

The late Samuel Goldwyn once said, "An oral contract isn't worth the paper it's written on." He was correct. Whether you and a friend are going together to

laim a filly for $5,000 or you're putting together a $10-million limited partner-
hip, it's important that you write down some sort of agreement. It can be scrib-
led on the back of a napkin in the former case, or it can be a 244-page legal
ocument in the latter case, but the fact remains you should write down: a) who's
oing to pay for what; b) who's going to have what management responsibilities;
) what's going to happen to the profits, if any, and; d) what happens if you have
disagreement and decide to dissolve the partnership.

In the case of limited partnerships, syndications, etc., this will all be set out for
ou in a long, complicated document. Read it! Don't just read the subscription
ocument, read the prospectus if it's a stock offering or the offering memoran-
um if it's a limited partnership. Look out for certain things which will almost
uarantee that you won't make money if you invest.

Be especially attentive to the qualifications of the people you'll be relying on to
ake the vital decisions which will mean profit or loss for your enterprise. The
ollowing is an actual paragraph from a prospectus on a thoroughbred partner-
ıip which sold out. It was listed under "Risk Factors" and it appeared in be-
veen "Operating Losses" and "Arbitrary Offering Price":

> *"Inexperienced Management.* No member of management
> of . . . the General Partner of the Partnership, has any experience in
> commercial thoroughbred breeding or farm management. Moreover,
> [the company] . . . has limited financial resources and a substantial
> portion of [the company's] operating budget for the foreseeable
> future is likely to be a direct result of this offering. Such inexperience
> and limited financial resources could have a materially adverse effect
> on the operations of the Partnership. . . ."

Believe it or not, this partnership raised $2-million.

Here are some other warning signs you should look for in a prospectus or of-
ring memorandum:

- Does the offering project a profit in the long term? It makes no sense to
  enter into a deal based on tax benefits alone. As a tax court judge said in
  1979, "As long as tax rates are less than 100 percent, there's no 'benefit' in
  losing money." If the primary goal isn't to show a profit, there's no way
  you'll ever make money. Besides, the IRS will probably disallow any write-
  offs associated with the enterprise, anyway. In the past year or so, they have
  been vigorous in attacking "tax shelter" deals, those which do not project a
  profit.

- A prospectus should at least contain some sort of specific business plan, and
  preferably that plan should include, at the very least, application of proceeds and an expense flow analysis. Income projections are very difficult in
  the current market, and some partnerships may not have them, but, if sales
  projections are included, the investor should be aware that they are simply
  projections and are subject to wide variations.

  We recently saw a prospectus for $5-million partnerships which did not
  contain any sort of pro forma and the business plan was, basically the partnership "will engage in business in all aspects ot the thoroughbred industry . . ."

161

While there is seldom any real legal way to hold the general partner's fee to the fire if a prospectus is written properly, a specific business plan and pro forma will at least give you something to point to in times of trouble

- Try to avoid a large front-end load. It is difficult enough to make money in the horse business without giving up 35% to 50% up front in commissions management fees, etc. In a recent survey of 16 offering memoranda, the amounts of the limited partners' contributions which actually went to the purchase of bloodstock ranged from 40% to 100% (additional contribu tions for expenses were to be assessed in the latter), with an average of les than 70% going for actual purchase of horses. In any substantial partner ship, 80% or better should go toward the purchase of horses.

- The general partner should not get rich until the limited partners have bee paid back. Most of the general partners in the survey were taking bi, management fees. The average, in fact, was $140,000 a year, while the to was $400,000 a year. Management should, we believe, be compensated onl nominally until all the limited partners have recouped their original invest ment. Then, as a reward for doing a good job, the general partner ca receive a percentage of the net proceeds.

- Self dealing. Many partnerships include purchasing horses from the genera partner, allowing the general partner to breed to his own stallions or buy th seasons which come with the shares he owns. Worse, they often permit general partner to sell seasons and horses back and forth from one partner ship to another and take a commission on the sale. All of these thing become very tempting if the general partner needs money, which he prob ably does or he wouldn't be forming the partnership in the first place. In sofar as the purchase of horses from the general partner, it doesn' necessarily have to be bad, but we'd advise getting an independent appraisa of the animals included in the deal because, whether honestly or not, ofte horse owners have an inflated value of the animals they own.

- Conflicts of interest. Undoubtedly, unless you participate in a partnershi in which no one has any previous connection to the industry, you'll be face with certain conflicts of interest, which isn't necessarily bad. While yo don't want someone to use the partnership to unload his own seasons an fill up his own stallions, you don't want a total stranger to the industry Most conflicts of interest are offset by useful contacts within the industry but you should bear them in mind while studying the offering memoran dum.

On the subject of conflicts of interest, it might be appropriate, here, t discuss the proposition of a "blind pool" vs. purchasing named horse which are already owned by the general partner. As mentioned above, if th horses are put into the partnership by the general partner, they could be in flated. On the other hand, there is the opportunity to have them appraise by an independent source. Most partnerships, though, are put together t raise capital for the general partner to take to the sales in order to purchas horses, and you don't know what you're going to get. In the latter case though, the prices will probably be dictated by the market, so it will be public knowledge what the horse is worth. What it all boils down to, we suppose, is whether or not the general partner is a person of integrity. If he isn't, you're not going to get an even break, either way.

Other Forms of Stretching Your Investment

Even before Wall Street and the other investors were beginning to gain awareness of the thoroughbred business, there were other ways of expanding our investment.

First, syndicators and others in the business began to offer deferred payment plans. Then banks, leasing companies, and other financial institutions began looking toward the business as a place for expansion, especially when the market was going up at a solid 30% a year and interest rates were 15% or better.

The first major trend toward offering terms or deferred payments came in the early to mid-'70s, as stallion syndication was becoming attractive to outside investors. Some of the innovators in the business reasoned, correctly, that a multiyear payout might prove beneficial to the people for whom they were syndicating the horses (capital gains were on a sliding scale in those days, with a maximum rate considerably higher than the current 20%). By offering terms, the syndicator could get a higher price per share than otherwise and, at the same time, make ownership of syndicate shares more attractive to outside investors.

They began offering variations on a basic theme, an initial payment, followed by three or four subsequent annual payments, depending on the syndicate manager. The rationale, at first, was that the purchaser of a share would be able to amortize the share before the horse was proven to be a failure at stud, if that were going to happen. In year one, the horse was just off the track and the syndicate manager could still promote him using the glitter of his race record; in year two the hype would surround the arrival of his first foals; year three would see his first yearlings coming to market; and year four would feature his first two-year-olds getting to the races. If they couldn't run, the stallion's seasons would begin to decline in value, but the shareholder would have paid for his share through the sale or use of seasons while they held their price, and the subsequent sale of seasons, even at a reduced rate, would be gravy.

This formula became even more attractive in 1981, when the ACRS (depreciation) guidelines were reduced to five years (see Chapter 7), and the depreciation of a share closely approximated the payment schedule for the share. For example, if one were to buy a share for $100,000 in 1984, the payment schedule and depreciation allowances would look something like this:

Year	Share Payment	Depreciation
1984	$20,000	$15,000
1985	$20,000	$22,000
1986	$20,000	$21,000
1987	$20,000	$21,000
1988	$20,000	$21,000
	$100,000	$100,000

In addition to the depreciation schedule matching the payment schedule, interest payments are tax deductible, so the purchase of syndicate shares became very popular form of outside investment in the late '70s and, especially, in the early '80s.

When breeders, owners, and other people began seeing how effective payment over time were becoming, and as prices continued to escalate, the trend caught on with other forms of bloodstock, until now you can get terms on almost an bloodstock purchase you make privately. As a large participant in the business is fond of saying, "The terms make the deal," and we have to agree. The terms can also create a great temptation to overextend yourself, though, and that, we'll remind you several times in this section, is very, very dangerous.

Bank Loans

Not too far behind the industry in offering leverage on horses came the bank They were in a very aggressive mode in those days, because interest rates were very high and they could afford to take a few risks. Prior to 1975, there were very few financial institutions which were willing to take a flyer on horses, but all of sudden, it seemed, banks all over the country were actively seeking investors who wanted to borrow money on horses. If there ever was a red flag waved in front of a bull, it was banks offering to lend money to people wanting to buy horse Some of the banks were not overly discriminate in selecting their loans, either For instance, one of the cited causes of the widely publicized failure of the Penn Square Bank in Oklahoma was a number of questionable horse loans, although in all fairness it must be said they were mostly quarter horse loans.

While a number of banks today still make loans of 50%, and occasionally up t 70%, on horses, they are much more discriminating about the people to whom they lend money. Indeed, the people to whom banks lend money are, quite properly, a more important consideration than the horses themselves, because while the prices of horses may accelerate rapidly, they can fall just as rapidly, and the bank will want to have people they can rely on to make up the difference if the horse, for some reason, declines drastically in value.

There are several factors you should bear in mind as you go to the bank seeking a loan on a horse. As mentioned, you, yourself, will make the most important difference in the bank's decision. An important factor will be your preparedness—you should have a definite business plan and/or projections of income and expenses, including when and how you plan to repay the loan. Be prepared with copies of income tax returns for the previous two or three years and a current, easily verifiable, financial statement (your financial statement should emphasize liquidity, if possible). Lastly, but very importantly, if you're not established and experienced in the business, you should bring some information on your advisors. It helps if you go to a bank where you're well known and if your regular bank absolutely does not give loans on horses, it will help you the long run if you begin to establish a relationship with one which does.

Finally, we have two other bits of advice for you when going to the bank. First, don't overvalue your horses; the bank will have an independent appraisal done on your horses and, if there is a large discrepancy, it'll send up a red flag. Second, banks are very reluctant to lend money on horses at the track, because, as mentioned in Chapter 4, title to a horse is carried by The Jockey Club Registration Certificate. Since the certificate must be on file at the racing secretary's office in order for the horse to race, this, in effect, causes the bank to make an unsecured loan since it does not have title to the horse. That doesn't give the banker much of a feeling of confidence.

The problem with bank financing today, as we see it, is the same as that of a partnership with a large front-end load, i.e. it's tough enough to make it in the horse business without adding on a 13% additional burden to your operation in the form of interest. However, if you decide leveraging is good for your business you should include the interest at a reasonable rate in your business plan.

Leases

The last form of alternative financing which merits discussion here is leasing. Leasing has been prevalent on the race track for a number of years as a way for people who are interested in racing, but not breeding, to have some fun with a well-bred horse who has some potential, while the breeder who is interested in breeding, but not racing, can benefit from the appreciation of the horse on the race track.

Leasing is becoming an increasingly popular proposition in the breeding industry, too, as more and more breeders find themselves in a cash bind on occasion and they want to generate some fairly immediate income without losing their best broodmare. There are, of course, certain advantages and disadvantages for both sides in a lease deal but, in general, the lessor (the person who owns the horse) comes out on the better end of the deal.

For the lessee, the advantages are that all expenses of the deal are deductible in the year they are paid, and the lease probably permits him to get a foal out of a mare whom he might not be able to touch otherwise. However, while he can get a guarantee that the mare is in foal at the time the lease is signed, he cannot get a live foal guarantee, because tax rulings have stated that a live foal guarantee removes all risk of loss, and therefore the lease money is being paid for the purchase of the foal and must be capitalized as such. Also, since the tax rules essentially rule out multiyear leases (renewals are permissible, though), the lessee is not necessarily tied for life to a mare who doesn't fit into his breeding program.

For the lessor, as mentioned, a lease permits some cash flow, without permanently divesting himself of a major and valued asset. Also, since he retains actual ownership of the horse, the lessor continues to take depreciation on it, even though it may be in the possession of the lessee.

Leases basically have been between individuals. During the past couple of years, leasing companies have sprung up for the wholesale purchase of horses for

165

people who will then lease them from the company. The brochure for one leasing company cites the benefits of leasing as permitting the lessee to:

"Conserve investments and other assets by making the lease payments out of earnings or other income.

"Be able to purchase more horses, or horses of better quality, than funds available permit.

"Permit investment of available funds in other needed items."

TRANSLATION: "We'll help you get in over your head."

In summary, there are advantages and disadvantages to participation in all forms of alternative ownership and/or financing. The important thing to remember, though, whether you're buying shares of common stock at $4.50, limited partnership units at $100,000, or taking out a million-dollar loan is to plan ahead, allow for contingencies, and, above all, stay within your means. Greed has probably caused more bankruptcies in the horse business than ineptitude.

Chapter 9

State-Bred Programs

During the past 25 years, 22 of the 31 states conducting racing have established incentive programs to encourage the establishment and growth of a substantial agricultural industry—thoroughbred breeding. With the nationwide expansion of racing dates to include winter racing in the North and summer racing in the South, the old, traditional racing circuits have tended to disappear. More and more stables (with the exception of their stars who continue to move about the country for racing opportunities) remain in one location or area on a year-round basis.

In various states, legislators and forward-thinking horsemen got together and realized that the racing industry in their respective states would become more and more dependent on local thoroughbred production to help fill races. From this concept, legislators determined that by developing incentive programs funded by a percentage of the tax revenue from mutuel handle at the race tracks, the state could help assure that its tracks had the necessary supply of runners for this expanded schedule.

In practice, state-funded breeding programs enhance local participation in breeding and racing thoroughbreds. You're more likely to become directly involved in racing and breeding if you can drive to the farm where your mares are located on Sunday afternoon, pat them on the forehead, and see the latest addition to your crop wobbling around on unsteady legs, or sneak out to the race track to see the horse you bred make his first start in the long march to the dream of a Kentucky Derby victory.

State-bred programs vary greatly in size and restrictions and the types of incen tives they offer, but basically there are four categories of incentive programs—1 awards for breeders of successful horses bred in the state; 2) awards to owners o successful state-breds in races in which they participate; 3) awards for owners o sires of successful state-breds; and 4) purses for races restricted to state-breds.

Awards for breeders of successful horses bred in the state are normally de scribed as breeders' awards because they are paid to the breeder of a successfu racehorse, regardless of who owns the horse at the time of the successful perform ance. The breeder of a horse is defined by The Jockey Club as the owner of the mare at the time she delivers the foal, and this is normally the person to whom the local breeders' association awards the incentive bonus.

Awards for owners of successful state-breds are found even in Kentucky, where the Kentucky Thoroughbred Development Fund provides a bonus over and above the normal purse, when a Kentucky-bred or Kentucky-sired horse wins a designated race, for example: at Keeneland an allowance race may carry a $15,000 purse with the stipulation that, if a Kentucky-bred or Kentucky-sired horse finishes first through fourth, an additional $2,500 in purse money is provid ed by the Kentucky Thoroughbred Development Fund. This bonus goes to the current owner of the horse, not to the breeder. Many other states provide owners' awards over and above breeders' and stallion awards.

A more recent development is the stallion award. This award is a type of breeders' award except that it goes to the owner of the sire of the successful state- bred. Normally, though, stallion awards go only to those successful in the higher level allowance and stakes races.

Interestingly enough, in almost all states the largest amount of incentive money provides purses for restricted races, as distinguished from breeders' awards or stallion awards. Restricted races allow a double incentive to horse owners. Not only are the races restricted to state-breds (which, by virtue of the restriction, reduces the competition), but the purses are much larger than purses for horses running under similar conditions in unrestricted races. The amounts involved are significant because of the emphasis they place on racing rewards for successful breeding. The original theory advanced behind the heavy emphasis placed on purse distribution was to encourage those who participate in racing to purchase the state-bred foals and to race them at tracks within the state. It also had the theoretical effect of making such foals more valuable at public auction since they would have the opportunity to race for sizable purses in restricted company.

In the majority of states this emphasis hasn't produced the desired result of a substantial commercial market for state-bred yearlings, but rather has increased foal production of mediocre horses who end up racing for their breeders after they have proven to be unmarketable. With a few exceptions, state breeding pro grams, with their self-imposed restrictions, have tended to operate more as agricultural subsidies than rewards for excellence. In many cases, however, the improvement of the breed aside, this has been accomplished and the state breeding programs can be considered a success as thoroughbred breeding farms and related services are substantial industry to a state, employing thousands of people in many cases. And the race tracks within the state have more horses to fill races, regardless of the questionable quality of some of those horses.

Incentives are most often distributed based on the percentage of the purse earned by a state-bred in a particular race. In some states, however, where the funds available are not elastic, the awards are determined on an annual basis, based on the horse or sire's relative performance for the year. The accompanying chart shows dollar amounts paid in 1983 in the four categories of incentives for each state-bred program.

Thoroughbred Breeder/Owner Incentive Programs
1983 Payments
(Pari-Mutuel States)

State	Breeders Awards	Owners Awards	Stallion Awards	Gross Purses for State-bred Restricted Races
Arizona	$ 328,374	$ ---	$ ---	$ 820,935
Arkansas	158,282	---	---	756,575
California	2,468,767	1,663,798	2,567,738	5,307,800
Colorado	118,682	59,341	19,780	234,177
Florida	2,528,614	---	381,246	3,250,425
Illinois	751,738	---	406,007	9,177,465
Kentucky	---	---	---	1,936,412*
Louisiana	1,741,848	---	280,140	7,769,922
Maryland	1,004,120	704,700	339,647	1,020,000
Massachusetts	170,734	17,684	59,756	230,000
Michigan	441,848	---	---	805,900*
Nebraska	465,458	170,785	64,096	1,957,770
New Jersey	1,708,174	269,124	295,686	3,367,759
New Mexico	531,345	472,307	82,653	---
New York	3,874,000	906,000	794,000	14,311,000
Ohio	412,196	---	137,570	2,099,910
Oregon	54,000	380,000	---	38,000*
Pennsylvania	902,095	239,469	234,343	1,237,400
South Dakota	3,500	107,400	---	27,500*
Washington	782,717	2,064,186	---	---
West Virginia	66,703	151,015	37,754	302,400

*Notes: **Kentucky** payments ($1,936,412) represent supplements paid to Kentucky sired/bred horses finishing fourth or better in designated races in the state. **Michigan** ($805,900), **Oregon** ($38,000), and **South Dakota** ($27,500) payments represent supplements paid by incentive program for restricted races. Total purse figures for restricted races not available.

State-Bred Incentive Programs

Arizona

An Arizona-bred is defined as a horse foaled in the state and is physically present within the state's borders for not less than six months during the first year of his life.

The breeder of an Arizona-bred which wins any race at a pari-mutuel meeting in the state receives a breeders' award equal to 40% of the purse earned. The owner of an Arizona-bred which wins any race at a pari-mutuel meeting in the state receives a bonus equal to 25% of the earned purse.

Arkansas

An Arkansas-bred is defined by the state program as a) a horse foaled in the state, out of a registered Arkansas mare which was bred to a registered Arkansas stallion, or b) a horse foaled in the state which is by an out-of-state stallion, provided that the mare arrives in Arkansas prior to December 31 of the year bred and remains in Arkansas to foal and is then bred back to a registered Arkansas stallion.

The breeder of an Arkansas-bred which finishes first through fifth in any race at a pari-mutuel meeting in the state receives a breeders' award equal to 10% of the earned purse. The owner of an Arkansas-bred which finishes first through fifth in any race restricted to Arkansas-breds receives a bonus on a pro rata basis as a purse supplement, depending upon money available. In addition, any funds remaining in the breeders' award fund at the end of the fiscal year following allocation of breeders' awards and owners' supplements are distributed equally among all qualified breeders. Due to this added distribution, the net breeders' awards percentage bonus may exceed 10% in any year.

California

A California-bred is a) a horse foaled in California after having been conceived in California, or b) a horse foaled in California, which may be by an out-of-state stallion, provided the mare remains in the state to be bred to a California stallion the following year. If the mare can't be bred for two consecutive breeding seasons but remains in California during that period, her foal is considered a California-bred. A California stallion is a sire that stands regularly in California and remains in the state while his progeny are running. Stallion award eligibility is lost if a stallion leaves California to stand elsewhere.

The breeder of a California-bred which finishes first, second, or third in any race at a pari-mutuel meeting in the state (except for fair meets) receives a breeders' award equal to 10% of the purse earned (exclusive of nomination, entry, or starting fees). The breeder of a California-bred which wins a graded stakes race outside of California carrying a purse value of $25,000 or more receives a breeders' award equal to 10% of the winner's share of the purse, up to a maximum of $7,500 for any one race.

The owner of a California-bred which wins a nonclaiming race, plus specially designated claiming races, at a nonfair pari-mutuel meeting in the state receives a bonus equal to approximately 15% of the winner's share of the purse, exclusive of nomination, entry, or starting fees. The exact percentage varies from meeting to meeting and may be supplemented to a maximum of 20% of the winner's share of the purse.

The owner of a California sire whose California-bred offspring wins a nonclaiming race, plus specially designated claiming races, at a nonfair pari-mutuel meeting in the state receives a stallion award. The benefits are paid to the stallion owner as of December 31 in a pro rata form based on the total amount earned by the stallion's progeny in qualifying races. The amount of the final award depends on the funds available, which normally amounts to approximately 15% of the qualifying winners' share of the purses. Included in the computation are graded stakes wins outside of California, with a maximum award of $7,500 for any one race. The maximum amount payable for any one race is 3% of the total stallion award funds available for the year in which that race is run.

At least one race per day must be restricted to California-breds at all pari-mutuel meetings.

Colorado

A Colorado-bred is a horse foaled in Colorado out of a registered mare which must be in the state and registered by September 1 of year bred. The mare cannot leave the state until the foal is born. The owner of a Colorado sire, for the purpose of qualifying for stallion awards, is the stallion owner at the time the foal is conceived.

Breeders of Colorado-breds receive awards on the basis of a point system for wins at tracks in the state. A stakes win is worth points equal to 55% of the winner's share of the purse. Points for each horse, or stallion, are totaled at the end of the racing season and the funds available for distribution are divided according to points won.

Owners of Colorado-breds receive awards determined by the same point schedule as the breeders' awards. Owners of sires of Colorado-breds receive stallion awards based on the same point basis as breeders of Colorado-breds.

The available funds are divided at the end of the race meeting—60% for breeders' awards, 30% for owners' awards, and 10% for stallion awards.

At least one race each racing day must be written for Colorado-breds at all pari-mutuel meetings.

Florida

A Florida-bred is a) a horse foaled in Florida whose dam is normally domiciled in Florida, or b) a horse foaled in Florida out of a mare normally domiciled elsewhere but bred to a stallion standing in Florida which did not stand outside of Florida during that calendar year.

The breeder of a Florida-bred which wins any overnight or stakes race at a pari-mutuel meeting in the state receives a breeders' award equal to 15% of the gross purse of that race.

The owner of a registered Florida sire of a Florida-bred that wins any stakes race at a track at a pari-mutuel meeting in the state receives a bonus equal to 15% of the gross purse of that race (including all added monies).

The owner of a Florida sire, for the purpose of stallion awards, is the stallion owner at the time the foal was conceived.

At least one race per day shall be written with Florida-breds as preferred entries at all pari-mutuel meetings.

Rexson's Hope, tenth in the 1984 Kentucky Derby, got there off one stakes win, a triumph at two in the $150,000 In Reality division of the restricted Florida Stallion Stakes.

Idaho

An Idaho-bred is a horse foaled in Idaho. Breeders and owners of Idaho-breds which win a race in the state receive a pro rata share of a fund administered by the Idaho Thoroughbred Breeders Association.

Illinois

An Illinois-foaled horse is one foaled in the state and sired by a stallion that stands outside the state, or by a stallion that stands in Illinois but is not registered annually with the Illinois Department of Agriculture. The dam must be in the state and inspected on or before December 1 of the year the foal is conceived, and must remain in the state continuously until the foal is born.

An Illinois-conceived and -foaled horse is a horse foaled in the state and sired by a registered Illinois stallion who was standing for service in the state at the time of conception. To qualify, the dam must be in the state at least 30 days prior to foaling and/or remain in the state at least 30 days after foaling.

The owner of an Illinois sire, for the purpose of participation in stallion awards, is the owner of the stallion at the time of conception. An Illinois stallion must be registered with the Illinois Department of Agriculture before he covers any mare in the state. He also must stand the entire season in Illinois and be at least 50% owned by Illinois residents. To qualify for stallion awards, the stallion may not stand outside the state during the calendar year in which the qualified foal wins an eligible race.

The breeder of an Illinois-bred (either foaled or conceived and foaled) which wins an open race at a pari-mutuel meeting in the state receives a bonus award equal to 12½% of the winner's share of the purse. The breeder of an Illinois-bred which finishes first through fourth in any race restricted to Illinois-breds at a pari-mutuel meeting in the state receives a bonus from a pool which is equal to approximately 7% of the purse earned.

The owner of an Illinois sire of an Illinois-bred which wins any race in the state carrying total purse money of at least $7,500 receives a stallion award equal to approximately 11% to 15% of the total purse.

At least one race per day must be restricted to Illinois-breds at all pari-mutuel meetings. Purse supplements are provided only to maiden allowance and

Largely because of his win in open company in the $577,725 Arlington-Washington Futurity in 1983, All Fired Up is one of the richest Illinois-breds of all time.

allowance races with conditions up to nonwinners of four races. Purse supplements must increase the purses by an average of 25%. The fund also provides purses for 30 stakes races annually for all categories of Illinois-breds.

Kentucky

A Kentucky-bred is a horse foaled in Kentucky. A Kentucky-sired horse is one that is sired by a registered Kentucky stallion standing the entire breeding season in Kentucky during the year of conception.

Purse supplements for Kentucky-sired and Kentucky-bred horses are provided from the Kentucky Thoroughbred Development Fund Supplement, in all stakes races, handicaps, allowance races, or other nonclaiming events in the state. These amounts are designated prior to the race, for eligible horses which finish first through fourth in those races. Supplements not earned are returned to the KTDF fund.

Louisiana

A Louisiana-bred is a horse foaled in the state by a mare permanently quartered in Louisiana. After producing a Louisiana-bred foal, the mare may be shipped out of state to be bred, provided she is returned to Louisiana to domicile no later than August 1. A mare which has her foal in Louisiana by an out-of-state stallion may qualify as a permanent resident, but she must be bred back to a stallion standing in Louisiana her first year of domicile. At no time can a mare be bred to an out-of-state stallion two consecutive years.

The owner of a Louisiana stallion, for the purpose of qualifying for stallion awards, is the owner at the time of conception. A Louisiana stallion must be permanently domiciled in the state and registered with the Louisiana Thoroughbred Breeders Association. Should he leave the state for any reason he forfeits his future stallion awards.

The breeder of a Louisiana-bred which finishes first through third in a race restricted to Louisiana-breds at a pari-mutuel meeting in the state receives a breeders' award equal to 20% of the purse earned. The breeder of a Louisiana-bred that finishes first in an open race at a track in the state earns a breeders' award equal to 10% of the purse earned. At the end of the fiscal year (July 1), the owner of a Louisiana stallion whose Louisiana-bred progeny wins a handicap, allowance, or stakes race at a pari-mutuel meeting receives a bonus based on the ratio of earnings to the total amount earned by the progeny of all qualified stallions from available funds.

Three races restricted to accredited Louisiana-breds must be written daily at all pari-mutuel meetings. One restricted race shall be a maiden special weight race.

Maryland

A Maryland-bred is a) a horse foaled in the state, the breeder of which is a resident of Maryland, or a person whose mares are permanently domiciled in the state; b) a horse out of a mare that conceived and foaled in Maryland; or c) a horse by an out-of-state stallion, out of a mare brought into the state to foal, and bred back to a Maryland stallion after foaling.

A Maryland sire is a registered sire standing in the state at the time of the foal's conception. A stallion leaving the state of Maryland for breeding purposes forfeits future stallion awards. The owner of a Maryland sire, for purposes of qualifying for stallion awards, is the owner at the time of conception. The breeder of a Maryland-bred which wins any race at a pari-mutuel meeting in the state receives a bonus equal to 15% to 20% of the winner's purse.

The owner of a Maryland-bred which wins any race at a pari-mutuel meeting in the state, other than stakes and claiming events, receives a bonus of approximately 25% of the winner's share of the purse.

The owner of a Maryland sire of a Maryland-bred that wins any race at a pari-mutuel meeting in the state receives a bonus equal to approximately 7½% to 10% of the winner's share of the purse. Awards are computed at the conclusion of each race meeting.

Massachusetts

A Massachusetts-bred is a horse foaled in the state a) out of a mare which is in the state continuously from October 15 of year bred to the date of foaling, or b) a horse foaled in the state out of a mare bred back to a Massachusetts stallion.

The owner of a Massachusetts sire, for the purpose of qualifying for the stallion awards, is the owner at the time of conception. A Massachusetts stallion is one which stands the entire breeding season in the state and is registered with the Massachusetts Department of Food and Agriculture.

The breeder of a Massachusetts-bred which finishes first through third in any race at a pari-mutuel meeting in the state receives a bonus equal to 25% of the earned purse.

The owner of a Massachusetts-bred which finishes first through third in any race at a pari-mutuel meeting in the state receives a bonus award equal to 5% of the earned purse.

The owner of a Massachusetts sire of a Massachusetts-bred which finishes first through third in any race at a pari-mutuel meeting in the state receives a stallion award equal to 15% of the earned purse.

The Massachusetts Department of Food and Agriculture estimates the funds to be available for purse supplements after payment of the breeder, owner, and stallion awards, and determines the schedule of restricted races based on that estimate.

Michigan

A Michigan-bred is a horse foaled in the state, out of a mare which has been in the state since December 1 of the year bred and remains until foaling. The mare must be registered with the Michigan Department of Agriculture by December 1. The mare can leave the state after foaling for the purpose of being bred to a stallion standing out of state, but must be domiciled in the state for not less than seven months total of the foaling year.

The breeder of a Michigan-bred which wins an open or restricted race in the state receives a bonus equal to 10% of the gross purse.

One race per day at each track must be restricted to Michigan-breds. Purse supplements are provided for restricted races.

Nebraska

A "Class A" Nebraska-bred is a horse conceived and foaled in Nebraska, sired by a stallion standing in Nebraska, owned or leased by a resident of Nebraska, and registered in the Nebraska Thoroughbred Registry.

175

A "Class B" Nebraska-bred is a horse foaled in the state which is by an out-of-state or unregistered stallion. For both Class A and Class B, the mare must be registered and must be in the state continuously for six months prior to foaling, although the period may be reduced to 90 days in the case of a mare which is 1) either registered as a broodmare with the Nebraska Registry but is being actively trained and raced outside the state and is returned to the state to remain there continuously 90 days prior to foaling, or 2) purchased at a nationally recognized thoroughbred bloodstock sale, entries for which are closed prior to September 1 of the year purchased. The owners of a horse (including all stockholders of corporate ownership) must have been bona fide citizens of Nebraska continuously from January 1 of the year of conception through the date of foaling in order for that horse to qualify as a Nebraska-bred.

The breeder of a Class A Nebraska-bred which wins any race at a pari-mutuel meeting in the state receives a breeders' award equal to 20% of the winning purse.

The breeder of a Class B Nebraska-bred which wins any race at a pari-mutuel meeting in the state receives a breeders' award of 10% of the winning purse.

At least one race per day must be written for Nebraska-breds at each track, and one stakes race for two-year-old Nebraska-breds must be written at each race meeting.

New Jersey

A New Jersey-bred is a) a horse foaled in the state whose breeder is a resident of the state or whose breeding stock is domiciled in the state; b) a horse foaled in the state which is by a registered New Jersey stallion; or c) the offspring of a mare sent into the state to foal and be covered by a registered New Jersey stallion after foaling.

The owner of a New Jersey sire, for the purpose of qualifying for stallion awards, is the owner of record at the time of conception.

A New Jersey sire is a stallion standing in the state and registered with the Breeders Association of New Jersey prior to the time of the offspring's conception.

The breeder of a New Jersey-bred which finishes first through fifth in any race at a pari-mutuel meeting in the state receives a bonus equal to 30% of the earned purse. If the New Jersey-bred was foaled but not conceived in New Jersey, the bonus is equal to 25% of the earned purse.

The owner of a New Jersey-bred which finishes first through fifth in any open race at a pari-mutuel meeting in the state receives a bonus equal to 10% of the earned purse.

The owner of a registered New Jersey stallion whose offspring finishes first through fifth in an overnight or stakes race at a pari-mutuel meeting in the state receives a bonus award equal to 10% of the earned purse.

At least one race per day at each track must be restricted to New Jersey-breds. Purses for restricted races shall be 25% higher than corresponding open races.

New Mexico

A New Mexico-bred is a horse foaled in the state and sired by a stallion which stands in the state and is registered with the New Mexico Horse Breeders Association. Also, the foal must be out of a mare registered with the NMHBA no later than September 1 of the year of conception and remains in the state during pregnancy and foaling (unless prior written approval for the mare to leave the state is obtained from the NMHBA).

The owner of a New Mexico sire, for the purpose of qualifying for stallion awards, is the owner at the time of conception.

The breeder of a New Mexico-bred which wins any race at a pari-mutuel meeting in the state receives a pro rata bonus award at the end of the award year (October 1) based on the funds available and the number of horses qualifying for such awards, plus a bonus from the racing association equal to 10% of the winner's share of the purse, except for stakes races where the sum equals 10% of the added money.

The owner of a New Mexico-bred which finishes first, second, or third in any race at a pari-mutuel meeting in the state receives a pro rata bonus award based on the funds available and the number of horses qualifying for such awards.

The owner of a New Mexico stallion which sires a New Mexico-bred winner of any race at a pari-mutuel meeting in the state receives a pro rata bonus award based on the funds available for such awards and the total earnings of that stallion's progeny during the year.

At least one race per day is restricted to New Mexico-breds.

New York

A New York-bred is a horse foaled in the state and:

A) If the horse was conceived in the state by a New York registered stallion, one of three criteria must be established: 1) the dam of the horse was quartered permanently in New York from August 16 of the year of conception until foaling; 2) the dam of the horse was bred back to a registered New York stallion in the year of foaling; or 3) the dam of the horse was permanently quartered in New York from August 16 of the year of foaling until it foals the following year, or, if not in foal, through December 31 of the year of foaling; or,

B) If the horse was not conceived in New York by a registered New York stallion, the dam must be bred back to a registered New York stallion *and* one of the following two criteria must be established: 1) the dam of the horse was permanently quartered in New York from August 16 of the year of conception until foaling; or 2) the dam of the horse was permanently quartered in New York from August 16 of the year of foaling until it foaled the following year or, if not in foal, to December 31 of the year of foaling.

An accredited New York sire is a stallion standing in New York at the time of breeding registered with the New York State Registry *and:* 1) owned by a resident of the state and standing the entire season in New York; or 2) owned by a resident of another state but standing the entire season in New York and leased by a resi-

The gray New York-bred Fio Rito captured the Grade I Whitney Stakes at Saratoga from Winter's Tale. Fio Rito won the majority of his races against state-breds and retired with earnings of $584,142.

dent of the state for not less than two years; or 3) owned jointly by a resident of New York and a resident of another state and standing the entire season in New York and leased by a resident of the state for not less than two years.

The owner of a New York stallion, for purposes of participating in stallion awards, is the owner at the time of conception.

The breeder of a New York-bred which earns any purse money at a pari-mutuel meeting in the state receives a bonus award equal to at least 15% of the earned purse. A fund surplus in any year may increase that award.

The owner of a New York-bred which earns purse money in certain non-claiming races in New York receives a bonus equal to as much as 40% of those earned purses. An owner of a New York-bred which earns money in claiming races with a claiming value of at least $20,000 receives a bonus equal to 20% of those earned purses.

The owner of a New York sire whose offspring earn any purse money at a pari-mutuel meeting in the state receives a bonus award equal to at least 10% of the earned purse. A fund surplus in any year may increase that award.

The fund also provides purses and purse supplements for races restricted to New York-breds.

Ohio

An Ohio-bred is a horse both conceived and foaled in Ohio. The sire must stand only in Ohio during the year in which the foal is conceived and must be registered with the Ohio Racing Commission. The dam must remain in Ohio hroughout the pregnancy and be registered with the Ohio Racing Commission.

An Ohio-foaled horse is a horse foaled in the state, out of a mare that a) ntered the state before July 15 of the year the foal was conceived and remained n the state throughout the pregnancy, or b) shipped into the state after July 15 of he year bred but was bred to an Ohio stallion after foaling. The mare must be egistered with the Ohio Racing Commission and remain in Ohio for one year ontinuously after foaling, or continuously through foaling to the cover of an)hio stallion, whichever occurs first.

The owner of an Ohio sire, for the purpose of qualifying for stallion awards, is he owner at the time of conception. An Ohio stallion is a stallion registered with he Ohio Racing Commission and standing in Ohio only.

The breeder of an Ohio-bred or Ohio-foaled horse which wins an open or

ˉhe filly Tah Dah won 14 stakes races in 1983-'84 as a two- and three-year-old. All those wins but one came against Ohio-breds, and she earned in excess of $250,000.

estricted event at a pari-mutuel meeting in the state receives a bonus equal to ₀0% of the earned purse.

The owner of an Ohio-sired horse which wins a race at a pari-mutuel meeting in he state receives a bonus award equal to 5% of the earned purse.

The Ohio Thoroughbred Race Fund provides 70% of the Ohio-bred stakes urses and supplements Ohio-bred overnight races according to a graduated scale ased on the quality of the race. An Ohio-bred is eligible for all stakes monies, /hile an Ohio-foaled horse is eligible for 75% of all stakes monies.

₀regon

An Oregon-bred is a horse foaled in Oregon.

The breeder of an Oregon-bred that wins any race at a pari-mutuel meeting in ₁e state with a daily mutuel handle of at least $150,000 receives a bonus award qual to 10% of the earned purse.

179

The owner of an Oregon-bred that finishes first through fifth in any race at an Oregon thoroughbred meet with a daily handle of at least $150,000 receives a bonus award calculated at the end of the meet.

At least one race per day at all tracks must be restricted to Oregon-breds.

Pennsylvania

A Pennsylvania-bred is a horse foaled in Pennsylvania and registered with the Pennsylvania Horse Breeders Association.

The owner of a Pennsylvania sire, for purposes of qualifying for stallion awards, must be the owner at the time of conception. A Pennsylvania sire is a stallion that stands in Pennsylvania and was registered with the PHBA at the time the offspring was conceived.

The breeder of a Pennsylvania-bred that wins any open race at a pari-mutuel meeting in the state receives a bonus award equal to 10% of the earned purse. The owner of a sire of a Pennsylvania-bred which finishes first through third in any race at a pari-mutuel meeting in the state receives a bonus award equal to 10% of the earned purse.

The breeding fund sponsors a schedule of approximately 12 stakes races for Pennsylvania-breds and also supplements purses of races restricted to Pennsylvania-breds. Purse supplements are proportioned according to the quality of the races and supplemental purses are up to 50% larger than purses for open events of corresponding quality.

The breeder of a Pennsylvania-bred which finishes first through third in any race at a pari-mutuel meeting in the state receives a bonus award equal to 20% of the earned purse.

South Dakota

A South Dakota-bred is a horse foaled in the state and bred by a bona fide resident of the state.

The breeder of a South Dakota-bred which wins any race at a pari-mutuel meeting in the state receives a bonus award equal to 5% of the winning purse.

One race per day must be restricted to South Dakota-breds.

Washington

A Washington-bred is a horse foaled in Washington.

The breeder of a Washington-bred which wins any race at a pari-mutuel meeting in the state receives a bonus award equal to a maximum of 20% of the earned purse.

The owner of a Washington-bred that finishes first through fourth in any race at a pari-mutuel meeting in the state receives a bonus award allocated on the basis of the purses won by each qualifying Washington-bred to the total of such purses won by Washington-breds.

At least one race at each track must be restricted to Washington-breds.

West Virginia

A West Virginia-bred is a horse foaled in West Virginia and bred by a bona fide resident of the state. A West Virginia sire is a stallion standing in the state and owned by a bona fide resident of the state. The owner of a West Virginia sire, for the purpose of qualifying for stallion awards, is the owner at the time of conception.

The breeder of a West Virginia-bred that wins any race at a pari-mutuel meeting in the state receives a bonus award equal to 10% of the winning purse.

The owner of a West Virginia-bred which wins any race at a pari-mutuel meeting in the state receives a bonus award equal to 10% of the winning purse, provided that the owner is a bona fide resident of the state.

The owner of a West Virginia sire of a West Virginia-bred that wins any race at a pari-mutuel meeting in the state receives a bonus award equal to 10% of the winning purse. There is legislation not yet passed that would create purse supplements for races restricted to West Virginia-breds. Stakes races will be supplemented through a 20% share of this fund and purses for overnight races would be supplemented using the remaining 80%.

State-bred incentive programs more often than not make the difference between profit and loss, or the difference between a home run and an ordinary sale for a local breeder. For the buyer of a state-bred yearling, the restricted races, particularly the stakes, allowances, and high price claiming races offer lucrative earning opportunities that can easily make the difference between profit and loss at the end of the year.

Some Examples of State-Bred Benefits

Texas Delta was sold as a yearling by Clear Creek Stud in August of 1983 for $18,000. Texas Delta is by Nile Delta, a stallion standing at Clear Creek Stud for a fee of $2,000 live foal, and he is out of a 16-year-old mare purchased several years earlier at private treaty for a modest sum. This was a profitable sale as a yearling, but since then it has turned into a real bonanza for the farm by virtue of breeders' awards that Texas Delta has earned. As a juvenile through November 15, Texas Delta has become a stakes winner of $95,578. In so doing, Texas Delta has already earned over $12,000 in breeders' awards for Clear Creek Stud, because he is an accredited Louisiana-bred. The benefit to the owners, Texas Racing Stable, is obvious in that they are able to run him in races restricted to accredited Louisiana-breds. You can see from the accompanying charts how much this has meant. In the Cross Lake Stakes, the purse supplement, because of the state fund, was $20,000. Texas Delta earned 60% of this. In the September 28 race, Texas Delta won a restricted allowance race with a purse of $14,500, of which $3,500 was a supplement. Again, 60% of this supplement went to Texas Racing Stable.

Nile Delta's owners (he is syndicated) also will reap substantial benefits from Texas Delta's success. Because his victories were allowance and stakes wins, a stallion award of approximately $5,000 will accrue to the syndicate from these two races alone and will be paid in August, 1985.

TENTH RACE

La. Downs

AUGUST 17, 1984

7 FURLONGS. (1.21⅗) 3rd Running CROSS LAKE STAKES, ALLOWANCE. $35,000 Added (includes $20,000 supplement). 2-year-olds, accredited Louisiana-bred. Weight, 120 lbs. Winners of an accredited $9,000 twice other than maiden or claiming, 3 lbs. additional. Non-winners of an accredited $9,000 once other than maiden or claiming allowed 2 lbs.; an accredited $6,000 other than maiden or claimng, 4 lbs.; maidens, 6 lbs. (Closed Saturday August 11 with 20 nominations, with $150 to pass the entry box on Wednesday, August 15, and $150 additional to start on Friday, August 17. Should this race not be divided and the entry number exceed the starting gate capacity, high weights will be preferred and an also eligible list will be drawn. Different owners will have equal draw according to weights. The second parts of same owner entries will have no consideration over a single interest. Failure to draw into the race cancels all fees.)

Value of race $39,350; value to winner $23,610; second $7,870; third $3,935; fourth $2,361; fifth $1,574. Mutuel pool $76,939. Exacta Pool, $101,165.

Last Raced	Horse	Eqt.A.Wt PP St	¼	½	Str	Fin	Jockey	Odds $1
2Aug84 8LaD2	Texas Delta	2 116 13 1	31½	1hd	13	18 Poyadou B	10.70
2Aug84 8LaD1	Snap A Buck	b 2 120 3 6	4½	4½	32	2½ Sam J D	2.60
13Jly84 8LaD6	Illustrious High	2 116 .8 8	6hd	62½	43	3nk Snyder L	7.10
4Aug8411LaD3	Red Soda Pop	2 120 2 9	9½	91	5hd	41½ Franklin R J	3.00
2Aug84 8LaD4	Native Robber	b 2 116 1 7	2hd	2½	2½	5hd Delahoussaye D J	30.50
2Aug84 8LaD9	Process Server	b 2 116 6 13	11hd	111½	73	66 Lively J	8.70
4Aug8411LaD6	No Brag Just Fact	b 2 116 12 4	51½	5½	6hd	7½ Ardoin R	8.70
2Aug84 3LaD1	Prince Beau	2 116 9 5	7hd	7½	81½	8nk Court J K	13.20
10Aug84 3LaD1	Kanstreak	b 2 116 7 14	132½	136	10hd	9nk Hightower T W	9.50
2Aug84 8LaD5	Jumping Rope	b 2 117 4 12	123	121½	91½	105½ Theriot B J	54.90
5Aug8411EvD5	Pacific Sun	b 2 116 5 10	10½	101	112	111 Guajardo A	f-31.70
28Jly84 9JnD4	Swiss Claim	2 116 11 3	8½	8hd	122½	124 Holland M A	31.70
2Aug84 3LaD	Dr. Joachim	2 114 14 11	14	14	14	133½ White J R	f-31.70
4Aug84 9JnD4	Bold Abuse	b 2 116 10 2	1hd	31	131½	14 Frazier R L	f-37.20

f—Mutuel field.

OFF AT 7:37. Start good. Won driving. Time, :22⅗, :45⅕, 1:10⅗, 1:24⅕ Track fast.

$2 Mutuel Prices:

11-TEXAS DELTA	23.40	7.80	4.20
3-SNAP A BUCK		4.00	3.20
7-ILLUSTRIOUS HIGH			4.40

$5 EXACTA (11-3) PAID $189.00

B. g, by Nile Delta—Snow Zeem, by Hillsdale. Trainer Schultz Robert D. Bred by Clear Creek Stud (La).

EIGHTH RACE

La. Downs

SEPTEMBER 28, 1984

6 ½ FURLONGS. (1.15) ALLOWANCE. Purse $14,500 (Includes $3,500 supplement). 2-year-olds, accredited Louisiana-breds which have not won two accredited races. Weight, 122 lbs. Non-winners of an accredited race other than claiming allowed 4 lbs.; maidens, 8 lbs.

Value of race $14,500; value to winner $8,700; second $2,900; third $1,450; fourth $870; fifth $580. Mutuel pool $52,223. Exacta Pool, $76,130.

Last Raced	Horse	Eqt.A.Wt PP St	¼	½	Str	Fin	Jockey	Odds $1
15Sep8411LaD4	Texas Delta	2 122 11 1	1½	12	16	15 Snyder L	1.90
31Aug84 3LaD2	Tricky Bond	2 122 5 9	11	11	6hd	21½ Herrera C	13.40
17Aug84 8LaD2	British Ruler	b 2 122 8 5	3hd	23	22	31 Pellerin R S	3.30
19Sep84 3LaD2	Ronic Wind	b 2 114 1 10	2hd	3hd	32½	4hd Poyadou B E	15.70
10Sep84 8EvD1	Mr. Jones Country	b 2 113 9 2	93	92½	51	54½ Melancon G5	39.40
8Sep8411LaD9	Process Server	b 2 122 7 4	7hd	71	7½	61½ Lively J	12.10
7Sep84 9LaD10	Kid Caneck	b 2 118 4 11	104	102½	107	72 Whited D E	61.10
21Sep84 6LaD8	Pacific Lark	2 122 2 8	62	5hd	8hd	8no Hightower T W	26.00
17Aug8410LaD5	Native Robber	b 2 122 3 6	4½	61½	92	91 Delahoussaye D J	29.40
15Sep8411LaD3	No Brag Just Fact	b 2 122 6 7	5hd	42½	4½	107 Ardoin R	2.40
8Sep84 9EvD1	Chris's Lil Kicker	b 2 118 10 3	85	81	11	11 Guajardo A	32.40

OFF AT 4:32. Start good. Won driving. Time, :22⅗, :45⅕, 1:10⅘, 1:17⅘ Track fast.

B. g, by Nile Delta—Snow Zeem, by Hillsdale. Trainer Schultz Robert D. Bred by Clear Creek Stud (La).

In the Cross Lake Stakes at Louisiana Downs (top chart), Texas Delta earned for his breeders, Clear Creek Stud, an award of $4,722. The syndicate members of Nile Delta will share the stallion award of $3,540. And the owners of the gelding were able to run him in a race restricted to Louisiana-breds that received a purse supplement of $20,000. Texas Delta followed with a win in an allowance race (bottom chart), which meant another $1,740 in breeders' awards and $1,300 to the Nile Delta syndicate.

R. J.'s Nijinsky is the first foal from the mare Greek Dazzler, purchased by Clear Creek Stud in Florida for $34,000. The colt brought only $9,700 at the Fasig-Tipton Louisiana sale. He was smallish and somewhat immature and that, coupled with a weak market, resulted in an unsatisfactory price. R. J.'s Nijinsky didn't start until three, probably because of his size and immaturity. At three through October 15, though, R. J.'s Nijinsky had won three of seven starts. He had earned $21,462 for his owners and almost $4,000 in breeders' awards for Clear Creek Stud. If he continues to run as well, the breeders' awards may well turn a loss into a profit!

FIFTH RACE	6 ½ FURLONGS. (1.15) CLAIMING. Purse $13,200 (includes $3,200 supplement). 3-year-olds,
La. Downs	accredited Louisiana-bred. Weight, 122 lbs. Non-winners of an accredited race since September 4 allowed 4 lbs.; since August 4, 8 lbs. Claiming price, $25,000. (Races where entered
OCTOBER 4, 1984	for $20,000 or less not considered.)

Value of race $13,200; value to winner $7,920; second $2,640; third $1,320; fourth $792; fifth $528. Mutuel pool $73,714.

Last Raced	Horse	Eqt.A.Wt	PP	St	¼	½	Str	Fin	Jockey	Cl'g Pr	Odds $1
19Sep84 8LaD1	R. J.'s Nijinsky	3 114	7	1	1hd	22	14	11	Ardoin R	25000	2.20
30Aug84 5LaD2	Lipan Magic	b 3 114	1	8	8	7hd	3hd	27	Hightower T W	25000	6.60
30Aug84 5LaD1	Garabaldi	3 114	6	4	4½	4½	67	3½	Court J K	25000	5.90
27Sep84 8LaD4	Shecky Jay	3 114	2	6	5½	5hd	5hd	4nk	Sorrows A G Jr	25000	17.60
21Sep84 2LaD4	Rampant Son	b 3 109	8	3	2½	1hd	22	51	Fox W I Jr5	25000	2.80
12Sep84 8LaD2	Fancy Star	3 118	4	7	6½	3½	4hd	66	Holland M A	25000	6.90
26Sep84 5LaD10	Reason To Rob	3 114	3	2	78	8	7½	714	Guajardo A	25000	5.40
21Sep84 2LaD3	Lolly M.	b 3 114	5	5	3½	63	8	8	Melancon G	25000	29.20

OFF AT 3:00. Start good. Won driving. Time, :22⅖, :46, 1:11¾, 1:18¼ Track fast.

$2 Mutuel Prices:	7-R. J.'S NIJINSKY	6.40	3.60	3.00
	1-LIPAN MAGIC		6.00	4.00
	6-GARABALDI			3.40

Dk. b. or br. c, by Baldski—Greek Dazzler, by Gleaming. Trainer Walker Charles W. Bred by Clear Creek Stud Inc & Partners (La).

R. J.'S NIJINSKY put away RAMPANT SON entering the stretch and held sway under pressure. LIPAN MAGIC wheeled at the start and was taken up, rallied outside of horses through the stretch and finished with good energy. GARABALDI held on well for third. SHECKY JAY was outrun. RAMPANT SON vied outside of the winner through the turn and tired. FANCY STAR tired. REASON TO ROB was outrun. LOLLY M. was through early.

Owners— 1, D'Agostino V; 2, Russell R S; 3, Salem C R; 4, Jerome F; 5, Gabriel H J; 6, Vanston & Folsom; 7, Lorino J; 8, Flying M Ranch.

Trainers— 1, Walker Charles W; 2, Robideaux Larry Jr; 3, Hallock George H; 4, Hudson Billy; 5, Leggio Andrew Jr; 6, O'Bryant Jim; 7, Schultz R Denton; 8, Melek Dawn.

As a result of the victory of R. J.'s Nijinsky in this claiming race, Clear Creek Stud will receive a breeders' award of $1,584. And the owner of the colt was able to run him in a race with a purse $3,200 larger than an unrestricted race with similar conditions.

Chapter 10

Theories, Systems, And Innovations

This chapter is about some of the theories, systems, and innovations you may run into during your experience in the horse business. To be perfectly honest, we don't necessarily feel that all of them are completely valid, but it is important to know about them.

Unfortunately, there is no "miracle formula" for breeding a good horse—if there were it would take a lot of the fun and mystery out of the business—and probably the best formula for breeding good horses, in our opinion, is one of the oldest: "Breed the best to the best and hope for the best."

Lately, because the price of horses has risen to such extremes, this has had to be revised to: "Breed the best you can obtain to the best you can afford and hope for he best." The basic formula is still probably the most valid one in existence.

We feel it important, however, to acquaint you with some of the more popular systems and theories of today, because you'll undoubtedly encounter someone who is a practitioner of one of them, and you can probably save yourself a little ime and, possibly some grief, by knowing in advance what they're talking about.

The theories range in complexity from the simple (Bold Ruler crossed well with Princequillo mares) to the extremely complex $(Y = 71,752 + 18,291 \ X_1 + 34,391 \ X_2 - 8,511 \ X_3 + 956 \ X_4 - 11,253 \ X_5)$.

We have no intention of passing judgment, one way or the other, on any theory or any system mentioned in this chapter. As a matter of fact, we feel that many of hem have some validity as a tool, but only as a tool, for picking out horses or leciding on a mating.

We'll state at the outset, though, that we feel many of the innovations which have been brought about by the computer in terms of pedigree research and equine biomechanics will go down in history as revolutionary advances for the business. However, we will give you a few things to think about with respect to all of them.

First, we'll bet you that we can find a horse, a good horse, to fit into any theory which has ever been thought up by the human mind. As a matter of fact, most of these theories were devised by people who were trying to figure out what makes a good horse good and so they'll be able to mention at least three or four really top horses which prove their theory.

Secondly, you'll notice that almost all of the breeding systems are based on prepotent sires. Those are sires which are especially strong in the transmission of a particular trait, usually a desirable one, to a vast majority of their offspring. In other words, they "stamp" their get. Those stallions often change the course of the breed, so they are the subject of many of the theories. And, for you feminists out there, stallions are usually chosen as the subject of breeding theories because they produce 40-50 offspring a year, while mares produce, you hope, one per year.

Finally, we can tell you one other thing with absolutely no fear of ever being proven wrong. If, as will inevitably happen, someone begins to talk of the infallibility of their system or, if someone says their system is the only answer to breeding or picking out good horses, run like hell. Avoid those people like the plague, and you'll wind up thanking us in the long run. As mentioned above, some of these theories may be of some help to you at some time, *but there is no magic formula for picking or breeding good horses.* If there were such a formula, the few with all the money would have all the good horses, and there'd be no John Henrys or Seattle Slews.

In the interest of fairness, we will present these theories and systems in alphabetical order.

Computerized Information and Record Keeping

As was mentioned in several previous chapters, the thoroughbred business is highly information-intensive. As a matter of fact, every horse appearing in *The Stud Book* today can be traced back to the Byerly Turk, the Godolphin Barb, the Darley Arabian, and the 60 or so English mares to whom they were bred to establish the thoroughbred breed. Furthermore, this is undoubtedly the most fully documented sport in the world, and not only can you tell what every thoroughbred who ever set foot on a race track won, you can tell where he was during every point of the race, how fast he ran, whom he beat and how much, what he paid, what weight he carried, etc. In short, everything that happened.

This information was and is, of course, very valuable in the purchase and mating of thoroughbreds. When we first started out in this business, people used to spend hours upon hours looking up pedigrees and race records on horses in whom they were interested.

In 1966, The Jockey Club began to enter into a computer all the racing and breeding information pertinent to the breed and, by 1970, they were generating pedigrees by computer. But their services were, in truth, available only to sales companies and individuals who were willing to wait for some considerable time for The Jockey Club Statistical Bureau to find the time to generate a pedigree or a race record for them.

Then, in the early '70s a company called Bloodstock Research and Statistical Bureau began offering a service which would revolutionize pedigree research and record keeping in the thoroughbred business. They offered a time-sharing computer through which anyone who had a compatible system could call up and generate a pedigree, race record or any one of a number of other valuable informational reports, within a matter of minutes.

Suddenly, research which used to take a trained person hours to generate could be called up within a matter of minutes, and at a very reasonable cost. For example, a catalog-style pedigree (one with full information, not the kind you get in a sales catalog) costs $14.50 generated by computer, whereas it used to cost a minimum of $25 from a pedigree service. If you did it yourself, you could count on spending about three hours of your time, at whatever value you place on it.

In addition, the computer permits a breeder to make certain analyses of stallions which would literally take weeks and even months to complete prior to the advent of the computer[1].

Perhaps the most difficult proposition in terms of obtaining information from the Bloodstock Research computer is making up your mind what you want. By just dialing the computer, entering your name and password, you have access to more than 50 different types of reports; in addition to which you can obtain race results from any major North American race track within minutes after a race is run; you can call up "The Thoroughbred Daily News," which is a brief synopsis of what's going on in the industry; or you can gain access to Bloodstock

---

A personal note from Kirkpatrick on the subject. In the late '60s, Bill Robertson, the late editor of *The Thoroughbred Record*, and I first started working on the system of stallion analysis currently used by that publication which compares a stallion's performance with the mares to whom he was bred to the performance of those same mares when they were bred to other stallions to see whether he is improving on his mares or vice versa, e.g.:

NORTHERN DANCER, 18 starts in 2 seasons, 14 wins, $580,647. Sire of 72 (108) SWs. Syndicated, standing at E. P. Taylor's Windfields Farm Maryland, Inc. near Chesapeake City, Maryland. Through 1983 sired 457 foals out of 346 mares which produced 1,966 foals by 499 other stallions.

	By NORTHERN DANCER (16)	Mares' Other Foals
Runners/Winners	274/ 218 (80%)	1,368/1,054 (77%)
Starts/Wins	5,941/1,027 (17%)	34,822/5,166 (15%)
Earnings	$14,655,291	$56,951,791
Avg Per Rnr/Index	$53,486/ 3.91	$41,631/ 3.03
Avg Per Start/Index	$ 2,467/ 4.52	$ 1,636/ 3.20

Statistics reflect North American racing only.

I performed this same statistical analysis on three stallions by hand. It took me 11 weeks to complete the research! The same analysis can be performed by the computer in two or three minutes. This particular form of analysis is available only from *The Thoroughbred Record* and not from Bloodstock Research, but I wanted to include this little story as a point of reference to the value of the computer in thoroughbred research.

Research's Thoroughbred Multiple Listing Service, which lists mares, seasons and shares which the company has for sale.

While it would be foolish in the space allocated here to attempt to list all the reports that are available, it is worthwhile to list all the major categories of reports that are available and discuss each of them briefly:

Race Records. The computer offers nine different types of tabulated race records, ranging in complexity from a single line which lists only starts, wins, seconds, thirds, money earned, and stakes wins and placings, to a year-by-year analysis of a horse's race track performance. Also, as a measure of a horse's class, Bloodstock Research has developed what they call the Standard Starts Index (SSI). Basically, it is a comparison of each horse's average earnings per start with the average earnings per start of every other horse of the same sex from the same crop. For example, if all the colts born in 1980 earned an average of $1,000 every time they started and a horse you were interested in was from that crop and he earned $2,500 every time he started he'd have an SSI of 2.5 or, if he earned $500 each time he ran, he'd have an SSI of .5. One more thing, if a horse has an SSI of 3.64 or better, he is designated as a superior runner and he ranks among the top 3% of all horses racing in North America. It is probably the best raw index of racing class available today.

Broodmare Produce Records. There are four different types of broodmare produce records, which offer varying forms of the pedigree and race record of the mare and of all her offspring.

Stallion Progeny Reports. The nine different stallion reports range from those which contain a tabulated race record of every one of the stallion's offspring who has ever started in a race to reports which list only his stakes winners, stakes-placed runners, and superior runners. Each stallion report also contains a summary at the end which includes such information as the stallion's number and percentage of starters, winners, stakes winners, stakes-placed horses, superior runners, earnings, average earnings (per start and per runner), average number of starts per year, and average number of years raced.

Catalog-Style Pedigrees. These pedigrees, as mentioned, are not edited to reflect the particular horse in its best light, so they are useful as a comparison to a sales catalog (see Chapter 4). There are 11 different types available in varying complexities, but they all basically tell you just about everything you'll need to know about a horse you're thinking about buying. There is one thing you should know about the catalog-style pedigrees and, for that matter, all the computer pedigrees, and that is they're a little weak in terms of foreign racing. For foreign racing, they include only stakes wins and placings, so a horse in a report can be a good, solid performer abroad and still show up as "unraced" in a report. It will indicate that the horse was sent abroad, however, and that should be a clue to you to look further for foreign racing and breeding statistics.

Broodmare Sire Reports. As you'll learn below, under the subject of "Nicks," it is often very useful to know what kind of producers the daughters of a particular sire make. There are three different kinds of broodmare reports, ranging from a one-page summary all the way to a full produce record on every daughter of a particular stallion. (Warning: the latter is going to be a long report and can be fairly costly.)

Previous Week's Stakes Results. Both foreign and domestic stakes results for the previous week can be obtained and they can be called up by the name of the race, by name of the first three finishers, or by the sire, dam, or broodmare sire of the first three finishers.

Sales Reports. These six types of reports are among the most useful reports you can obtain from the computer, especially when you're headed for a breeding stock sale. What you can get is the selling price for any horse sold at public auction, *since 1975*, listed by sire, dam, horse, broodmare, broodmare sire, and/or covering sire.

In addition to the pedigree and other services offered on the Bloodstock Research computer, they offer time sharing for farm accounting and herd health, or, if you invest in a personal computer, they offer software packages for the same purposes. As a matter of fact, there are quite a number of companies currently offering software for farm accounting and herd health and, while we've not tried all of them, most of them seem to be pretty good.

If you're not involved in the business to the point at which you feel that you can justify the purchase of a computer, many of the state breeders' organizations (see Appendix) have computers nowadays, and they sell pedigrees to members at cost or a little above.

However, you don't have to get too involved in the horse business to make a terminal cost effective. The cheapest terminal is only $495, and the company requires only that you spend a minimum of $50 a month with them, so you can get off very reasonably.

For further information, contact:

Bloodstock Research Information Services
P.O. Box 4097
Lexington, Kentucky 40544
Phone: (606) 223-4444

In addition to Bloodstock Research, there are two other companies now offering computerized buying and selling of bloodstock, predominantly stallion seasons and shares. Membership in each is a valuable information tool regardless of whether or not you do much buying and selling. The two are:

International Seasons and Shares Information Exchange. As the name implies this company offers seasons and shares which are priced on a computer system, similar to a multiple listing service. Season prices are published and the agents from whom they are available are listed, so you can deal with the agents on a direct basis. This service also is hooked up to the racing division of British PressTel, so they offer European race results nearly as quickly as you can get North American race results. It operates with terminals that are compatible with those of the other companies, so, if you're a member and have your access code, you can get information from ISSIE with the same computer you use for Bloodstock and Matchmaker. For more information, contact:

International Seasons and Shares Information Exchange
P.O. Box 1957
Lexington, Kentucky 40593
Phone: (606) 278-5491

Matchmaker Breeders' Exchange. This is sort of an over-the-counter market for seasons and shares, with bid and ask prices published on a weekly basis, or, once again, if you're a member, you can gain access to the information through the same terminal you use for Bloodstock Research and ISSIE. There is one thing to remember with respect to Matchmaker, though, and that is *all seasons are sold with no guarantee whatsoever*, not even the guarantee that the stallion in question will be alive when your mare is ready to be bred. As a consequence, you should figure that the seasons listed as being sold are at a price about 60% of what they'd be on a live foal basis. Membership to Matchmaker, if you meet the rather stringent qualifications they've established for membership, is $400 a year. For further information, contact:

Matchmaker Breeders' Exchange
333 West Vine Street (Suite 1630)
Lexington, Kentucky 40507
Phones: (800) 522-2348 and (606) 259-0451

Dosage Systems

In the 1920s, a French cavalry officer, Col. J. J. Vuillier, wrote a book in which he analyzed the pedigrees of certain prominent racehorses of the time through the 12th generation, which meant he had to account for 4,096 ancestors for each. The end result was Vuillier's Dosage system, which stated that certain sires were desirable in the makeup of great thoroughbreds and, if the pedigree of a particular sire were lacking in any of the required bloodlines, the deficiency should be made up by breeding him to mares which contained a high proportion of the missing line. Vuillier managed the breeding operation of the Aga Khan with great success, and his matings produced such horses as *Blenheim II, *Bahram, *Mahmoud, and *Nasrullah. Geneticists, however, citing Galton's Law, quite properly felt that going back 12 generations was a bit extreme, considering that each ancestor in the 12th generation was contributing only 1/4,096th of the genetics of each horse in question.

Vuillier's system was refined and updated in the late '50s and early '60s by an Italian lawyer, Dr. Franco Varola, who identified 100 stallions as being especially important in changing or influencing the direction of the breed. These stallions were called "Chefs-de-Race" by Varola, who also divided them into five categories, depending upon their degree of speed or staying ability. The categories ranged from "Brilliant" for the sprinters, through "Intermediate," "Classic," and "Solid," to "Professional," the latter category of which were ires imparting the most stamina. In addition to reducing the formula to a more reasonable four generations, Varola refined the dosage theory to include a measure of balance, i.e. if you were picking a mating for a "Brilliant" sire, you'd be wise to add a little stamina by picking something from the "Classic" or "Professional" categories. As with Vuillier, Varola made no allowance for the position which a sire occupies in a pedigree, i.e. a horse in the fourth generation was given the same weight as one in the first generation, despite the fact that his influence can logically be only 1/8th as much.

In the late '60s, Leon Rasmussen, the breeding expert and columnist for the *Daily Racing Form*, began to analyze and expand on the Varola system. He was joined, early in 1980, by Steven A. Roman, Ph.D., who, with Rasmussen, added another 54 chefs-de-race, and developed a numerical system of weighting the position of the chefs-de-race according to their category and, more importantly, their position in the pedigree being analyzed. For instance, in deference to Galton, Roman gives a total of 16 points for a chef-de-race in the first generation, eight for the second, four for the third, and two for the fourth. Further, Rasmussen and Roman felt that not all stallions could be categorized into a single category, so if a horse fit into two categories, he is listed in both and his influence in the pedigree of his offspring is divided and put half into each category.

All this expansion, sophistication, and numerical identification has resulted in the development of three dosage indices—the Dosage Profile (a series of five numbers which reflects the proportions of aptitudinal characteristics in each category), the Dosage Index (a ratio of speed to stamina, with speed being represented by higher numbers and stamina by lower numbers), and the Center of Distribution (a measure of balance in a pedigree, with the point of perfect balance being 0).

If you are interested in pursuing the Dosage systems, particularly the Roman system, it is fully explained by Dr. Roman in *The Thoroughbred Record* of April 18, 1984 (pp. 1979-1984). The Varola system was explained by Leon Rasmussen in a three-part series in *The Record*, September 9, 16, and 23, 1967.

Gait Analysis

As the techniques of photography and computer science advanced spectacularly through the decade of the '70s, scientists began combining those techniques to improve the performance of human athletes.

Shortly thereafter, a genuine genius—and self-styled "racehorse nut"—George W. Pratt, Ph.D., a professor of electrical engineering and computer science at MIT, began employing these advanced techniques of photography, actually cinematography, and computerized analysis to study the stride of horses.

Before going further, it should be noted that Dr. Pratt has also developed a noninvasive technique of measuring bone strength in the horse; he has developed an instrumented horseshoe which measures the force of a horse's hoof as it strikes the surface of a race track; he has developed a method of testing race track consistency; and he has developed a forceplate which shows, basically, the onset of lameness in a horse's leg.

191

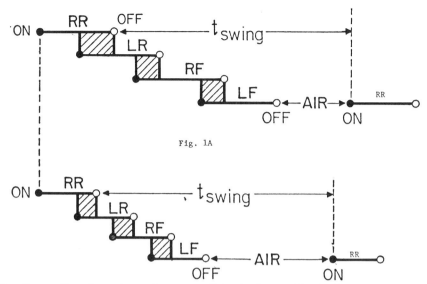

Fig. 1A

Dr. George Pratt has advanced sportsmedicine in thoroughbreds through his research on gait analysis. Figure 1A represents the timing sequence for the stride at gallop starting with the right rear (RR). Solid dots represent the times at which the leg comes down, open dots the times it lifts off. The swing and airborne times are indicted. Figure 1B is the timing sequence for the same left lead stride, but at a faster speed. The stance times of each leg (the distance between the closed and open dots) are shorter, the airborne time longer, but the swing time is unchanged.

In the gait analysis, a horse is galloped, at a two-minute clip or better, past a high-speed camera which records his action at a speed of 600 frames per second. The film is played on a screen, frame by frame, and the elements of the horse's stride are entered into the computer where they are analyzed.

The data from the computer provides a profile of each horse's stride, including stride length, step length, and air time. Those characteristics are then compared against the strides of some of the good and great horses of recent times, including Secretariat, Genuine Risk, Spectacular Bid, and Lord Avie.

The differences between an Eclipse Award winner and a $5,000 plater, Dr. Pratt writes, are:

"The better the horse, the more nearly his legs come down like the spokes of a wheel. The periods when two legs are on the ground at the same time, that is when they overlap, are as brief as possible. . . .

"Secondly, the superior horse not only has a highly efficient stride, but he has the conformation and physical stamina to maintain his action in the face of ever-increasing fatigue. . . .

"This means that when the horse tires, fatigue modifies the timing of his stride, drastically lowering its mechanical efficiency. Hence an even bigger effort is demanded and even though the tired horse has slowed down, he is forced to spend more and more time in the air than when fresh and running faster. He has to 'climb.' . . ."

Dr. Pratt is honest enough to admit that gait analysis, still in its nascent stages, is far from foolproof. He cites horses with "a super gait" who turned out to have

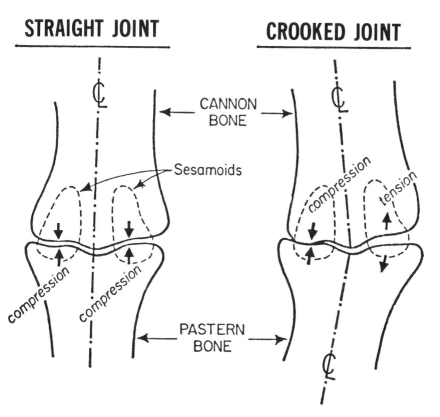

STRAIGHT JOINT

CROOKED JOINT

CANNON BONE

Sesamoids

compression

tension

compression

compression

PASTERN BONE

Load shared over entire joint surface

Load concentrated on half the joint surface

Dr. Pratt's research has revealed that uneven loading, as may be experienced on turns, can seriously overload the weight bearing capacity of the joint. The left diagram illustrates the fetlock joint when the load is shared over the whole joint surface; the diagram on the right when a lateral bend in the leg causes the load to be applied to half the joint surface.

little or no success on the race track and horses which have been rated as having inefficient strides who have turned out to be stakes winners. But the system is being constantly changed.

Dr. Pratt's technique of gait analysis was largely founded through the Association for the Advancement of Sports Potential, which patented the system and donated it to MIT.

While we promised at the outset of this chapter not to make any judgments on any of the theories and systems presented, we're going to make an exception here. Dr. Pratt's work is, in our opinion, not only fascinating, but is extremely useful. In addition, it provides a great deal of heretofore unrealized insight into a horse's way of going, soundness, and lameness. As a consequence, we'd like to urge you to get copies of several of Dr. Pratt's articles which have appeared in *Th* *Thoroughbred Record* over the past few years, most notably:

"Remarks on Lameness and Breakdown," October 26, 1977 (pp. 1486-1489);
"Biomechanics of a Race Horse (Gait Analysis and Measurement of Bone Strength)," March 7, 1979 (pp. 768-772);
"Analyzing Track Characteristics," February 20, 1980 (pp. 771-776).

Also, Susan Rhodemyre did an article on Dr. Pratt and gait analysis in *Th* *Record* issue of March 10, 1982. For additional information we'd suggest yo* contact:

The Association for the Advancement of Sports Potential
P.O. Box 185
Unionville, Pennsylvania 19375
Phone: (215) 793-1881

Heartbeats

Over the past few years a number of people, laymen as well as veterinarians have begun to listen to the hearts of horses at sales.

Needless to say, heart size and efficiency are important determinants in a horse's overall ability, or, at least, his ability to perform to capacity. As a matte of fact, the heart is so important that the term "heart" is often used in the jargo* of the industry as a catchall phrase for courage, intelligence, ability, will to win etc.

By listening to the heart of a yearling, a veterinarian might pick up some glar ing defect which might militate against the horse's living up to his ability. Som leading equine practitioners also warn that, as with every theory and system, on can very easily find truly excellent racehorses whose hearts sound defectiv through a stethoscope. There's a very real danger of turning down a horse whic* will turn out to be a top racehorse.

At the time this is written, veterinarians believe there is some promise in the us of ultrasound in the prediction of athletic ability, but that is in its very earl stages.

Inbreeding, Line Breeding, and Outcrossing

Inbreeding can be defined as the mating of related individuals, especially i order to reproduce desired characteristics. Actually, all thoroughbreds are inbre to a certain extent, since the breed descends from three stallions and approx imately 60 mares. Today, inbreeding usually refers to the same horse appearing i a pedigree more than once in the first five generations.

While inbreeding, in the latter sense, has been practiced with impunity i thoroughbreds over the past century as a shortcut to attainment of a specifi desired characteristic of a particular sire or mare, there may be certain dangerou side effects. Just as inbreeding causes a concentration of desirable traits, it ca also cause a similar concentration of undesirable ones, such as unsoundness, in fertility, and, probably most often, mental problems.

One of the most infamous cases of inbreeding producing mental problems oc-
curred with a filly named Mata Hari, who was one of the top racemares of the
mid-1930s. As a matter of fact, she was a champion filly at two and three and
earned $66,699 in the days when that was a whole lot of money. Mata Hari was
inbred 3x4 to Hastings, which meant that Hastings appeared in the third and
fourth generation of her pedigree. Her pedigree looked like this:

			Commando	Domino
		Peter Pan		Emma C.
			*Cinderella	Hermit
	Peter Hastings			Mazurka
			Hastings	Spendthrift
		Nettie Hastings		*Cinderella
			Princess Nettie	His Highness
Mata Hari				Nettie
			Fair Play	Hastings
		Man o' War		*Fairy Gold
			Mahubah	*Rock Sand
	War Woman			*Merry Token
			Uncle	*Star Shoot
		Topaz		The Niece
			Ruby Nethersole	*Star Ruby
				Nethersole

As you can see, Mata Hari was also inbred 3x4 to *Cinderella, but that apparently was not part of
the problem.

The problem was that while Hastings was a source of great talent, he was also a
source of notoriously bad temper. As a matter of fact, Mata Hari's mating was
determined, not by hours of study, but by the fact that Mata Hari's dam, War
Woman, refused to leave the farm when she was due to be bred to a prominent
stallion, so they bred her instead to Peter Hastings, who stood at her owner's Dix-
iana Farm.

At any rate, Mata Hari's exceptional abilities were exceeded only by her foul
temper, and she was the scourge of the race track, when she was racing, and the
breeding farm when she was at stud.

Mata Hari, incidentally, went on to produce the full brothers Spy Song, who
was also a high-class racehorse and top sire, and Mr. Music, who was unraced,
but turned out to be one of the few unraced horses to be successful at stud.

Line breeding can be described, generally, as inbreeding outside the fourth
generation, and it is considered to be less volatile than strict inbreeding. It is
defined, in *Genetics of the Horse*, as "an attempt to get as much blood of a
stallion or mare into the animals of the herd as possible, while at the same time inbreeding is held as low as possible. . . . Studies with most animals have shown
that mild inbreeding with rigid selection usually results in initial improvement
but, when inbreeding of 25 to 50 percent is reached, some loss in vigor usually occurs. . . ."

When the loss in vigor or fertility begins to occur, or the mental problems increase, it may be time to outcross, which is try to find a mating in which the same
horse doesn't appear more than once in the first four generations. Since many of
the detrimental genes are apparently recessive, this is supposed to bring about

what is called "hybrid vigor." Hybrid vigor, however, diminishes rapidly in succeeding generations, so one might wind up "throwing out the baby with the bath water."

Bruce Lowe System

While the Bruce Lowe system is seldom used today, and nobody who uses i apparently, admits it, you are still liable to hear about it.

Bruce Lowe was a student of pedigrees who moved to the U.S. from Australia but, after meeting with little or no success moved to England where he traced the tail-female lines of winners of the English Derby, the English Oaks, and the S Leger to the earliest recorded female ancestress of each winner.

He found that all of them traced to 43 mares, and he numbered the families according to the number of winners of those three classics. The female line with the most winners of those classics was designated as Family Number 1, while the rest of the families were numbered in descending order of classic winners to Family Number 43.

Perhaps due to his lack of acceptance in this country, Lowe was rather contemptuous of the U.S. families, so he did not include them in his system.

If you're interested in learning more about the Bruce Lowe system, Leo Rasmussen described it fully in *The Thoroughbred Record*, June 17, 1967.

Measuring

Another "innovation" in the selection of horses for purchase is measuring them. While this is really nothing new (Indians reportedly measured their ponies in attempts to predetermine ability), the addition of computerization to the equation has brought measuring of horses in an attempt to determine their potential a new level of complexity and sophistication.

Today's systems of measurement are, in essence, an attempt to quantify numerically the basic quality that all horsemen feel is essential to good conformation—balance.

The developer and leading practitioner of measuring horses today is a man named Ken Trimble, who consulted with structural engineers, mechanic engineers, and space engineers, apparently, and has attempted to apply the principles of each discipline to develop a method of physical measurements of horse.

He and the practitioners he has trained throughout the country take a tape measure and make some 25 measurements on every horse they analyze (see illustration). These measurements are then analyzed and adjusted by a subjective measurement they call body texture, to come up with a "balance index," which a numerical indication of a horse's balance and basic engineering, and, therefore its potential. The index is stated on a scale from 0 to 100, and a score of 95 or better is supposed to indicate superior potential; 90 to 94.9 should indicate "an ability to win under the right conditions"; and an index below 90 indicates very little potential. The body texture is made by manual palpation and is graded A + , A—, or B. All these letters and numbers are then combined and compared to to

196

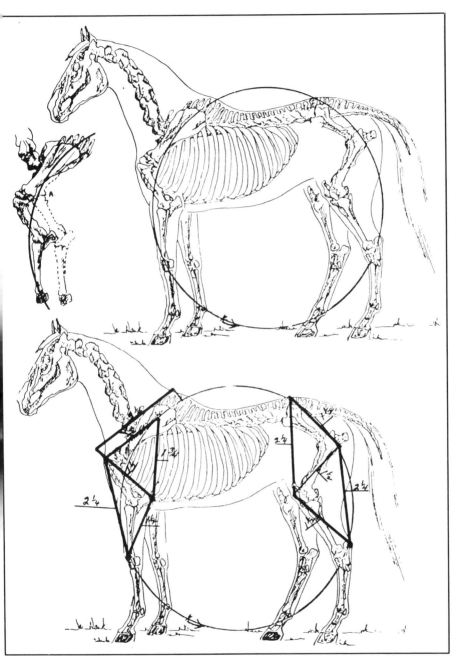

Techniques of measuring. The illustration on the top shows the circle which touches on the ten points where extreme tension is exerted when a horse is in motion. The illustration on the bottom shows triangles, the size of which determine 1) the amount of power a horse can produce; 2) the ability of the front end to stride in harmony with the rear end; 3) the distance a horse is able to stride.

197

tension points which all fall "on a perfect circle" in a great racehorse. If the horse is not properly balanced, they say, some of those points will fall inside or outside the perfect circle.

Not surprisingly, this system is not confined to picking horses for racing; it also has breeding applications. The horses to be mated are assigned a set of three conformation numbers, called a "breeding bubble," and one of five genetic types: "A," "B," "C," "D," or "E." Those factors are also analyzed with similar breeding bubble and genetic types for the mare to determine an ideal mating.

If you're interested in pursuing the measurement system further, it was discussed fully in an article in *The Record* of June 29, 1983 (pp. 3128-3140).

Nicks

A "nick" is a pattern of breeding which has (or is perceived to have) produced an exceptional proportion of good horses over time, for instance, the cross of Bold Ruler with *Princequillo mares, which was mentioned at the beginning of this chapter.

Often as not, as in the case of Bold Ruler and *Princequillo mares, a nick may be established by a very successful stallion standing at a farm with a preponderance of a certain type of mare. Students of breeding are always looking for trends of some sort, though, and, as a consequence, they occasionally find ones where they don't exist.

Once again, the entrance of the computer on the scene has changed the complexion of the system of nicks. As a matter of fact, the previously mentioned Bloodstock Research offers a very successful mating service for mares which has reportedly produced the likes of Interco, Miss Oceana, and Lucky Lucky Lucky. It is, in truth, a very, very sophisticated analysis of nicks.

When you get a mating on your mare from the Bloodstock Research mating service, you'll basically be getting a computer analysis of the success or failure of various crosses or nicks in terms of producing superior runners. The report will give you a percentage value on the chances of your mating producing a superior runner. For example, if you have a daughter of Soandso and you want to breed her to Thusandsuch, or a son of Thusandsuch, it'll tell you you have a 24% chance of winding up with a superior runner or you've got 1% chance of winding up with a superior runner.

As a matter of fact, nicks quite often may be more useful in telling you what doesn't work than what does work.

If you have a computer hookup with Bloodstock Research, you can do the same thing yourself. All you need to do is pull up one of their broodmare sire reports for the sire of the mare you're trying to mate. Then you go through it carefully and note which sires cross well with the broodmare sire in question and that should give you some sort of clue as to the crosses that seem to work. If you're making more than $3.85 an hour, however, it's probably more cost efficient to have the computer do the calculations for you.

Ultrasound

As mentioned a couple of times in this chapter, new techniques of measuring various functions in the horse by ultrasound have been springing up rapidly in the business. It began with Dr. Pratt measuring bone density in the forelegs of horses via ultrasound. That was followed, very quickly, by early detection of pregnancy in mares with the use of ultrasound. This has proven very useful, not only because pregnancy can be diagnosed as early as 15 days after breeding, but veterinarians also believe this might be useful in the detection of twins.

Then, as mentioned, some other veterinarians believe that ultrasonic evaluation of the equine heart might prove to be a more valuable indicator of potential than listening to it.

This has all transpired within the last couple of years, and we feel the uses of ultrasound could be virtually unlimited.

$Y =$

Finally, there's the aforementioned

$$Y = 71,752 + 18,291 \, X_1 + 34,391 \, X_2 - 8,511 \, X_3 + 956 \, X_4 - 11,253 \, X_5.$$

This was a formula, published in 1981, for figuring out the estimated price of a yearling (Y), when:

$X_1 =$ Number of stakes winners produced by the first dam;

$X_2 =$ Assumes the first dam is a stakes winner herself;

$X_3 =$ Date of foaling, indicated by the number of months that have elapsed since January 1;

$X_4 =$ Number of stakes winners produced by the third dam;

$X_5 =$ Assumes the first dam raced and was a nonwinner.

To be perfectly honest, we'd just as soon wait in suspense and find out what the yearling brings when it sells.

Chapter 11

Plans For Investment

Now that you are "fully acquainted" with the thoroughbred business, it is time for you and your advisor to begin working out your plan of investment for the business.

Your plans, primarily, will be based on the cost estimates which are contained in Chapter 6. But before you get into those plans, we would like to reiterate several points and add a few more which should help you in deciding which course to take in the business.

First, be conservative. The cost estimates we included in Chapter 6 are accurate but, as always seems to happen, you'll probably come up with more expenses than anticipated. So, don't come up with a business plan that extends you to the limit. Leave a little room for the extras that will inevitably crop up. *Do not, ever, overextend yourself.* You may leverage your investment from time to time, but don't leverage yourself to the point where you've got to do better than most people in the business are doing just to keep up your interest payments.

Second, be sure you pick a plan which is suited to your temperament. If you want action, and you want it *now*, claim or buy a horse, so you'll have something running and then expand your involvement from there, rather than pursuing some of the longer-term forms of investment.

Third, with respect to "longer-term" investments, don't put all your eggs in one basket—don't expect to get into the business with one horse and make money; you've got to be in this business over the long term. You should plan to invest over a minimum of at least three years and, more probably, five years before you expect to receive any substantial return on your investment.

Fourth, don't buy anything because it's cheap—it won't be in the long run. A our good friend Dr. B. W. Pickett of Colorado State University is fond of saying "The sweetness of low price is never equal to the bitterness of low quality." Tha applies to the horse business, today, more than it ever has in its history.

Fifth, don't back into any segment of the business. By that we mean don't ge into the breeding business because one of your fillies didn't turn out at the rac track . . . or vice versa. We'll discuss that more, further on.

Sixth, don't invest without investigating. The more you find out about your in vestment *before* you put your money into it, the less likely you are to be subjecteu to unpleasant surprises and, therefore, the less likely you are to be unhappy witl your investment.

Now, on to the plans. What we intend to do, here, is simply set out the pros and cons of several scenarios for you, without going too deeply into specifics because the range of the business is so broad, nowadays, that it is virtually im possible to make projections for income, without an idea of the range of the business in which you'll be dealing.

Claiming Runners

This will probably be one of the most common forms of entry into th thoroughbred business. It has several advantages and disadvantages, but the three primary advantages are:

1) You get immediate action and a fairly immediate opportunity for return on investment. When you claim a horse, despite the fact that he'll be "in jail" for 30 days (see Chapter 3), you can run him back, usually within a week to ten days. This gives you some fun right away, and a chance to get some of your investment back, immediately.

2) Reasonable certainty as to the value of the horse which you own. As you've also learned if you read Chapter 3, claiming horses seldom run very far above or below their worth as a racehorse.

3) Low unit cost for getting into the game. Approximately 75% of all claiming races are run for prices of $10,000 or less, which means that you can pick up the horses very reasonably.

There are, however, disadvantages to beginning your participation in the thoroughbred business at the claiming level. Primary among them is that there probably won't be any significant appreciation of your investment, which woulc help you convert straight income into capital gains. Also, a $7,500 claiming horse eats just as much as John Henry, gets sick or hurt just as often (if not more often), and doesn't generate nearly the same returns.

Finally, fillies who are found in claiming races very seldom are the type whc will be an asset to your broodmare band—and there's absolutely *no way* a coli who is running in the claiming ranks is going to attract sufficient interest to be a decent stallion prospect, unless he moves way, way up. Consequently, when your claiming horse is through racing, there is usually going to be little or no residua value.

Buying Yearlings and Two-Year-Olds to Race

This route, of course, will be more expensive than claiming horses, because it will be a minimum of 60 to 90 days before your horse will be ready to run (and nine months or more, if you purchase a yearling), before you have any chance of return. These are very expensive times, too, since yearling breaking and training at the track are among the most expensive propositions in the business on a per diem basis.

However, this method of getting into the business also has its advantages. Since you're purchasing at auction, you will be getting your horse, by and large, at market value—at least insofar as pedigree and conformation are concerned.

Further, its value as a racehorse is not established as yet so, if it can run, there is ample room for appreciation which can generate capital gains for you. Also, you can bring the horse along at its own pace . . . which will make a tremendous amount of difference in his overall welfare and worth.

Breeding Homebreds to Race

This can be the most rewarding form of participation in the business, but it also is the most expensive and requires the most patience. It is probably the last course you should undertake, insofar as your early participation in the business is concerned, because it is so long before you receive any return on your investment.

Say you purchased a broodmare in November of 1984 with a view toward racing the resulting offspring. You'd be looking at 2½ years of doing nothing but paying bills before you'd see your horse under silks—and, even then, you wouldn't have the satisfaction of knowing that you picked out the mating that resulted in an Eclipse Award-winning two-year-old that you now own. If you own a mare and pick out the mating yourself, you can add another six months to the equation.

Remember, too, less than 2% of all horses that are born ultimately turn out to be stakes winners, so your chances of success breeding homebreds as an early endeavor in the business are very slim. Leave that section of the business up to the Phippses and the Mellons.

Purchasing a Mare in Foal

Lately, many people have been gaining entry into the horse business through purchase of a mare who is in foal at one of the many breeding stock sales around the country. This, as you'll recall if you remember John Finney's quote from Chapter 6, used to be the safest route for entering the business, and it probably still is . . . it's just not the leadpipe cinch it used to be.

Depending upon the area of the country where you keep your horses and the expertise of the farm where your mare is boarded, you can expect to average four live foals in five years, down to less than 50% live foals at some places. Throughout the thoroughbred business, according to The Jockey Club, only 55% of the mares who are bred each year produce foals that are registered as thoroughbreds. That's pretty tough sledding, if you're trying to make money. A we've been emphasizing throughout, though, the better the place you keep you mare, the better your chances are of getting a live, healthy, marketable foal.

Here, once again, it will be some considerable time and no little expense befor you begin to see a return on your investment. If you sell the foal as a yearling, i will probably be approximately 22 months before you see any return or, as men tioned above, if you intend to race the offspring of your mare, it will probably b more like 2½ years before you have any chance of return. Even if you purchase a mare who is in foal at the time you buy her, you'll have to put at least one mor stud fee into her before you see any return, and, if you breed to a stallion whose fee is due September 1 of the year bred, you might have to put two stud fees in he before you have any return.

On the subject of safe investments in the business, the safest, up until about two years ago, was the purchase of stallion shares. Most share payments are spread out over time and the time usually nearly matches the depreciation schedule for the share, so, if you're in the 50% tax bracket, you're paying only 5C cents on the dollar, if you don't get any return on the share. Also, since the owner of a share normally gets an extra season at least every four years, you'd have enough income coming in to pay for the share as your own payments came due. On today's market, though, many stallion seasons are very depressed and the seasons are bringing half, or less than half, of what the seasons were worth when the stallions were first syndicated, so the situation is very difficult.

This brings us to another admonition: *do not buy stallion shares unless you have mares you want to breed to the stallion.* Also, don't overbuy—a pretty good formula for a small operation is one share for three mares. If you go more deeply than that, you're going to limit the selection of mates for your mares too much.

While we're hanging crepe, this is as good a time as any to elaborate further on our earlier admonition against *backing* into racing. If you do decide to purchase a broodmare and breed for the market, and, as often happens, your yearling doesn't turn out to be everything you'd hoped, don't keep it and race it, thereby increasing the severity of the beating you're going to take on it. Take the little lumps and don't turn them into big lumps.

Here's a rule of thumb for placing reserves on your sales yearlings: you and your advisor appraise your sales yearling and agree on an appraisal; then take 60% of that appraisal and make it your reserve. The marketplace is a very tough judge of horseflesh, but the race track is even tougher. Don't stick with your mistakes.

Buying or Claiming a Filly as a Broodmare Prospect

This might be the best way of all to get into the business, because it affords you some immediacy of action, while offering you the long-term benefits of getting into breeding. It, too, can be expensive, though.

First, we admonish you, once again, don't *back* into this program, go into it consciously. Don't go into breeding because you bought a filly, and she can't run and isn't worth keeping in training. This will lead you to owning a broodmare you wouldn't have on a bet if you were going into the business with breeding on your mind.

There are, however, a number of well-bred fillies who can run well in allowance company and have some black type in their immediate families. Occasionally, but only very rarely, do they turn up in claiming races, so you'll probably have to pay a bit of a premium for them. However, what you'll be doing is buying a filly who'll provide you with some fun if she can run a little (don't buy her if she can't), and she'll be a filly who can produce some foals which should sell well, if she or her family improves. It's a satisfying way to get into the business, especially if you can afford to buy, say, two good fillies a year for three years.

This way, too, can get expensive, because you have to factor in stud fees in the first two years off the track before you begin to see any yearling income, but it offers some of the satisfaction of most of the programs above.

In Conclusion

Throughout this book we have tried to give you a background and basic knowledge of the thoroughbred business to help you have as pleasant an experience in the business as is possible without the luck of buying a Seattle Slew, a John Henry, or a Lord Avie.

This business has evolved rapidly from a small "clubby" business after World War II to a highly sophisticated, multibillion-dollar business today, with a lot of participants who are in it only because they smell big bucks and are hungry to get ahold of a few. Don't you be the one they get ahold of.

The thoroughbred business is in a state of flux, right now. A serious oversupply of yearlings has brought auction sales prices down everywhere but at the very top of the market and, at the top of the market there are only ten or 12 buyers, so that can be a tremendously volatile place, too.

Broodmare prices and stud fees are primarily a function of yearling prices and we expect them to come down, too, in the next few years. Additionally, a lot of mares and some stallions at the bottom end of the ladder—mares and stallions that should never have been in production in the first place because of poor pedigree, lack of ability, and bad conformation—will have to go out of production completely before the market begins to stabilize again.

Legalization of racing in such states as Texas, Georgia, and Tennessee could change the outlook temporarily, but we believe it will only slow the shakeout that must occur before the industry can return to full health, as we believe it inevitably will.

For newcomers to the business, though, there is a plus side to all of this. During the next few years, you'll be able to get more yearling or more broodmare for your money, as those who were not committed to the business and those who overextended themselves drop out.

So, if your long-range plan goes beyond the next two or three years, which it should, with the proper advice you should be in an excellent position to profit handsomely from this trend.

At the risk of being thought didactic, we're going to end this book the way we started it, with the five rules for getting into the horse business.

This time, though, we'll add another: have fun and good luck!

Rules For Entering The Horse Business

1) Learn about the business. Foolishly, many people go into the business without really understanding what they're getting into. Study horse magazines and other sources of information.

2) Obtain sound, honest advice. The person you choose as your advisor in the horse business will make the difference between a pleasant and an unpleasant experience; between profit, loss and ruin. You must find a competent, knowledgeable and, most importantly, honest counselor—someone who is compatible with you and your needs. There's absolutely no way that a person who is not spending a majority of his or her time in the business can do justice to an investment without good advice.

3) Work out a plan for your investment. Establish your goals and determine how much you want to spend toward obtaining them. You should make a complete assessment of the tax and other financial ramifications of your plan. Then stick to your plan.

4) Emphasize quality. You don't necessarily have to pay a million dollars for a horse or invest a million in the business to become a success. However, you should buy the best-quality stock available for your price range. Probably the leading cause of failure in the horse business is that the investor attempts to buy a bunch of cheap horses and hopes to get lucky. Forget it! Cheap horses cost as much to keep as expensive ones—maybe more—and don't produce nearly the return.

5) Be patient. Don't become discouraged when you don't win the Kentucky Derby with the first horse you buy. That has happened only once (Hoop, Jr., 1945) and may not happen again for a long time!

Glossary

Acepromazine—The most common of all tranquilizers, often used in small quantities during vanning or other instances where a horse may become agitated, such as hair clipping or dental work. Also known as Ace.

Added money—Money added by the racing association to the amount paid by owners in nomination, eligibility, and starting fees. All added-money races in North America are stakes races.

Allowance race—An event other than claiming, for which the racing secretary drafts certain conditions.

Allowances—Weights and other conditions of a race.

Also eligible—Horse officially entered, but not permitted to start unless field is reduced by scratches below specified number.

Apprentice allowance—Weight concession to an apprentice rider. This varies among states. Usual allowance is five pounds. A horse whose weight under conditions for a race otherwise would be 115 pounds carries 110 pounds, if ridden by an apprentice.

Backstretch—Straightaway part of the track on far side between turns. Also a slang term to describe the stable area.

Bandage—Strips of cloth wound around the lower part of horses' legs for support or protection against injury.

Bar shoe—A horseshoe in which the heels are connected by a bar, rather than being open as a normal shoe. The purpose of the bar is to keep the hoof from spreading on impact and is normally used when a horse has a foot problem, such as a quarter crack. Its presence adds weight to the horse's foot and impedes his traction, which results in some loss of efficiency during running.

Barren—A term denoting the status of a mare who has not conceived after bein bred.

Bit—Metal bar in a horse's mouth by which he is guided and controlled. Ther are many types with varying degrees of severity.

Black type—Boldface type used in sales catalogs to distinguish horses who hav won or placed in a stakes race. If a horse's name appears in boldface type, a capital letters, he has won at least one stakes. If it appears in boldface typ capital and lower-case letters, he has placed in at least one stakes.

Bleeder—Horse that bleeds from lungs after or during a workout or race.

Blinkers—Device to limit a horse's vision and prevent him from swerving fror objects, other horses, etc., on either side of him. Many types with varyin degrees of limitation.

Blister—A horse is blistered for one of many reasons, one being as a direc counterirritant to pain or to assist in the removal of a synovial deposit.

Blood typing—A procedure implemented by The Jockey Club, it is the identifica tion of a horse from its blood type. Each horse has in its blood certain in dividual characteristics to help identify and verify the parentage. A thoroughbred mares and stallions are blood-typed.

Blood worms—Parasites that get into the bloodstream.

Bloodlines—The genealogy of a horse.

Bloodstock—Thoroughbred horses and interests therein.

Bloodstock agent—A broker who represents the purchaser or seller (or both) o thoroughbreds at public or private sale, generally in exchange for a commis sion.

Blow out—Exercising a horse for a short distance at a moderate pace, normally day or two before a race.

Bog spavin—Puffy swelling on the inside and slightly to the front of the hock Caused by overwork or strain.

Bone spavin—Bony growth inside and just below the hock. Even with good hock a bone spavin may occur as a result of undue concussion or strain, causin lameness.

Book—The group of mares being bred to a stallion in one given year. If he at tracts the maximum number of mares allowed by his manager (usually abou 46), he has a full book.

Bots—A stage of a worm which attaches to the lungs of a horse. The yellow egg seen on a horse's legs are ingested and become bots. The ultimate form is th bot fly.

Bottom line—Thoroughbred's breeding in female, or distaff, side.

Bowed tendon—Damage to the deep flexor tendon, superficial flexor tendon, o both, located below the knee (or hock on back leg) and running behind th cannon bone, usually in a front leg. Often caused by a bad step, poor confor mation, or strain. A bowed tendon requires a long layoff and can mean th end of a horse's racing career.

Brace (or bracer)—Rubdown liniment used on a horse after a race or exercise.

Break (a horse)—To accustom a young horse to racing equipment and carrying rider, usually done as a yearling in the fall.

Breakage—At pari-mutuel betting tracks, the rounding off to a nickel or dime, a required by state laws, in paying off winning tickets. If breakage is to th nickel, the bettor on a horse which should pay, say, $6.91, receives $6.90. I

210

breakage is to the dime, the payoff on a $6.91 horse would be $6.80. Generally, the breakage is split between the track and the state in varying proportions.

Breakdown—When a horse suffers a severe injury resulting in lameness.

Bred—A horse is bred at the place of his birth. Also, the mating of a horse.

Breeder—The owner of the foal at the time the foal is born.

Breeding farm—A farm for thoroughbreds used for breeding and/or potential racing stock.

Breeding right—The right to breed one mare to one stallion for one or more breeding seasons, generally not including an ownership interest in the stallion.

Breeze—Work a horse at a brisk pace.

Broken wind—Breakdown of the air vesicles of the lungs, usually caused by strain or excessive feeding before exercise.

Broodmare—Female thoroughbred used for breeding.

Broodmare prospect—A filly or mare that has not been bred.

Bucked shins—Inflammation of the periosteum on the front of the cannon bone. It is confined chiefly to young horses, although it is possible for older horses to buck shins. It is not a serious ailment, but requires a layoff of about three weeks from training routine. Known as bucked because of humped or bucked appearance on front of cannon bone.

Bug—Apprentice allowance.

Butazolidin (Bute)—A slang term for Phenylbutazone (see Phenylbutazone).

Buy-back—A horse put through public auction which did not reach his reserve and so was retained by the consignor. Also called charge-back.

Cannon bone—The bone located between the knee or hock and the fetlock (ankle). A common site of fracture in racehorses.

Champion—In the U.S., a horse voted best of its division in a given year by members of the *Daily Racing Form*, Thoroughbred Racing Associations, and National Turf Writers Association, and thus earner of an Eclipse Award. In other countries, either voted upon in a similar fashion or topweighted on a published year-end handicap list.

Chute—Extension of backstretch or homestretch to permit straightaway run from the start.

Claiming race—An event in which each horse entered is eligible to be purchased at a set price. Claims must be made before the race and can be made only by persons who have had a horse claimed at that same meeting or who have received a claim certificate from the stewards. Claiming races are generally of a lower class than allowance races; also, the lower the claiming price, the lower the class.

Clerk of scales—Official whose chief duty is to weigh the riders before and after race to insure proper weight being carried.

Clocker—The track employee who is on duty during morning training hours to identify the horses during their morning workouts, time them, and report to the public their training activities. Each track normally has several clockers, often employed by the *Daily Racing Form*.

Clubhouse turn—The first turn past the finish line, where the clubhouse is usually located.

Coggins test—A test named after its developer, Dr. Leroy Coggins, to determine whether or not a horse is a carrier of swamp fever. This test, almost universally required today, has essentially wiped out this disease among thoroughbreds.

Cold water bandages—Bandages used when a horse is put in an ice tub to "freeze" his legs prior to a race. These bandages are normally left on after the horse is taken out of the ice tub while walking to the paddock in order to keep the legs cold.

Colors—The individual owner's racing silks, jacket, and cap, worn by riders to denote ownership of horse. All colors are different and most are registered with The Jockey Club.

Colt—A male thoroughbred horse (other than a gelding or ridgeling) which has not reached its fifth birth date or has not been bred.

Combiotic—The most common antibiotic used in horses, a combination of penicillin and streptomycin. Normally effective on many illnesses.

Condition book—Publication produced by a race track that lists the races to be run, usually covering a period of two weeks. Horsemen use the book to decide in what race to enter a horse, based upon its eligibility for the event. If the minimum number of horses are not entered, meaning the race did not fill, it will not be contested and a substitute race is written and used in its place.

Conformation—The physical makeup or qualities of a thoroughbred horse; it physical appearance and structural makeup.

Consignor—The seller of a horse at public auction. The consignor can be the horse's owner or the owner's agent.

Contract rider—Jockey under contract to specific stable or trainer.

Controlled medication—A widely used term today to mean that some drugs primarily Phenylbutazone and Lasix, are permissible under controlled circumstances which allow veterinary administration of predetermined dosage at predetermined intervals prior to race time. These dosages and circumstances vary from state to state. The National Association of Racing Commissioners has come out strongly urging national guidelines on the subject but to date they have not been adopted.

Cooling out—Restoring the horse to normal body temperature and heart rate usually by walking, after he becomes overheated in a workout or race.

Coupled—Two or more horses running as a single betting unit. Also known as an entry.

Cover—A single breeding of a mare to a stallion. If a mare were bred to a stallion three times before becoming pregnant, then she was covered three times Cover date in a sales catalog refers to the last time a mare was bred that season.

Cradle—A device normally made of a series of connected sticks and rods which strapped around the horse's neck to prevent him from reaching some part of his extremities. Normally used after a horse has been blistered, or fired, to prevent the horse from scratching the affected area, which could result in serious infection.

Cribber or crib-biter—Some horses develop a habit of swallowing air. A crib biter or "cribber" swallows air by taking hold of the manger or other object with his teeth. It is discouraged by using creosote, covering objects with metal, or using a cribbing strap around his neck.

Cuppy track—A surface which will break under a horse's hooves; usually such a surface will be sandy in nature.

Curb—A painful swelling and thickening of one or all of the ligaments or tendons at the lower part of the hock. The swelling is seen on the rear legs, from the point of the hock to the cannon bone. It is common in young jumping horses.

Cushion—Top layer of the race track. Normally three to four inches in depth, maintained to absorb the concussion of horse's legs uniformly during running.

Dam—Mother of a horse. In a pedigree, the first dam is the horse's mother; the second dam is the first dam's mother; and the third dam is the second dam's mother.

Dead heat—Two or more horses finishing on even terms.

Declared—Horse withdrawn from a stakes race in advance of scratch time on the day of the race.

Derby—A stakes race for three-year-olds.

Detention barn—The barn where horses are required to go until blood tests or urine samples have been taken for testing (see Spit box).

Dogs—Barriers placed on a track away from the inside rail to indicate that the inside strip of the track is not to be used during morning workouts to preserve the surface. Workouts around these barriers are noted, and the times are correspondingly slower, due to the longer distance it adds on the turns.

Driving—Strong urging by rider.

Dwelt—Tardy in breaking from gate.

Easily—Horse running or winning without being pressed by rider or opposition.

Eighth—An eighth-mile; a furlong; 220 yards; 660 feet.

Eligible—Qualified to start in a race, according to conditions.

Entrance fee—Money paid to start a horse. Usually required only in stakes or special events.

Entry—Two or more horses owned by the same stable interest or trained by the same person, and running as a unit in the betting. Also known as a coupling or coupled.

Exercise boy—Rider who exercises horses during morning workouts.

Fetlock—A horse's ankle, located above the pastern and below the cannon bone.

Field—One or more starters running coupled as single betting unit. Usually horses calculated to have small chance to win are grouped in the "field."

Filly—A female thoroughbred horse which has not reached its fifth birth date or has not been bred.

Firing—A medical treatment used on horse's legs to encourage healing by increasing circulation. The method consists of numbing the horse's leg and creating a number of pin-size holes in the horse's leg with a hot electrically heated tool. Also known as pin firing.

First turn—Bend of track beyond starting point. Usually same as clubhouse turn.

Flat race—Contest on level ground as opposed to a hurdle race, a steeplechase, or harness race.

Flatten out—When a horse drops his head almost on straight line with his body while running. Indicates exhaustion.

Foal—A baby horse. Also, the process of giving birth. A pregnant mare is termed in foal.

Foal heat—The first time a mare comes into season after giving birth, about nine days afterward (also called nine-day heat).

Foal sharing—An arrangement between the owner of a stallion share or season and the owner of a broodmare to breed them and (generally) to share the foals, by either owning one-half interest in each foal or owning every other foal the broodmare produces.

Founder—See Laminitis.

Fractional time—Intermediate time made in race, as at quarter-mile, half-mile, three-quarters, etc.

Free handicap—Race in which no liability is incurred for entrance money, stakes, or forfeit until acceptance of weight. Also, a term used to describe an end-of-the-year assessment of individual horses expressed in weight, or pounds.

Freshening—To rest a horse after he becomes jaded from racing or training.

Full brother (sister)—Horses who have both the same sire and dam.

Furlong—One-eighth of a mile; 220 yards; 660 feet.

Furosemide—A diuretic medication often used to treat bleeders at race tracks. Legal under restricted conditions in many states. Commonly called by its brand name, Lasix.

Gallop—A type of gait; a fast canter. To ride horse at that gait.

Gallop boy—A rider who normally exercises horses during training hours on days when they are not exercised for speed. Some gallop boys do also ride horses during works.

Gelding—Male horse who has been castrated.

Get—Progeny of a sire.

Girth—Band around the body of horse to keep the saddle from slipping.

Good bottom—Track that is firm under its surface which may be sloppy or muddy.

Good track—Condition of track surface between fast and slow as surface dries out.

Granddam—Grandmother of a horse.

Grandsire—Grandfather of a horse.

Green osselet—An osselet that is just beginning to develop.

Groom—An employee who works on the backstretch for a trainer and is the person actually in charge of taking care of the horses. A groom may take care of anywhere from three to six horses, depending on the circumstances.

Half brother (sister)—Horses who have the same dams. The term does not apply to horses who share only the same sire.

Halter—Like a bridle, but lacking bit. Used in handling horses around stable and when they are not being ridden.

Halterman—One who claims a horse on a routine basis.

Hand—Four inches. Unit used in measuring the height of all horses, from withers to ground.

Hand ride—Urging a horse with the hands and not using a whip.

Handicap—Event in which the racing secretary determines the weight to be carried by each horse according to his assessment of their ability. The better the horse the more weight he would carry to give each horse a theoretically equal chance of winning. Overnight handicaps (nonstakes handicaps) generally are considered of a higher class than claiming races, but of a lower class than stakes, although some stakes are run under handicap conditions.

Handicapper—One who handicaps races, officially or privately; expert who makes selections for publication. Also; name given to racing secretary who assigns weights for handicaps at his track.

Handicapping—Study of all factors in past performances to determine the relative qualities of horses in a race. These factors include distance, weight, track conditions, trainers, owners, riders, previous race record, breeding, idiosyncrasies of the horses, etc.

Handily—Working or racing with moderate effort. Not under the whip.

Handle (mutuel)—Amount of money bet on a race, a daily card, or during meeting, season, or year.

Head—One unit of measurement of distance between horses in a race. Approximately an eighth of a length.

Health certificate—A standard form certificate concerning a horse's health, which is universally required for interstate travel.

Horse—In broad terms, any thoroughbred regardless of sex. Specifically, an entire male, five years old or older, or any male who has been bred.

Hots—Horses after a workout or race, before cooling out.

Hotwalker—A person or a mechanical device to lead a horse after exercise to cool it down.

Hung—Horse tiring, but holding position. Usually used in negative context, a horse not being able to pass another horse.

Icing—Standing a horse in a tub of ice water or applying ice pack to its legs to deaden pain.

Identifier—The person assigned the job of identifying all horses coming to the paddock prior to a race. The identifier uses the registration form, which has the color, sex, markings, and age of the horse, as well as its tattoo number.

In foal—Pregnant.

In foal contract—An agreement by the owner of a stallion share or season that all or a portion of the stud fee will be refunded, or will not become due, if the mare does not produce a live foal.

In hand—When horse is running under moderate control at less than his best pace. With speed in reserve at call of rider.

Inquiry—An investigation into the running of a race or claim of foul, brought by a racing official (or by one rider against another).

Interfering—A gait imperfection, occurring when one front foot hits the other while the horse is in motion, or when one rear foot strikes the other. Corrective shoeing may help.

Interval training—A relatively new method of training which involves considerably more exercise than the traditional training methods used for thoroughbreds today. Interval training has evolved from human interval training in sports medicine and is in its early stages of development.

Laminitis—A fever in the feet of a horse. This can be a very debilitating disease and one that is the subject of a great deal of research. This condition is also known as founder. The fever causes swelling and the coffin bone, which is the lowermost bone of the foot, actually is forced to rotate downward, making a horse a chronic cripple. The most common causes are digestive disturbance or stress.

Lasix—A brand name for furosemide.

Layup—A racehorse sent away from the race track to recuperate from injury or illness or to be rested.

Lead—The leading leg of a horse. A horse usually leads with his inside leg around turns and with his opposite leg on straightaways.

Lead pony—Horse or pony that heads parade of field from paddock to starting gate. Also horse or pony who accompanies a starter to the post to quiet him.

Leg up—Helping jockey to mount his horse. Also strengthening horses' legs by exercise. Sometimes used as a slang expression for giving help of some sort.

Length—Length of a horse from nose to tail, about eight feet. Distance between horses in a race. Calculated as one-fifth of a second in terms of time.

Magnetic field therapy—A new method of therapy being used in horses to encourage rapid healing. This therapy is based on similar therapy in humans which is used to encourage unions of fractures. This is relatively new for thoroughbreds and while many are very pleased with its results, others question its therapeutic value.

Maiden—A racehorse of either sex that has never won a race. Also, a female horse that has never been bred. Refers also to a classification of race open only to horses that have never won a race. Straight (nonclaiming) maiden races are considered of a higher class than maiden claiming races.

Maiden race—Race for nonwinners.

Mare—Female thoroughbred five years old or older, or younger if she has been bred.

Morning line—Odds quoted in the official program at the track and are the odds at which betting opens.

Mudder—Horse that runs best on muddy or soft track.

Muzzle—Nose and lips of a horse. Also a guard placed over horse's mouth to prevent his biting.

Near side—Left side of a horse. Side on which he is mounted.

Neck—One unit of measurement of distances between horses in races. Approximately equal to a quarter-length.

Nerved—Operation that severs nerve to enable horses to race without pain. Prohibited in many states except for nerving in the heel area.

Nom de course—Assumed name of an owner or racing partnership.

Nominator—Person who paid nomination fee when entering a horse for a race in the future.

Nose—One unit of measurement of distances between horses in races. The smallest such unit.

Not sold—In sales results, a horse that went through the auction ring but did not change owners, usually because the consignor did not receive a price high enough (see Reserve).

Oaks—Stakes event for three-year-old fillies.

Objection—Claim of foul lodged by rider, patrol judge, or other official. At some tracks it is termed "Inquiry."

Odds-on—A payoff that would be less than even money.

Off side—Right side of horse.

Official—Sign displayed when result is confirmed. Or, racing official.

On the bit—When a horse is eager to run.

Open sale—A sale in which the only qualification for entry is the payment of a fee.

Osselet—Calcification deposit in the area of the fetlock joint which creates an impediment of movement of that joint. Depending upon severity, it can be very debilitating.

Overreaching—Toe of hind shoe striking foreleg on the heel, or back of coronet.

Overnight line—Odds quoted on horses the night before a race.

Overweight—Surplus weight carried by a horse when a rider cannot make the required poundage. Limited to five pounds or less.

Ownership registry—The registration arm of The Jockey Club which now registers the owners of all stallions and broodmares and requires ownership to be transferred when these horses change hands.

Paddock—Structure or area where horses are saddled and paraded before post time.

Paddock judge—Official in charge of paddock and saddling routine.

Paint—A medication used on the legs of horses.

Palpation—The physical entrance by a veterinarian through the anus of a mare to feel or "palpate" her ovaries and uterus to determine breeding soundness, follicular activity (readiness to breed), uterine condition, or pregnancy.

Parentage verification—A horse whose parents have been verified by blood typing. This is becoming more prominent in high-priced yearlings to insure the integrity of the sale (see Blood typing).

Pari-mutuel—Form of wagering existing at all U.S. tracks today in which odds are determined by the amount of money bet on each horse. In essence, the bettors are competing against each other, not against the track, which acts as an agent, taking a commission on each bet to cover purses, taxes, and operating expenses.

Patrol judges—Officials who observe progress of race from various vantage points around running strip.

Pedigree—A written record of a thoroughbred's immediate ancestors. Usually one that gives four generations, called a four-cross pedigree.

Penalties—Extra weight a horse carries, according to conditions of a race.

Phenylbutazone—A nonsteroidal anti-inflammatory medication legal in certain amounts for horses in many states. Normally administered 24 to 48 hours before race time.

Photo finish—Result of a race so close that the placing judges cannot decide it with the naked eye and must consult a photograph.

Pin firing—See Firing.

Placed—Finishing second or third in a race. A stakes-placed horse is one who has finished second or third in a stakes but has not won a stakes. Not to be confused with betting terms place (second) and show (third).

Placing judge—An official who, in conjunction with other officials, determines the order of finish of a race.

Plater —Horse who runs in claiming races.

Plates—Shoes horses wear in races. Racing plates.

Pole—Markers at measured distances around the track, and identified by distance from the finish line.

Pool—Total money bet on entire field, to win, place, and show.

Post parade—Horses going from paddock to starting gate (post), parading past the stands.

Post position—Position in the starting gate from which horse breaks. Positions are numbered from the rail outward.

Post time—Designated time for race to start.

Preferred list—Horses with prior rights to starting for various reasons.

Prep (or prep race)—Training; an event preliminary to another, usually more important, engagement.

Produce—The offspring of a mare.

Produce race—For the produce of horses named or described at time of entry.

Producer—A term applied to a mare only after one of her offspring wins a race.

Public trainer—One whose services are not exclusively engaged by one owner and who accepts horses to train for a daily fee.

Purse—A race for money or other prize to which the owners do not contribute.

Quarter crack—A crack in a horse's hoof wall near the heel on either side. This area of the hoof wall is known as the quarter and a crack in it is debilitating depending upon its severity and the extent to which it penetrates upward toward the coronet band. It can be the result of a concussion or poor shoeing, or it may be hereditary and result from weak hoof walls.

Quarter pole—Marker one-quarter of a mile from finish.

Race-day medication—Medication given on race day. Most medications, with the exception of Lasix, are prohibited in almost all racing jurisdictions.

Racing secretary—Official who drafts conditions for races, writes condition book, and usually serves as handicapper.

Receiving barn—Structure at some tracks where ship-ins, and, in some cases, all horses entered are isolated for a certain period before post time. Used to minimize chances of tampering.

Reserve—The minimum amount for which a consignor will allow his horse to change hands at public auction.

RNA—Reserve Not Attained. Used by some sales companies rather than Not Sold or Charge Back.

Restricted race—A race restricted to certain starters either because of their place of birth, or their previous winnings.

Ridgeling —Male horse with only one descended testicle.

Run down—The result of a horse with weak pasterns hitting them on the track in a race or workout.

Run-out bit—Special type of bit to prevent horse from bearing out or in.

Saddle cloth—Cloth under saddle on which number denoting post position is displayed during races.

Saliva test—Laboratory test to determine whether horse has been drugged. Seldom used today.

Scale of weights—Fixed imposts to be carried by horses in a race, determined according to age, sex, season, and distance.

Schooling—Accustoming a horse to starting from gate and racing practices.

Schooling list—Horses required by the starter to undergo further education in the starting gate.

Select portion—The portion of the thoroughbred market comprised of yearlings whose pedigrees can generally be expected to qualify them for consideration for admission to the select sales. Also meaning that part of a sale which is restricted to the better bred or better conformed, as opposed to open to all horses.

Select sale—A public auction in which the entrants have been chosen on specified criteria, usually high-quality pedigrees and good conformation.

Sesamoids—Two small bones located at the back of the fetlock and held in place by ligaments. With stress and fatigue in a race, they can fracture. Although a horse can return to the races after such a fracture, it more often than not means the end of the racing career.

Shadow roll—A device normally made of sheepskin which goes over a horse's nose to keep him from seeing shadows on the ground. Some horses tend to jump shadows or become nervous at what they see, and the shadow roll is a method of limiting the horse's vision downward in the same manner that blinkers limit his vision to the sides.

Shedrow—The aisleway in the barn.

Short—A horse needing more work or racing to attain best form.

Silks—Jacket and cap worn by riders.

Sire—A stallion who has produced a foal which has won a race.

Sixteenth—One-sixteenth of a mile; a half-furlong; 110 yards; 330 feet.

Slipped—A pregnancy aborted or resorbed spontaneously. A mare who had been bred, conceived, and then aborted.

Snip—Small patch of white hairs on the lip or nose of a horse.

Sound—A term used to denote a thoroughbred's health and freedom from disease or lameness.

Sound for breeding—A mare having two normal ovaries, normal uterus, and genital tract. It does not normally mean that the mare is free from uterine infection. In stallions it indicates fertility.

Speedy cut—Injury to knee or hock caused by strike from opposite foot.

Spit box—Place where saliva, urine, and/or blood tests are taken from a horse for testing following a race (see Detention barn).

Splint—A hard swelling below the knee or hock indicating damage to the splint bones, two bones on either side of the cannon bone, or their connecting ligaments.

Stakes—The highest class of race at any racing jurisdiction. A race in which an entry fee is paid by the owners of the horses starting and those entry fees are added to the purse. Often all of such entry fees go to the winner. (Entry fees are not required for any other type of race.) Also, invitational races (no entry fee required) with a large purse (usually $50,000 or more) are regarded as stakes races. Stakes races qualify horses for black type in sales catalogs.

Stakes producer—A mare who has at least one foal who has won or placed in a stakes race.

Stall walker—Horse that constantly frets and moves in his stall.

Stallion—Entire male horse used for the purpose of breeding.

Stallion prospect—An entire male horse who has not been bred.

Stallion season—The right to breed one mare to a particular stallion for one particular season.

Stallion share—An undivided fractional interest in a stallion, which customarily entitles the owner to breed one broodmare to the stallion each year, plus an occasional extra season, depending upon the syndicate agreement (syndicate agreements usually provide for 40 shares).

Standard starts index (SSI)—A statistic to compare a horse's racing class based on earnings per start per year. It is calculated and divided into male and female categories. Any horse earning the average for his or her sex has an SSI of 1.00. A horse with an SSI of 2.00 would have earned twice the average per start of his crop, one with 0.50 would have earned half the average, etc.

Star—Small patch of white hair on horse's forehead.

Starter—Racing official in charge of the starting gate. A horse who runs in a race.

Starter allowance—A particular kind of race written to allow claiming horses who have improved from their earlier form to run in a nonclaiming event. Conditions of starter allowance races allow horses who have previously started for a certain lower-level claiming price to run under allowance conditions. These races are normally found at longer distances.

Starter handicap—The same type of race as a starter allowance, except that the horses are assigned their weights by the handicapper rather than determining them from allowance conditions.

Starting gate—Mechanical device having partitions for horses into which they are confined until the starter releases doors in front to start race.

Stayer—Stout-hearted horse; one who can race long distances.

Stewards—The three individuals who uphold the rules of racing at a race track. They are answerable to the state racing commission and their decisions can be appealed to that body.

Stickers—Calks on shoes which give horse better traction in mud or on soft track.

Stifle—The joint of a horse's rear leg composed of the femur, tibia, and kneecap.

Stimulant—An illegal foreign substance given to a horse to increase his normal physical activity temporarily for the purpose of improving his racing performance.

Stocking—White legs below knee.

Strangles—The slang name for distemper in a horse. Distemper can result in death when "bastard" strangles result, or can be relatively mild resulting in nothing more than a minor abscess in the area of the lower jaw. The term derives from the fact that in severe cases it occurs in the area of the windpipe and can strangle a horse.

Stretch—Straightaway portion of race track in front of the grandstand. More particularly the homestretch.

Stride—Manner of going. Distance progressed after each foot has touched ground once. More broadly, a step.

Stud—Male horse used for breeding. Also a breeding farm.

Stud Book—The registry and genealogical record of the breeding of thoroughbreds, maintained by The Jockey Club. Only thoroughbreds of accepted lineage are eligible for inclusion.

Stud fee (or service fee)—A fee for the right to breed a mare to a stallion during the breeding period.

Subscription—Fee paid by owner to nominate horse for stakes or maintain eligibility for it.

Substitute race—A backup race that is carded and/or run when a regularly scheduled race does not fill or is canceled.

Suckling—Thoroughbred still nursing his dam.

Tack—Riders' racing equipment. Applied also to stable gear.

Take (mutuel)—Commission deducted from mutuel pools which is shared by track, horsemen, and state.

Teasing—A method using a stallion to court a mare to determine whether or not she is in heat, and encourage her to come into heat. Often farms have a stallion specifically for this purpose called a teaser, and he is usually not the stallion to whom the mare will be bred.

Thoroughbred—A distinctive breed of horse used for flat and steeplechase racing. Generally, a thoroughbred must be registered with The Jockey Club of the United States, or a similar registry in other countries, to participate in sanctioned events.

Tongue strap—Strap or tape bandage used to tie down horse's tongue to prevent it from choking him in race or workout. Also known as a tongue tie.

Top line—Thoroughbred's breeding on sire's side.

Top weight—Highest poundage carried by any horse in a particular race.

Totalizator—Intricate machine which sells betting tickets, records total of straight, place, and show pools and amount bet on each horse in the three categories; shows odds to win on each horse in field and complete payoff after finish.

Track record—Fastest time at various distances made at a particular course.

Tranquilizer—A foreign substance given to a horse to relax him.

Triple Crown—In the United States, the Kentucky Derby, Preakness Stakes, and Belmont Stakes. In England, the Two Thousand Guineas, Epsom Derby, and St. Leger.

Turf—Grass as opposed to dirt racing surfaces. When capitalized denotes the entire racing industry.

Twitch—A device, generally consisting of a stick with loop of rope at one end, which is placed around horse's upper lip and twisted to curb fractiousness.

Under contract—Rider or trainer formally signed to a particular stable or person for specified time and compensation.

Under wraps—Horse under stout restraint in race or workout.

Untried—Not raced or tested for speed.

Unwind—Gradually withdrawing horse from intensive training preparatory to retiring him or her temporarily or permanently.

Upset price—The minimum amount at which bidding may start at a public auction and which varies depending on the sale.

Urinalysis—Laboratory test of urine to determine whether horse has been drugged.

Valet—Person who attends riders and keeps their wardrobe and equipment in order.

Walk hots—To cool out a horse after a workout or race.

Walkover—Race which scratches down to only one starter who merely gallops the required distance. A formal gesture required by rules of racing.

Warming up—Galloping horse on way to post.

Washy—Horse who breaks out in a nervous sweat before a race.

Weanling—A thoroughbred after being weaned until he becomes a yearling on the New Year's Day following his foaling.

Weaving—Swaying motion in a stall.

Weight for age—Fixed scale of weights to be carried by horses according to age, sex, distance of race, and month.

Wind puffs—A filling normally found to the rear and above the ankle in the area of the suspensories and are soft fluid fillings. Normally the result of strain.

Withers—A point where the neck of the horse meets the shoulders and turns into the back. The point at which the horse is measured for height.

Work—To exercise a horse. A workout.

Work horse—One used to accompany another of better quality in workout.

Yearling—Thoroughbred between the first New Year's Day after being foaled and the following January 1.

How To Read
The *Daily Racing Form*

In several chapters of this book, we have mentioned that thoroughbred racing is the most fully documented sport in the history of mankind. The reason is that the *Daily Racing Form* publishes charts of every race run in North America and, from those charts, you can tell precisely what happened to every horse in the race at every point in the race.

From those charts, the *Racing Form* also produces an abbreviated version setting forth what each horse did and those are published in the *Form* on the day that horse is to race, in the form of past performances.

Obviously, most of the readers of this book are no doubt racing fans already, so you know how to read the past performances and the charts, but, for those of you who may not be familiar with them, we are including an abbreviated key to each of them for your edification.

Incidentally, there is now a competitor to the *Racing Form,* operating at some tracks in the East, called *Sports Eye,* and it is, in our opinion, an excellent competitor for an excellent paper. With certain differences, the explanations that apply to the *Racing Form* are also valid for *Sports Eye.*

How to Read a Chart

Basically, charts are self-explanatory, but there are several areas which might merit some comment, and some tricks for understanding them that are perhaps worth noting.

As an example of an interesting chart, we have chosen the one from a race which we have mentioned twice earlier in the book, the $1-million claiming race which was held at Hollywood Park on Breeders' Cup Day, November 10, 1984. This particular chart was chosen, incidentally, not only because the race was mentioned elsewhere in the book, but because it is illustrative of many of the things you'll find in the charts of stakes races, as well as claiming races.

NINTH RACE
Hollywood
NOVEMBER 10, 1984

1 ⅛ MILES.(Turf). (1.46) 5th Running of THE SEABISCUIT CLAIMING STAKES. $100,000 added. 3-year-olds and upward. By subscription of $100 each which shall accompany the nomination, $500 to pass the entry box and $500 additional to start, with $100,000 added, of which $20,000 to second, $15,000 to third, $7,500 to fourth and $2,500 to fifth. Weights, 3-year-olds, 121 lbs.; older, 124 lbs. Claiming price $1,000,000; for each $100,000 to $500,000 allowed 2 lbs. Starters to be named through the entry box by closing time of entries. Trophies will be presented to the winning owner, trainer and jockey. Closed Wednesday, October 31, 1984 with 34 nominations.
Value of race $117,300; value to winner $72,300; second $20,000; third $15,000; fourth $7,500; fifth $2,500. Mutuel pool $448,852. Exacta Pool $608,220.

Last Raced	Horse	Eqt.A.Wt	PP	St	¼	½	¾	Str	Fin	Jockey	Cl'g Pr	Odds $1
25Oct84 $^{8}SA^{2}$	Zoffany	4 114	2	4	1^{hd}	1^{hd}	1^{hd}	$1^{\frac{1}{2}}$	$1^{1\frac{1}{4}}$	Lipham T	500000	6.10
28Oct84 $^{8}SA^{6}$	Late Act	b 5 124	12	12	12	10^{hd}	$10^{1\frac{1}{2}}$	$8^{2\frac{1}{2}}$	2^{1}	Maple E	1000000	1.90
19Oct84 $^{8}SA^{2}$	Johnotable	4 114	5	2	5^{2}	$3^{1\frac{1}{2}}$	$3^{1\frac{1}{2}}$	$2^{\frac{1}{2}}$	3^{hd}	McCarron C J	500000	5.10
29Aug84 $^{8}Bel^{5}$	Strong Dollar	4 117	7	10	$11^{1\frac{1}{2}}$	12	$11^{\frac{1}{2}}$	9^{2}	$4^{1\frac{1}{2}}$	Pincay L Jr	600000	7.70
12Oct84 $^{5}Eng^{1}$	Gouverno	5 114	8	11	9^{hd}	$8^{\frac{1}{2}}$	$8^{1\frac{1}{2}}$	7^{hd}	5^{nk}	Eddery P	500000	33.80
25Oct84 $^{8}SA^{1}$	Pol And Dic	5 114	11	8	7^{1}	6^{1}	4^{hd}	6^{hd}	$6^{\frac{1}{2}}$	Shoemaker W	500000	3.90
31Oct84 $^{5}SA^{1}$	Wise Strategy	b 4 114	4	1	$3^{1\frac{1}{2}}$	4^{hd}	5^{hd}	4^{1}	$7^{1\frac{3}{4}}$	Hawley S	500000	f-12.80
10Oct84 $^{8}SA^{8}$	Momento II	4 114	9	7	6^{hd}	$9^{1\frac{1}{2}}$	9^{hd}	10^{4}	8^{hd}	Barrera G	500000	f-12.80
27Oct84 $^{5}SA^{1}$	Truce Maker	b 6 115	3	3	$2^{3\frac{1}{2}}$	2^{1}	$2^{\frac{1}{2}}$	$3^{\frac{1}{2}}$	9^{nk}	Valenzuela PA	500000	21.60
14Oct84 $^{10}LaD^{10}$	Shamtastic	4 120	1	5	4^{hd}	5^{hd}	6^{hd}	$5^{1\frac{1}{2}}$	$10^{3\frac{1}{2}}$	Cordero A Jr	800000	21.00
2Nov84 $^{8}SA^{5}$	Fleet Joey	3 113	6	6	$8^{\frac{1}{2}}$	$11^{1\frac{1}{2}}$	12	11^{2}	$11^{4\frac{1}{2}}$	Stevens G L	500000	33.30
4Oct84 $^{8}SA^{6}$	Iron Leader	4 115	10	9	$10^{\frac{1}{2}}$	7^{1}	7^{1}	12	12	Sibille R	500000	f-12.80

f—Mutuel field.

OFF AT 4:00. Start good. Won driving. Time, :23⅕, :47⅕, 1:10⅗, 1:33⅘, 1:46⅗ Course firm.

$2 Mutuel Prices:

2-ZOFFANY	14.20	6.40	4.20
10-LATE ACT		4.00	3.00
4-JOHNOTABLE			3.80

$5 EXACTA 2-10 PAID $199.50.

B. c, by Our Native—Grey Dawn Girl, by Grey Dawn II. Trainer Gosden John H M. Bred by Carpinelli & Henwood Bros (NJ).

ZOFFANY set or forced the pace outside TRUCE MAKER to the final furlong, disposed of that one in the final sixteenth and held LATE ACT safe. The latter, outrun for six furlongs, went to the middle of the course entering the stretch and closed strongly. JOHNOTABLE, in good position from the outset, moved to contention when roused leaving the backstretch, vied for the lead into the final furlong but hung near the end. STRONG DOLLAR also outrun for six furlongs, rallied very wide and closed strongly. GOUVERNO rallied wide around the final turn and finished willingly. POL AND DIC rallied to contention leaving the backstretch but flattened out in the stretch. WISE STRATEGY veered outward after the start, raced forwardly after being brought under control, lodged a bid in the upper stretch but hung in the final sixteenth. TRUCE MAKER vied for the lead most of the trip but faltered in the final furlong. FLEET JOEY showed little. MASSERA (8) AND PROOF (11) WERE WITHDRAWN AND ALL WAGERS ON THEM WERE ORDERED REFUNDED.

Owners— 1, Bodie-Bodie-Speelman; 2, Greentree Stable; 3, Goodman H V; 4, Haefner W; 5, Jay Dee Stables; 6, Port S L; 7, Mdwvw Fm & Vntra Stb; 8, Hunt N B; 9, Fogelson Greer G; 10, Caston Jr & Ruback; 11, Vaughan Stable; 12, Sangster R E.

Trainers— 1, Gosden John H M; 2, Reinacher Robert Jr; 3, Stidham Michael; 4, Russell John W; 5, Mathews S G; 6, Whittingham Charles; 7, Whittingham Michael; 8, Whittingham Charles; 9, Whittingham Michael; 10, Lukas D Wayne; 11, Vaughan Kay; 12, Gosden John H M.

Overweight: Strong Dollar 1 pound; Truce Maker 1; Fleet Joey 2; Iron Leader 1.

Scratched—Massera (3Nov84 $^{7}SA^{1}$); Proof (3Nov84 $^{8}Haw^{1}$).

Here are what the elements of the chart mean:

NINTH RACE
Hollywood
NOVEMBER 10, 1984

This is self-explanatory. It was the ninth race at Hollywood Park on November 10, 1984.

1 ⅛ MILES.(Turf). (1.46)

This tells you the distance of the race, the course it is run on (there will be a notation when a race is run on a turf course or on the inner dirt track, but there's no notation when the race is run on the main dirt track), and the track record for that distance on that particular racing surface.

5th Running of THE SEABISCUIT CLAIMING STAKES.

In some handicaps and all stakes races, the name of the race is included as part of the chart.

$100,000 added.

This is the money which is put up by the track to make the race more attractive to good horses.

3–year–olds and upward.

This tells you which horses are eligible to run in the race. What this particular notation means is that any horse who is older than two, regardless of sex or race record, can be entered in this race, if his owners are willing to pay the nomination and entry fees. Common restrictions include sex (normally races for fillies and mares, with no males allowed), state where foaled, and ability ("non-winners of two races other than maiden or claiming," etc.).

By subscription of $100 each which shall accompany the nomination.
$500 to pass the entry box and $500 additional to start, with $100,000 added, of which $20,000 to second, $15,000 to third, $7,500 to fourth and $2,500 to fifth.

This shows the payment schedule that owners had to meet in order to make their horses eligible to run in this race, along with what they could expect to get back if their horse finished second through fifth (the winner's share is determined by the number of horses which are kept eligible at each point and by the number of runners, because all the fees put up by owners go to the winner of this race).

Weights, 3–year–olds, 121 lbs.; older, 124 lbs.

These are the weights that must be carried by each of the runners. As explained in Chapter 3, younger horses (and females in most instances) are given weight allowances.

Claiming price $1,000,000; for each $100,000 to $500,000 allowed 2 lbs.

This not only sets forth the claiming prices (prices at which you can buy the horses in the race), it has bearing on the amount of weight each horse will carry. By entering your horse at a lower claiming price, you can get weight off, which will enhance his chances of winning, but the lower claiming price often will increase the chances of his being claimed. It's a delicate balance in most instances. In this race, the winner, Zoffany, got ten pounds off (which undoubtedly made the difference between winning and losing) by being entered for $500,000, rather than the $1,000,000 at which Late Act was entered.

Starters to be named through the entry box by closing time of entries.

This means that, if there are more horses which want to run than there are slots in the starting gate, the ones who will be permitted to start will be chosen at the time of entry by any one of a number of methods (see Chapter 3). It also means that if a horse scratches, its place will not be taken (in most stakes races) by another horse from an "also eligible list."

Trophies will be presented to the winning owner, trainer and jockey.

This is noted because in most stakes races the only one who gets a trophy is the owner.

Closed Wednesday, October 31, 1984 with 34 nominations.

This was the closing date for original nominations, and, as you can see, there were 34 nominees.

Value of race $117,300; value to winner $72,300; second $20,000; third $15,000; fourth $7,500; fifth $2,500.

Most of this was stated above, but you can see that the winner got all the money which was put up by the owners ($17,300), plus 55% of the added money.

Mutuel pool $448,852. Exacta Pool $608,220.

This is how much money was bet on the race. The mutuel pool is how much was bet on win, place, and show wagering, and the exacta pool was a separate pool in which bettors had to pick the first two finishers in the correct order of finish.

Last Raced	Horse	Eqt.A.Wt	PP	St	¼	½	¾	Str	Fin	Jockey	Cl'g Pr	Odds $1
25Oct84 8SA2	Zoffany	4 114	2	4	1hd	1hd	1hd	1½	11¼	Lipham T	500000	6.10
28Oct84 8SA6	Late Act	b 5 124	12	12	12	10hd	101½	82½	21	Maple E	1000000	1.90

The line which is set off by rules is merely a partial explanation of what appears below it in the chart. Here's what each notation means and, since the winner led all the way we'll follow along with the second horse, Late Act.

28Oct84 8SA6

This not only tells you that Late Act's last race previous was on October 28, 1984, but it tells you that it was the eighth race (8) at Santa Anita (SA) and that he finished sixth (6) in that race.

Obviously, the next item on the line is the name of the horse, and that is followed by a "b" under the heading of "Eqt." That means the horse was "equipped" with blinkers.

Following the "A" column, which lists the age of the horse and the "Wt," which lists the actual weight the horse carried, you'll see seven sets of numbers, the first of which represents the post position from which Late Act was breaking, while the remainder represent the position of the horse in the field at the various points of call listed above. Each one is followed by a superior number *which indicates how far the horse in question was in front of the next horse at that particular call*, e.g.:

12 12 10hd 101½ 82½ 21

The thing to remember here is that, if you want to find out how far a particular horse was behind the pace, you have to go through every other horse in the chart that was in front of your horse at any point of call in the race. For example, at the stretch call (which, incidentally, is a furlong from the finish), Late Act was eighth. The margins in front of him were ½ length, ½ length, ½ length, one length, 1½ lengths, a head, and a head, which adds up to his being about 4¼ lengths behind the leader. Of course, at the finish, you have all the horses in order, so you don't have to search around much to find out how far a horse was beaten, but in the body of the race it's a little more complicated.

Next is the name of the jockey which is also self-evident in this particular race; but, if an apprentice is riding, the amount of his apprentice allowance—either seven, five, or three pounds—appears as a superior number following his name, e.g.:

Shoemaker W5

The claiming price column is also simple. It states the price for which any horse in the race can be claimed.

The "Odds $1" column shows what the odds on the horse were, and there are only two things to note here: if an entry is running in the race, the horses in the entry will be designated by an "a-" in front of each of their names or, if as is the case in this race there is a mutuel field, it will be designated by "f-" in front of the names of the horses in the field (usually the field consists of the horses given the least chance to win).

The line below the positions of all the horses on the chart says:

OFF AT 4:00. Start good. Won driving. Time, :23⅕, :47⅕, 1:10⅗, 1:33⅘, 1:46⅗ Course firm.

This is one of the most important lines on the chart. The first notation is the local time the gate opened. "Start good. Won driving," is important because it tells you that none of the horses were left in the gate and the winner was still under a full head of steam when he crossed the finish line. Occaionally, you'll see "Won easily" or "Won handily" which means the winner was so far ahead that he was able to coast across the finish line. The times noted here are the times for the horse who was in front of the field at the particular call for which the time is cited (generally every quarter of a mile, and then the finishing time). If you want to find out how fast your horse ran a particular segment of the race, you figure out how far he was behind the leader at that point and then add ⅕ of a second to the published time for each length he was trailing the leader at that call.

With certain exceptions, the rest of the chart is also self-explanatory. The mutuel payoffs are always stated in terms of the minimum bet available, $2 for a straight bet or $5 for an exacta. The next line gives the breeding of the winner, the trainer of the winner, the breeders of the winner, and the state where he was bred.

The narrative which follows next is very important, because it is an analysis of the race through the eyes of a true expert, the *Daily Racing Form* chartcaller. They have a man at every track and he is a trained professional, who can give you insight, through this narrative, as to whether or not the horse has had any trouble during the race.

The race narrative is followed by lists of the owners and trainers of all the horses in the race, arranged in the order in which their horses finished. That is followed by another important part of the chart, "Overweights," which tell you how much more weight some of the horses in the race were carrying than they could have carried under the actual conditions of the race, if the jockey were light enough.

Finally, there are the scratches. While the narrative, in this instance, would give you the impression that Massera and Proof were scratched at the gate, noting, "MASSERA (8) AND PROOF (11) WERE WITHDRAWN AND ALL WAGERS ON THEM WERE ORDERED REFUNDED," that was not the case in this race. The money was refunded because there was advance wagering the day before the race, and the two of them were scratched the morning of the race.

(Continued)

How To Read Past Performances

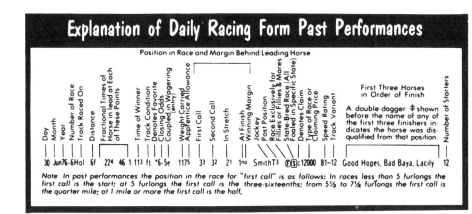

Explanation of Daily Racing Form Past Performances

Position in Race and Margin Behind Leading Horse

Day	Month	Year	Number of Race	Track Raced On	Distance	Fractional Times of Horse in lead at Each of These Points	Time of Winner	Track Condition	Closing Odds	Coupled in Wagering (entry)	Weight Carried	Apprentice Allowance	First Call	Second Call	In Stretch	At Finish	Winning Margin	Jockey	Post Position	Race Exclusively for Fillies or Fillies & Mares	State-Bred Race (All Foaled in Specific State)	Denotes Claim	Type of Race or Claiming Price	Speed Rating	Track Variant	First Three Horses in Order of Finish / A double-dagger ‡ shown before the name of any of the first three finishers indicates the horse was disqualified from that position.	Number of Starters

30 Jun76-6Hol 6f 22⁴ .46 1.11³ ft *6-5e 1175 3³ 3² 2¹ 1ⁿᵒ SmithT³ ⓇⓈc12000 81-12 Good Hopes, Bad Baya, Lacily 12

Note In past performances the position in the race for "first call" is as follows: In races less than 5 furlongs the first call is the start; at 5 furlongs the first call is the three-sixteenths; from 5½ to 7½ furlongs the first call is the quarter mile; at 1 mile or more the first call is the half.

Key to Symbols, Abbreviations in Past Performances

FOREIGN-BRED HORSES

An asterisk (*) preceding the name of the horse indicates foreign-bred. (No notation is made fo horses bred in Canada and Cuba.)

MUD MARKS

✳—Fair mud runner   ✕—Good mud runner

⊗—Superior mud runner

COLOR

B—Bay   Blk—Black   Br—Brown   Ch—Chestnut   Gr—Gray

Ro—Roan   Wh—White   Dk b or br—Dark bay or brown

SEX

c—colt   h—horse   g—gelding   rig—ridgling   f—filly   m—mare

PEDIGREE

Each horse's pedigree lists, in the order named, color, sex, age, sire, dam and grandsire (sire of dam

BREEDER

Abbreviation following breeder's name indicates the state, Canadian province, place of origin c foreign country in which the horse was foaled.

TODAY'S WEIGHT

With the exception of assigned-weight handicap races, weights are computed according to the cond tions of the race. Weight includes the rider and his equipment, saddle, lead pads, etc., and takes in account the apprentice allowance of pounds claimed. It does not include a jockey's overweight, which is announced by track officials prior to the race. The number of pounds claimed as an apprentice allowance is shown by a superior (small) figure to the right of the weight.

TODAY'S CLAIMING PRICE

If a horse is entered to be claimed, the price for which he may be claimed appears in bold face type to the right of the trainer's name.

RECORD OF STARTS AND EARNINGS

The horse's racing record for his most recent two years of competition appears to the extreme right of the name of the breeder and is referred to as his "money lines." This lists the year, number of starts, wins, seconds, thirds and earnings. The letter "M" in the win column of the upper line indicates the horse is a maiden. If the letter "M" is in the lower line only, it indicates the horse was a maiden at the end of that year.

TURF COURSE RECORD

The horse's turf course record shows his lifetime starts, wins, seconds, thirds and earnings on the grass and appears directly below his money lines.

LIFETIME RECORD

The horse's lifetime record shows his career races, wins, seconds, thirds and total earnings. The statistics, updated with each start, include all his races—on dirt, grass and over jumps—and are located under the trainer's name.

DISTANCE

a—preceding distance (a6f) denotes "about" distance (about 6 furlongs in this instance).

FOREIGN TRACKS

◆ —before track abbreviation indicates it is located in a foreign country.

RACES OTHER THAN ON MAIN DIRT TRACK

[•]—following distance denotes inner dirt course.
Ⓣ—following distance indicates turf (grass) course race.
[T]—following distance indicates inner turf course.
[S]—following distance indicates steeplechase race.
H]—following distance indicates hurdle race.

TRACK CONDITIONS

ft—fast	fr—frozen	gd—good	sl—slow	sy—sloppy
	m—muddy		hy—heavy	

Turf courses, including steeplechase and hurdles:

hd—hard	fm—firm	gd—good	yl—yielding	sf—soft

SYMBOLS ACCOMPANYING CLOSING ODDS

* (preceding)—favorite   e (following)—entry
f (following)—mutuel field

APPRENTICE OR RIDER WEIGHT ALLOWANCES

Allowance indicated by superior figure following weight—117[5].

ABBREVIATIONS USED IN POINTS OF CALL

no—nose   hd—head   nk—neck

DEAD-HEATS, DISQUALIFICATIONS

♦—following the finish call indicates this horse was part of a dead-heat (an explanatory line appears under that past performance line).

†—following the finish call indicates this horse was disqualified. The official placing appears under the past performance line. An explanatory line also appears under the past performance of each horse whose official finish position was changed due to the disqualification.

‡—before the name of any of the first three finishers indicates the horse was disqualified from that position.

POST POSITION

Horse's post position appears after jockey's name—Smith T³.

FILLY OR FILLY-MARE RACES

Ⓕ—preceding the race classification indicates races exclusively for fillies or fillies and mares.

RESTRICTED RACES

Ⓢ—preceding the race classification denotes state-bred races restricted to horses bred in a certain state (or a given geographic area) which qualify under state breeding programs.

Ⓡ—preceding the race classification indicates races that have certain eligibility restrictions other than sex or age.

RACE CLASSIFICATIONS

10000—Claiming race (eligible to be claimed for $10,000). Note: The letter c preceding claiming price (c10000) indicates horse was claimed.

M10000—Maiden claiming race (non-winners—eligible to be claimed).

10000H—Claiming handicap (eligible to be claimed).

⁰10000—Optional claiming race (entered NOT to be claimed).

10000⁰—Optional claiming race (eligible to be claimed).

Mdn—Maiden race (non-winners).

AlwM—Maiden allowance race (for non-winners with special weight allowances).

Aw10000—Allowance race with purse value.

HcpO—Overnight handicap race.

SplW—Special weight race.

Wfa—Weight-for-age race.

Mtch—Match race.

A10000—Starter allowance race (horses who have started for a claiming price shown, or less, as stipulated in the conditions).

H10000—Starter handicap (same restrictions as starter allowance).

S10000—Starter special weight (same restrictions as starter allowance). Note: Where no amount is specified in the conditions of the "starters" race dashes are substituted, as shown below:

A——————— H——————— S———————

50000S—Claiming stakes (eligible to be claimed).

STAKES RACES

In stakes race, with the exception of claiming stakes, the name or abbreviation of name is shown in the class of race column. The letter "H" after name indicates the race was a handicap stakes. The same procedure is used for the rich invitational races for which there are no nomination or starting fees. The letters "Inv" following the abbreviation indicate the race was by invitation only.

SPEED RATINGS

This is a comparison of the horse's final time with the track record established prior to the opening of the racing season at that track. The track record is given a rating of 100. One point is deducted for each fifth of a second by which a horse fails to equal the track record (one length is approximately equal to one-fifth of a second). Thus, in a race in which the winner equals the track record (a Speed Rating of 100), another horse who is beaten 12 lengths (or an estimated two and two-fifths seconds) receives a Speed Rating of 88 (100 minus 12). If a horse breaks the track record he receives an additional point for each one-fifth second by which he lowers the record (if the track record is 1:10 and he is timed in 1:09⅗, his Speed Rating is 102). In computing beaten-off distances for Speed Ratings, fractions of one-half length or more are figured as one full length (one point). No Speed Ratings are given for steeplechase or hurdle events, for races of less than three furlongs, or for races which the horse's speed rating is less than 25.

When Daily Racing form prints its own time, in addition to the offical track time, the Speed Rating is based on the official track time.

Note: Speed Ratings for new distances are computed and assigned when adequate time standards are established.

TRACK VARIANTS

This takes into consideration all of the races run on a particular day and could reflect either the quality of the competition, how many points below par the track happened to be, or both. The Speed Rating of each winner is added together, then an average is taken based on the number of races run. This average is deducted from the track par of 100 and the difference is the Track Variant (example: average Speed Rating of winners involved is 86, par is 100, the Track Variant is 14). When there is a change in the track condition during the course of a program the following procedure is employed in compiling the Variant: races run on dirt tracks classified as fast, frozen or good, and those listed as hard, firm or good on the turf, are used in striking one average. Strips classified as slow, sloppy, muddy or heavy on the dirt, or yielding and soft on the turf, are grouped for another average. If all the races on a program are run in either one or the other of these general classifications only one average is used. The lower the Variant the faster the track or the better the overall quality of the competition. Note: A separate Track Variant is computed for races run on the turf (grass), straight course races, and for races run around turns at distances of less than 5 furlongs.

TROUBLE LINES

When a horse experiences trouble in a race, this information is reported, with the date of the incident, in a capsule description directly below the past performance line for that race.

WORKOUTS

Each horse's most recent workouts appear directly under the past performances. For example, Jly20 Hol 3f :38b indicates the horse worked on July 20 at Hollywood Park. The distance of the work was 3 furlongs over a fast track and the horse was timed in 38 seconds, breezing. A "bullet" • appearing before the date of a workout indicates that the workout was the best of the day for that distance at that track.

Abbreviations Used In Workouts

b—breezing   d—driving   e—easily   g—worked from the gate   h—handily   bo—bore out ⓣ—turf course   Tr—trial race   tr.t following track abbreviation indicates horse worked on training track.

(Continued)

Abbreviations and Purse Value Index

For North American Tracks

The following table may be used as an adjunct to Daily Racing Form's past performance feature of showing the value of allowance race purses. The number following the name of each track (except hunt meets) represents the average net purse value per race (including stakes and overnight races), rounded to the nearest thousand, during the track's 1983 season. A comparision thus can be made of the value of an allowance purse in a horse's current past performances with the average value of all races at that track the preceding season. The purse value index in the track abbreviation table will be changed each year to reflect the values of the previous season. If no purse value index is shown in the following table, the track did not operate a race meeting last year.

AC — (Agua) Caliente, Mexico—3
Aks — Ak-Sar-Ben, Neb.—11
Alb — Albuquerque, N. Mex.—7
AP — Arlington Park, Ill.—12
Aqu — Aqueduct, N.Y.—22
ArP — Arapahoe Park, Colo.
AsD — *Assiniboia Downs, Canada—4
Atl — Atlantic City, N.J.—6
Ato — *Atokad Park, Neb.—1
Bel — Belmont Park, N.Y.—28
Bil — *Billings, Mont.—1
BM — Bay Meadows, Cal.—11
Bmf — Bay Meadows Fair, Cal.—10
Bml — Balmoral Park, Ill.—3
Boi — *Boise, Idaho—1
Bow — Bowie, Md.—9
BRD— *Blue Ribbon Downs, Okla.
CD — Churchill Downs, Ky.—11
Cda — *Coeur d'Alene, Idaho—1
Cen — Centennial Race Track, Colo.—2
Cls — *Columbus, Neb.—4
Crc — Calder Race Course, Fla.—9
CT — *Charles Town, W. Va.—3
Dar — Darby Downs, Ohio—4
       (formerly Beulah Race Track)
DeD — *Delta Downs, La.—3
Del — Delaware Park, Del.
Det — Detroit Race Course, Mich.—6
Dmr— Del Mar, Cal.—19

Dmf— Del Mar Fair, Cal.—9
EIP — Ellis Park, Ky.—4
EnP — †Enoch Park, Canada
EP — *Exhibition Park, Canada—6
EvD — *Evangeline Downs, La.—3
Fai — †Fair Hill, Md.
FE — Fort Erie, Canada—6
Fer — *Ferndale, Cal.—2
FG — Fair Grounds, La.—9
FL — Finger Lakes, N.Y.—5
Fno — Fresno, Cal.—4
Fon — *Fonner Park, Neb.—4
FP — Fairmount Park, Ill.—4
GBF — *Great Barrington, Mass.—2
GD — †Galway Downs, Cal.
GF — *Great Falls, Mont.—1
GG — Golden Gate Fields, Cal.—11
GP — Gulfstream Park, Fla.—16
Grd — *Greenwood, Canada—10
GrP — *Grants Pass, Ore.—1
GS — Garden State Park, N.J.
HaP — *Harbor Park, Wash.—1
       (formerly listed as Elma)
Haw— Hawthorne, Ill.—9
Hia — Hialeah Park, Fla.—10
Hol — Hollywood Park, Cal.—27
HP — *Hazel Park, Mich.—5
Imp.— *Imperial, Cal.
JnD — *Jefferson Downs, La.—5

Jua — Juarez, Mexico
Kee — Keeneland, Ky.—17
Key — Keystone Race Track, Pa.—8
LA   — *Los Alamitos, Cal.—10
LaD — Louisiana Downs, La.—13
LaM — *La Mesa Park, N. Mex.—2
Lar — Nuevo Laredo, Mexico—2
Lat — Latonia, Ky.—5
Lbg — *Lethbridge, Canada
LnN — *Lincoln State Fair, Neb.—3
Lga — Longacres, Wash.—6
Lrl — Laurel Race Course, Md.—9
MD   — *Marquis Downs, Canada—2
Med — Meadowlands, N.J.—13
Mex — *Mexico City, Mexico
MF   — *Marshfield Fair, Mass.—2
Mth — Monmouth Park, N.J.—12
Nmp — *Northampton, Mass.—2
NP   — *Northlands Park, Canada—5
OP   — Oaklawn Park, Ark.—16
OTC — †Ocala Training Center, Fla.
Pay — †Payson Park, Fla.
Pen — Penn National, Pa.—4
Pim — Pimlico, Md.—10
PJ   — *Park Jefferson, S.D.—1
Pla — *Playfair, Wash.—2
Pln — Pleasanton, Cal.—9
PM   — Portland Meadows, Ore.—2
Pmf — Portland Meadowls Fair, Ore.
Poc — *Pocono Downs, Pa.
Pom — *Pomona, Cal.—11
PP   — Pikes Peak Meadows
PR   — Puerto Rico (El Comandante)
Pre — *Prescott Downs, Ariz.—1
Rap — *Rapid City, S.D.—1
RD   — River Downs, Ohio—4
Reg — *Regina, Canada—2
Ril — *Rillito, Ariz.—1
Rkm — Rockingham Park, N.H.
Rui — *Ruidoso, N. Mex.—4
SA   — Santa Anita Park, Cal.—25
Sac — Sacramento, Cal.—5
Sal — *Salem, Ore. (Lone Oak)—1
San — *Sandown Park, Canada—2
Sar — Saratoga, N.Y.—28
SFe — *Santa Fe, N. Mex.—3
SJD — San Juan Downs, N. Mex.
SLR — †San Luis Rey Downs, Cal.

Sol — *Solano, Cal.—7
Spt — *Sportsman's Park, Ill.—11
SR   — *Santa Rosa, Cal.—7
Stk — Stockton, Cal.—5
StP — *Stampede Park, Canada—5
Suf — Suffolk Downs, Mass.—6
SuD — *Sun Downs, Wash.—1
Sun — Sunland Park, N. Mex.—3
Tam — Tampa Bay Downs, Fla.—3
Tdn — Thistledown, Ohio—5
Tim — *Timonium, Md.—5
TuP — Turf Paradise, Ariz.—3
Vic — *Victorville, Cal.
Was — Washington Park, Ill.
Wat — Waterford Park, W. Va.—2
WO   — Woodbine, Canada—14
YM   — Yakima Meadows, Wash.—1

Hunt Meetings

Aik — Aiken, S. C.
AtH — Atlanta, Ga.
Cam — Camden, S. C.
Clm — Clemmons, N.C.
Fai — Fair Hill, Md.
Fax — Fairfax, Va.
FH   — Fair Hills, N.J.
Fx   — Foxfield, Va.
Gln — Glyndon, Md.
GN   — *Grand National, Md.
Lex — Lexington, Ky.
Lig — Lignonier, Pa.
Mal — Malvern, Pa.
Mid — Middleburg, Va.
Mon — Monkton, Md.
Mor — Morven Park, Va.
Mtp — Montpelier, Va.
Oxm — Oxmoor, Ky.
PmB — Palm Beach, Fla.
Pro — Prospect, Ky.
PW   — Percy Warner, Tenn.
RB   — Red Bank, N.J.
SH   — Strawberry Hill, Va.
SoP — Southern Pines, N.C.
StL — St. Louis, Mo.
Try — Tryon, N.C.
Uni — Unionville, Pa.
War — Warrenton, Va.
Wel — Wellsville, Pa.

Tracks marked with (*) are less than one mile in circumference. †Training facility only.

Race Tracks And Racing Organizations

Race Tracks

ARIZONA

Prescott Downs	Prescott	(602) 445-0220
Rillito Downs	Tucson	(602) 888-2115
Turf Paradise	Phoenix	(602) 942-1101

ARKANSAS

Oakland Park	Hot Springs	(501) 623-4411

CALIFORNIA

Bay Meadows	San Mateo	(415) 574-RACE
Del Mar	Del Mar	(619) 755-1141
Ferndale	Ferndale	(707) 786-9511
Fresno	Fresno	(209) 255-3081
Golden Bear/Cal-Expo.	Sacramento	(916) 924-1103
Golden Gate Fields	Albany	(415) 526-3020
Hollywood Park	Inglewood	(213) 419-1500
Los Alamitos Race Course	Los Alamitos	(714) 995-1234
Pleasanton	Pleasanton	(415) 846-2881
Pomona	Pomona	(714) 623-3111
Santa Anita	Arcadia	(213) 574-7223
Santa Rosa	Santa Rosa	(707) 545-4200
Solano	Vallejo	(707) 644-4401
Stockton	Stockton	(209) 466-5041

COLORADO

Arapahoe Downs	Littleton	(303) 798-0612

DELAWARE

Delaware Park	Stanton	(302) 994-2521

FLORIDA

Calder Race Course	Miami	(305) 625-1311
Gulfstream Park	Hallandale	(305) 454-7000
Hialeah	Hialeah	(305) 885-8000
Tampa Bay Downs	Oldsmar	(813) 855-4401

IDAHO

Coeur D'Alene	Coeur D'Alene	(208) 664-5940
Les Bois Park	Boise	(208) 384-8785

ILLINOIS

Arlington Park	Arlington Heights	(312) 255-4300
Balmoral Park	Crete	(312) 672-7544
Fairmount Park	Collinsville	(618) 345-4300
Hawthorne Race Course	Cicero	(312) 372-0222
Sportsman's Park	Cicero	(312) 242-1121

KENTUCKY

Churchill Downs	Louisville	(502) 636-3541
Ellis Park	Henderson	(502) 683-0266
Keeneland	Lexington	(606) 254-3412
Latonia Race Course	Florence	(606) 371-0200

LOUISIANA

Delta Downs	Vinton	(318) 589-7441
Evangeline Downs	Lafayette	(318) 896-6185
Fair Grounds	New Orleans	(504) 944-5515
Jefferson Downs	Kenner	(504) 466-8521
Louisiana Downs	Bossier City	(318) 742-5555

MARYLAND

Bowie Race Track	Bowie	(301) 262-8111
Laurel Race Course	Laurel	(301) 725-0400
Pimlico	Baltimore	(301) 542-9400
Timonium	Timonium	(301) 252-0200

MASSACHUSETTS

Great Barrington	Great Barrington	(413) 528-3030
Marshfield	Marshfield	(617) 934-2217
Northampton	Northampton	(413) 584-2237
Suffolk Downs	East Boston	(617) 567-3900

MICHIGAN

Detroit Race Course	Livonia	(313) 525-7300
Hazel Park	Hazel Park	(313) 566-1595

MONTANA

Montana State Fair	Great Falls	(406) 452-6401
Yellowstone Exhibition	Billings	(406) 252-9366

NEBRASKA

Ak-Sar-Ben	Omaha	(402) 556-2305
Atokad	South Sioux City	(402) 494-3611
Columbus	Columbus	(402) 564-3274
Fonner Park	Grand Island	(308) 382-4515

NEW HAMPSHIRE

Rockingham Park	Salem	(603) 898-2311

NEW JERSEY

Atlantic City	Atlantic City	(609) 641-2190
Garden State Park	Cherry Hill	(609) 488-8181
Monmouth Park	Oceanport	(201) 222-5100
The Meadowlands	East Rutherford	(201) 935-8500

NEW MEXICO

Albuquerque	Albuquerque	(505) 265-1791
La Mesa Park	Raton	(505) 455-2761
Ruidoso Downs	Ruidoso	(505) 378-4431
Santa Fe Downs	Santa Fe	(505) 471-3311
Sunland Park	Sunland Park	(505) 589-1131

NEW YORK

Aqueduct	Queens	(212) 641-4700
Belmont Park	Elmont	(516) 488-6000
Finger Lakes	Farmington	(716) 924-3232
Saratoga	Saratoga	(518) 584-6200

OHIO

Darby Downs	Grove City	(614) 875-3434
River Downs	Cincinnati	(513) 232-8000
Thistledown	North Randall	(216) 662-8600

OKLAHOMA

Blue Ribbon Downs	Sallisaw	(918) 775-4418

OREGON

Portland Meadows	Portland	(503) 285-9144
Salem	Salem	(503) 378-3247

PENNSYLVANIA

Commodore Downs	Fairview	(814) 474-2641
Keystone Race Track	Bensalem	(215) 639-9000
Penn National	Grantville	(717) 469-2211

SOUTH DAKOTA

Park Jefferson	Jefferson	(605) 966-5511

WASHINGTON

Longacres	Renton	(206) 226-3131
Playfair Race Course	Spokane	(509) 534-0505
Yakima Meadows	Yakima	(509) 248-3920

WEST VIRGINIA

Charles Town	Charles Town	(304) 725-7001
Waterford Park	Chester	(304) 387-2400

CANADA

Assiniboia Downs	Winnipeg, Man.	(204) 885-3330
Exhibition Park	Vancouver, B.C.	(604) 254-1631
Fort Erie	Fort Erie, Ont.	(416) 871-3200
Greenwood	Toronto, Ont.	(416) 698-3131
Northlands Park	Edmonton, Alb.	(403) 471-7379
Stampede Park	Calgary, Alb.	(403) 261-0214
Woodbine	Toronto, Ont.	(416) 675-6110

Racing Organizations

AMERICAN TRAINERS ASSOCIATION
President: Mitchell C. Preger
Contact: John V. Hennegan, Asst. Sec.
P.O. Box 6702
Towson, MD 21204

HORSEMEN'S BENEVOLENT & PROTECTIVE ASSOCIATION
Contact: Ed Flint, Pres.
6000 Executive Blvd.,
Suite 317
Rockville, MD 20852
(301) 881-7191

THE JOCKEY CLUB
Chairman: Ogden Mills Phipps
Contact: Hans Stahl, Exec. Dir.
380 Madison Ave.
New York, NY 10017
(212) 599-1919

JOCKEYS' GUILD, INC.
President: William Shoemaker
Contact: Nick Jemas, Man. Dir.
555 Fifth Ave., Rm 1501
New York, NY 10017
(212) 687-7746

NATIONAL ASSOCIATION OF STATE RACING COMMISSIONERS
President: Billy Vessels
Contact: Warren D. Schweder,
Exec. V.P.
P.O. Box 4216
Lexington, KY 40504
(606) 278-5460

NATIONAL TURF WRITERS ASSN.
President: Dan Farley
Contact: Mike Barry, Exec. Sec.
2362 Winston
Louisville, KY 40205

RACE TRACK CHAPLAINCY OF AMERICA, INC.
President: Rev. Daniel G. Sommer
Contact: Sam Ed Spence, Exec. Dir.
P.O. Box 18988
Fort Worth, TX 76118
(817) 379-5957

RACETRACKS OF CANADA
President: Jack Cruickshank
Contact: Rod Seiling, Exec. V.P.
555 Burnamthorpe Road,
Suite 607
Etobicoke, Ontario M9C 2Y3
Canada
(416) 622-6561

RACING FANS CLUB OF AMERICA
Contact: Milton S. Forman, Pres.
P.O. Box 6158
Philadelphia, PA 19115
(215) 342-2821

THOROUGHBRED CLUB OF AMERICA
President: Robert N. Clay
Contact: Maud H. Thornton,
Exec. Mgr.
P.O. Box 8147
Lexington, KY 40533
(606) 277-8202

THOROUGHBRED OWNERS & BREEDERS ASSOCIATION
President: Shirley Taylor
Contact: Mrs. Linda J. Cowasjee,
Exec. Dir.
P.O. Box 358
Elmont, NY 11003
(516) 488-2260

THOROUGHBRED RACING ASSOCIATIONS OF NORTH AMERICA, INC.
President: Morris J. Alhadeff
Contact: J. B. Faulconer, Exec. V.P.
3000 Marcus Ave., Suite 2W4
Lake Success, NY 11042
(516) 328-2660

THOROUGHBRED RACING PROTECTIVE BUREAU
Contact: Clifford W. Wickman, Pres.
P.O. Box 3557
New Hyde Park, NY 11042
(516) 328-2010

UNITED THOROUGHBRED TRAINERS OF AMERICA, INC.
President: Martin L. Fallon
Contact: Ruth LeGrove, Sec./Treas.
19363 James Couzens Hwy.
Detroit, MI 48235
(313) 342-6144

Libraries

KEENELAND LIBRARY
Contact: Doris Jean Warren, Librarian
Keeneland Race Course
Box 1690
Lexington, KY 40592
(606) 254-3412

NATIONAL SPORTING LIBRARY
Contact: A. Mackay-Smith, Curator
P.O. Box 1335
Middleburg, VA 22117
(703) 687-6542

WILLIAM P. KYNE MEMORIAL THOROUGHBRED RACING LIBRARY
Contact: Rusty Mathieson, Librarian
Bay Meadows Race Course
P.O. Box 5050
San Mateo, CA 94402
(415) 574-7223

NOTE: Most state breeders' organizations maintain a library, all of varying degrees of completeness.

State Breeders Organizations

ARIZONA THOROUGHBRED BREEDERS
ASSOCIATION
P.O. Box 35055
Phoenix, AZ 85069
Telephone: (602) 942-1310

ARKANSAS THOROUGHBRED BREEDERS
AND HORSEMEN'S ASSOCIATION
P.O. Box 1665
Hot Springs, AR 71901
Telephone: (501) 624-6328

CALIFORNIA THOROUGHBRED
BREEDERS ASSOCIATION
P.O. Box 750
Arcadia, CA 91006
Telephone: (818) 445-7800

COLORADO THOROUGHBRED BREEDERS
ASSOCIATION
5300 S. Federal
Littleton, CO 80120
Telephone: (303) 798-3846

FLORIDA THOROUGHBRED BREEDERS
ASSOCIATION
4727 N.W. 80th Avenue
Ocala, FL 32675
Telephone: (904) 629-2160

GEORGIA HORSE FOUNDATION
P.O. Box 52903
Atlanta, GA 30355
Telephone: (404) 261-0612

IDAHO THOROUGHBRED BREEDERS
ASSOCIATION
P.O. Box 841
Meridian, ID 83642
Telephone: (208) 888-4560

ILLINOIS THOROUGHBRED BREEDERS
FUND PROGRAM
Illinois Department of Agriculture
Springfield, IL 62706
Telephone: (217) 782-4231

241

KENTUCKY THOROUGHBRED OWNERS AND BREEDERS
P.O. Box 4158
Lexington, KY 40544
Telephone: (606) 277-1122

LOUISIANA THOROUGHBRED BREEDERS ASSOCIATION
P.O. Box 24650
New Orleans, LA 70184
Telephone: (504) 947-4676

MARYLAND HORSE BREEDERS ASSOCIATION
Box 427
Timonium, MD 21093
Telephone: (301) 252-2100

MASSACHUSETTS THOROUGHBRED BREEDERS' ASSOCIATION
One Washington Mall
Boston, MA 02108
Telephone: (617) 723-8100

MICHIGAN DEPARTMENT OF AGRICULTGURE
Fairs and Racing Division
Lewis Cass Building, 5th Floor
Lansing, MI 48909
Telephone: (517) 373-1095

MINNESOTA THOROUGHBRED ASSOCIATION
918 Marie Avenue
South St. Paul, MN 55075
Telephone: (612) 455-2214

NEBRASKA THOROUGHBRED BREEDERS ASSOCIATION
Box 2215
Grand Island, NE 68802
Telephone: (308) 384-4683

THOROUGHBRED BREEDERS' ASSOCIATION OF NEW JERSEY
118 Abbington Drive
East Windsor, NJ 08520
Telephone: (609) 443-5404

NEW MEXICO HORSE BREEDERS ASSOCIATION
P.O. Drawer 5649
Santa Fe, NM 87502
Telephone: (505) 345-1113

NEW YORK THOROUGHBRED BREEDER
253 Hempstead Turnpike
Elmont, NY 11003
Telephone: (516) 354-7600

OHIO THOROUGHBRED OWNERS AND BREEDERS
812 Race Street
Cincinnati, OH 45202
Telephone: (315) 241-4589

OKLAHOMA HORSEMEN'S ASSOCIATIO
2720 N. Classen
Oklahoma City, OK 73106
Telephone: (405) 521-8540

OREGON THOROUGHBRED BREEDERS ASSOCIATION
P.O. Box 17248
Portland, OR 97217
Telephone: (503) 285-0658

PENNSYLVANIA HORSE BREEDERS ASSOCIATION
203 N. Union Street
Kennett Square, PA 19348
Telephone: (215) 444-1050

SOUTH DAKOTA RACING COMMISSION
State Capitol
Pierre, SD 57501
Telephone: (605) 773-3179

TENNESSEE THOROUGHBRED OWNERS AND BREEDERS ASSOCIATION
Suite 1300, Plaza Tower
Knoxville, TN 37929
Telephone: (615) 637-7777

TEXAS THOROUGHBRED BREEDERS ASSOCIATION
P.O. Box 14967
Austin, TX 78761
Telephone: (512) 458-6133

WASHINGTON HORSE BREEDERS ASSOCIATION
P.O. Box 88258
Seattle, WA 98188
Telephone: (206) 226-2620

WEST VIRGINIA THOROUGHBRED BREEDERS ASSOCIATION
P.O. Box 670
Charles Town, WV 25414
Telephone: (304) 725-2276

Bibliography

Valuable References

American Produce Records; 1930-. Bloodstock Research and Statistical Bureau, Lexington. 12 volumes. Annual.

American Racing Manual, The; Daily Racing Form, Hightstown, New Jersey, 19___. Annual. 1754 pp.

Book of the Horse, The; Macgregor-Morris, Pamela, Ed.; G. P. Putnam's Sons, New York, 1979. 208 pp.

Drugs and the Performance Horse; Tobin, Dr. Thomas; Charles C. Thomas Publisher, Springfield, Illinois, 1981. 438 pp.

Sources of Books

J. A. Allen and Company
1 Lower Grovesnor Place
London, SW1, England

Breakthrough Publications, Inc.
Millwood, NY 10546

Harris Books
12000 Old Georgetown Road
Suite N-1209
Rockville, MD 20852

Pegasos Press
535 Cordova Road
Suite 163
Santa Fe, NM 87501

The Uncommon Market
900 North Broadway
Lexington, KY 40505

The Book Stable
3326 Tomahawk Trail
Fort Wayne, IN 46804

Equine Medicine and Surgery; American Veterinary Publications, Santa Bar bara, California, 1963. 797 pp.

Horse Industry Directory; American Horse Council, Washington, D.C., 19____ 76 pp.

Illustrated Veterinary Encyclopedia, The; Equine Research Publications Grapevine, Texas, 1975. 650 pp.

Racehorses of 19____; Portway Press, Ltd., Halifax, Yorkshire, England. An nual.

Veterinary Treatments and Medications for Horsemen; Equine Research Publica tions, Grapevine, Texas, 1977. 555 pp.

Reference—Legal and Accounting

Equestrian Bookkeeper; Weekly, Wood Publications, Inc., Rancho Santa Fe California.

Horse Owners and Breeders Tax Manual, The; American Horse Council Washington, D.C. Annual. 800+ pp.

Horse Syndication Manual; Wood Publications, Inc., Rancho Santa Fe, Califor nia. 450 pp.

Law for the Horse Breeder; Wood Publications, Inc., Rancho Santa Fe, Califor nia.

Racing Law; Humphreys, John O.; National Association of State Racing Com missioners, Lexington, 1963. 358 pp.

General Reading—Breeding and Pedigree Theory

Bloodstock Breeding; Leicester, Sir Charles; J. A. Allen and Co., London, England, 1957. 482 pp.

Breeding the Racehorse; Tesio, Federico; J. A. Allen and Co., London, England 1958. 130 pp.

Genetics of the Horse; Jones, W. E. and Bogart, Ralph; Caballus Publishers, Fort Collins, Colorado, 1973. 356 pp.

Great Breeders and Their Methods, The; Hewitt, Abram S.; Thoroughbred Publishers, Inc., Lexington, 1982. 390 pp.

Names in Pedigrees; Palmer, Joe H.; Thoroughbred Owners and Breeders Association, Lexington, 1939. 328 pp.

Sire Lines; Hewitt, Abram S.; Thoroughbred Press, Lexington, 1977. 595 pp.

Thoroughbred Pedigrees Simplified; Napier, Miles; J. A. Allen and Co., Lon don, England, 1973. 76 pp.

Typology of the Racehorse; Varola, Francisco; J. A. Allen and Co., London, England, 1974. 242 pp.

General Reading—History and Biography

All the Way; Atkinson, Ted; The Citadel Press, New York, 1961. 192 pp.

Harness Horse Racing; Wrensch, Frank A.; D. Van Nostrand, New York, 1951. 219 pp.

History of Horse Racing, The; Longrigg, Roger; Stein and Day, New York, 1972 318 pp.

Hyperion; Derby, The Earl of; J. A. Allen and Co., London, England, 1957. 164 pp.

Kentucky Derby, The: The First 100 Years; Chew, Peter; Houghton-Mifflin, Boston, 1974. 303 pp.

Various Titles; Francis, Dick; Harper and Row, New York. Horse racing mysteries.

World of Horses, A; Reynolds, James; Creative Age Press, New York, 1947. 255 pp.

General Reading—Training, Conditioning, and Veterinary

Anatomy of the Horse, The; Way and Lee; J. B. Lippincott Co., Philadelphia, 1965. 214 pp.

Applied Animal Nutrition; Crampton and Harris; W. H. Freeman and Co., San Francisco, 1969. 754 pp.

Are Your Horses Trying?; Rickaby, Fred; J. A. Allen and Co., London, England, 1967. 191 pp.

Art and Science of Horseshoeing, The; Greely, R. Gordon; J. B. Lippincott Co., Philadelphia, 1970. 176 pp.

Conditioning to Win; Wagoner, Don; Equine Research Publications, Grapevine, Texas, 1974. 312 pp.

Feeding to Win; Wagoner, Don; Equine Research Publications, Grapevine, Texas, 1973. 314 pp.

Fit Race Horse, The; Ivers, Tom; Esprit Racing Team, Ltd., Cincinnati, Ohio. 300 pp.

Harness Horse Lameness; Levman, Martin I., D.V.M.; Horseman's Veterinary Publishing Co., Toronto, Canada, 1982. 164 pp.

Horse, The: From Conception to Maturity; Rossdale, Peter D.; California Thoroughbred Breeders Association, Arcadia, California, 1972. 224 pp.

Horseshoeing Theory and Hoof Care; Emery, Leslie, Miller, Jim, and Van Hoosen, Nyles; Lea and Febiger, Philadelphia, 1977. 257 pp.

Lame Horse, The; Rooney, Dr. James R.; Wilshire Book Company, North Hollywood, California, 1974. 233 pp.

Progress in Equine Practice—Book Number One in the Modern Veterinary Reference Series; Catcott, E. J., D.V.M., PhD and Smithcors, J. F., D.V.M., PhD (Edited by); American Veterinary Publications, Inc., Wheaton, Illinois, 1966. 595 pp.

Progress in Equine Practice—Volume II, Book Number Eleven in the Modern Veterinary Reference Series; Catcott, E. J., D.V.M., PhD and Smithcors, J. F., D.V.M., PhD (Edited by); American Veterinary Publications, Inc., Wheaton, Illinois, 1970. 640 pp.

Race Horse Training; Collins, Robert W.; The Thoroughbred Record, Lexington, 1972. 312 pp.

Reproduction in Farm Animals; Hafez, E.S.E.; Lea and Febiger, Philadelphia, 1974. 440 pp.

Training for Fun; Daingerfield, Keene Jr.; The Thoroughbred Record Company, Lexington, 1948. 230 pp.

Training Thoroughbred Horses; Burch, Preston M.; The Blood-Horse, Lexington, 1953. 130 pp.

Veterinary Diagnosis and Treatment; Jorgenson, G. E., A. B., D.V.M.; D. Appleton and Company, New York/London, 1925. 341 pp.

Periodicals—National

Backstretch, The, 19363 James Couzens Highway, Detroit, Michigan 48235. Quarterly, $6.00 annually.

Blood-Horse, The, P. O. Box 4038, Lexington, Kentucky 40544. Weekly, $68.75 annually. Plus the following excellent supplements: "Stallion Register for 19___," (included) annual; "Principal Winners Abroad, 19___," (included) annual; "Auctions of 19___," (included) annual.

Daily Racing Form, The (Eastern Edition), 10 Lake Drive, Hightstown, New Jersey 08520. Daily newspaper, $1.75 daily, $920.40 annually first class, $546.00 annually second class.

Daily Racing Form, The (Midwest Edition), 731 Plymouth Court, Chicago, Illinois 60605. Daily newspaper, $1.75 daily, $927.00 annually first class, $546.00 annually second class.

Daily Racing Form, The (Western Edition), 170 South Bimini Place, Los Angeles, California 90004. Daily newspaper, $1.75 daily, $873.00 annually first class, $546.00 annually second class.

Derby, P. O. Box 5418, Norman, Oklahoma 73070. Monthly, $18.00 annually.

Equine Sportsmedicine, Animal Health Divisions, E. R. Squibb & Sons, Inc., Veterinary Learning Systems, Inc., 50 Hightstown Rd., P. O. Box 277, Princeton Junction, New Jersey 08550. Complimentary.

Equine Sports Medicine News, P. O. Box 38206, Cincinnati, Ohio 45238. Monthly, $40.00 annually.

Equine Veterinary Data, P.O. Box 1127, Wildomar, California 92395. 24 times a year, $95 annually.

Equus, Equus Subscription Dept., P. O. Box 932, Farmingdale, New York 11737. Monthly, $20.00 annually.

Horse Digest, The, XIT Robinwood Publishing Co., P. O. Box 918, Farmingdale, New York, 11737. Monthly, $18.00 annually.

Horseman's Journal, The, 6000 Executive Blvd., Suite 317, Rockville, Maryland 20852. Monthly, $24.00 annually.

Journal of Equine Veterinary Science, Journal of Equine Veterinary Science, P. O. Box 1127, Wildomar, California 92395. Bimonthly, $30.00 annually.

Racing Update, P. O. Box 11052, Lexington, Kentucky 40511. 24 issues a year, $200.00 annually.

Speedhorse, The, P. O. Box 1000, Norman, Oklahoma 73070. Monthly (quarter horses), $20.00 annually.

Sports Eye, 18 Industrial Park Drive, Port Washington, NY 11050. Daily newspaper, $1.25 daily, $295.00 annually.

Sports Illustrated, 541 N. Fairbanks Court, Chicago, Illinois 60611. Weekly.

Spur, Spur, Inc., P. O. Box 85, Middleburg, Virginia 22117. Bimonthly, $16.00 annually.

Thoroughbred Record, The, P. O. Box 4240, Lexington, Kentucky 40544. Weekly, $60.00 annually. Plus the following excellent supplements: "Sire Book (Season of 19___)," (included) annual; "Breeders Book (Season of 19___)," (separate, $15.00) annual.

Turf and Sport Digest, 511 Oakland Ave., Baltimore, Maryland 21212. Monthly, $8.00 annually.

Periodicals—Regional

Arizona Thoroughbred, P. O. Box 35055, Phoenix, Arizona 85069. Bimonthly, $9.00 annually.
British Columbia Thoroughbred, 4023 E. Hastings Street, North Burnaby, B. C. V5C251, Canada. Eight issues a year, $25.00 annually.
Canadian Horse, The, P. O. Box 172, Rexdale, Ontario M9W SL1, Canada. Monthly, $24.00 annually.
Florida Horse, The, P. O. Box 2106, Ocala, Florida 32678. Monthly, $35.00 annually.
Idaho Thoroughbred, The, P. O. Box 841, Meridian, Idaho 83642. Quarterly, $10.00 annually.
Illinois Racing News, 111 Shore Drive, Hinsdale (Burr Ridge), Illinois 60521. Monthly, $18.00 annually.
Louisiana Horse, P. O. Box 2098, Hammond, Louisiana 70404. Bimonthly, $9.00 annually.
Maryland Horse, The, P. O. Box 4, Timonium, Maryland 21093. Monthly, $18.00 annually.
New York Thoroughbred, 575 Lexington Avenue, Suite 2605, New York. Quarterly, free to NYTBA members.
Ohio Thoroughbred, 812 Race Street, Cincinnati, Ohio 45202. Quarterly, $8.00 annually.
Oregon Horse, The, P. O. Box 17248, Portland, Oregon 97217. Quarterly, $8.00 annually.
Texas Thoroughbred, The, P. O. Box 14967, 6207 Sheridan Avenue, #303, Austin, Texas 78761. Monthly, $18.00 annually.
Thoroughbred of California, The, 201 Colorado Place, Arcadia, California 91006. Monthly, $24.00 annually.
Washington Horse, The, P. O. Box 88258, Seattle, Washington 98188. Monthly, $25.00 annually.

Periodicals—International

Australian Thoroughbreds, Suite 4, 179 Elizabeth Street, Sydney 2000, Australia. Bimonthly.
Courses et Elevage, Union Nationale, Interprofessionale du Cheval, 51 Rue Dumont d'Urville, 75116, Paris, France. Bimonthly.
European Racehorse, The, Oakfield House, Perrymount Road, Hayward Heath, West Sussex RH16 3 DH, England. Quarterly.
Horse and Hound, King's Reach Towers, Stamford St., London SE1 9GS, England. Weekly.
New Zealand Blood-Horse, The, P. O. Box 3967, Auckland, New Zealand. Monthly.
Pacemaker International, P. O. Box 90 King's Road, London SW3 4 UN, England. Monthly, or: P. O. Box 24288, Lexington, Kentucky 40524. Other Publications: "Pattern Races," monthly; "Sires for 19____," annual; "Directory of the Turf, 19____."

South African Horseman, The, P. O. Box 78220, Sandton 2146, South Africa. Bimonthly.

Stud and Stable, 59 High Street, Ascot, Berkshire SL5 7HP, England. Monthly.

Turf e Fomento, Avenida Linneu de Paula Machado, 775, Sao Paulo, Brazil. Bimonthly.

Books From Shelves

Ainslie's Complete Guide to Thoroughbred Racing; Ainslie, Tom; Simon & Schuster, Inc., New York, 1968. 470 pp.

All About Thorobred Horse Racing; Swilder, David T.; Hialeah Guild Publishers, Miami, Florida, 1967. 189 pp.

American Horse, The; Nagler, Barney; The MacMillan Company, New York, 1966. 182 pp.

Anatomy and Conformation of the Horse; Edwards, Gladys Brown; Dreenan Press, Ltd., Croton-On-Hudson, New York, 1973. 218 pp.

Anatomy of the Horse, The; Stubbs, George; J. A. Allen and Co., London, England, 1965. 146 pp. (The original 1766 edition and illustrations, with a modern veterinary paraphrase by McMunn, James, FRCS, LRCP, MRCVS, assisted by Ottaway, C. W., PhD, FRCVS.)

Anatomy of the Horse, The; Way, Robert F., V.M.D., M.S., and Lee, Donald G., V.M.D.; J. B. Lippincott Company, Philadelphia and Montreal, 1965. 214 pp.

Beauty of the Horse, The; Isenbart, H. H. and Nowas, C. & V.; The Viking Press, New York, 1972. 70 pp.

Big Red of Meadow Stable; Nack, William; Arthur Fields Books, Inc., New York, 1975. 342 pp.

Biomechanics of Lameness in Horses; Rooney, James R., D.V.M.; Williams and Wilkins Company, Baltimore, 1969. 259 pp.

Book of the Horse, The; Macgregor-Morris, Pamela (Consultant Editor); G. P. Putnam's Sons, New York, 1979. 208 pp.

Both Sides of the River; Asbury, Dr. Eslie; The Thoroughbred Press, Inc., Lexington, 1984. 283 pp.

Bred for the Purple; Seth-Smith, Michael; Leslie-Frewin, London, England, 1969. 286 pp.

Champions; Magee, Michael and Bayes, Pat; William Morrow and Company, Inc., New York, 1980. 121 pp.

Classic Lines: A Gallery of the Great Thoroughbreds; Reeves, Richard Stone and Robinson, Patrick; Oxmoor House, Inc., Birmingham, Alabama, 1975. 170 pp.

Classic Lives; Silver, Caroline; Harcourt Brace Jovanovich, Inc., New York, 1973. 250 pp.

Complete Horseshoeing Guide, The; Wiseman, Robert F.; University of Oklahoma Press, Norman, Oklahoma, 1968. 238 pp.

Derby; Cox, Millard; J. A. Allen and Co., London, England, 1974. 164 pp.

Derby, The; Levy, Bill; The World Publishing Company, Cleveland and New York, 1967. 150 pp.

Down the Stretch; Winn, Col. Matt J.; Smith & Durrell, New York, 1944. 292 pp.

Encyclopedia of the Horse, The; Hope, Lieutenant-Colonel C. E. G. and Jackson, G. N. (Edited by); The Viking Press, Inc., New York, 1973. 236 pp.

Equine Medicine and Surgery: A Text and Reference Work; Catcott, E. J., D.V.M., PhD, and Smithcors, J. F., D.V.M., PhD (Edited by); American Veterinary Publications, Inc., Wheaton, Illinois, 1972. 960 pp.

Equus; Vavra, Robert; William Morrow and Company, Inc., New York, 1977. 224 pp.

Fair Exchange; Finney, Humphrey S.; Charles Scribner's Sons, New York, 1974. 175 pp.

Family Library of Horses, The; Hartley-Edwards, Elwyn; Octopus Books, Limited, London, England, 1981. 80 pp.

Feeds and Feeding - Abridged; Morrison, Frank B.; The Morrison Publishing Company, Clinton, Iowa, 1961. 696 pp. Ninth edition.

Fireside Book of Horse Racing, The; Woods, David F. (Edited by); Simon & Schuster, Inc., New York, 1963. 341 pp.

Genetics of the Horse; Jones, William E., D.V.M., PhD and Bogart, Ralph, PhD; Copyright, 1971 by the authors. 356 pp.

Great Racehorses in Art; Fairley, John; The University Press of Kentucky, 1984. 224 pp.

Grooming Horses; Collins, Robert W.; The Blood-Horse, Lexington, 1959. 122 pp. Reprinted by The Thoroughbred Record Co., Lexington, 1971.

Growth and Nutrition in the Horse; Willoughby, David P.; A. S. Barnes and Co., Inc., Cranbury, New Jersey, 1975. 194 pp.

Harper's Encyclopedia for Horsemen; Taylor, Louis; Harper & Row Publishers, New York, Evanston, San Francisco, London, 1973. 558 pp.

History and Romance of the Horse; Alexander, David; Cooper Square Publishers, Inc., New York, 1963. 128 pp.

History of Horsemanship, A; Chenevix-Trench, Charles; Doubleday and Company, Inc., Garden City, New York, 1970. 320 pp.

History of the Thoroughbred in California; Fleming, Mary; California Thoroughbred Breeders Association, Arcadia, California, 1983. 224 pp.

History of Thoroughbred Racing in America, The; Robertson, William H. P.; Prentice-Hall, Inc., Englewood Cliffs, New Jersey, 1964. 621 pp.

Hoofprint on My Heart, A; Coleman, Jim; McClelland and Stewart, Limited, Toronto-Montreal, 1971. 256 pp.

Hoofprints of the Century; Excerpts from America's oldest journal of horse racing and breeding, *The Thoroughbred Record,* and its predecessor publications, *The Livestock Record* and *Kentucky Live Stock Record,* as compiled and annotated by William Robertson (covering 1875-1919 and 1966-1974) and Dan Farley (1920-1965, 1975). 110 pp.

Horse, The; Seth-Smith, Michael (General Editor); Octopus Books, Limited, London, England, 1979. 479 pp.

Horse Gentlemen, The; Harrison, Stanley; The Thoroughbred Press, Inc., Lexington, 1951. 88 pp.

Horses' Injuries; Strong, Charles L.; Arco Publishing Company, Inc., New York, 1973. 118 pp.

Horse Owner's Vet Book, The; Straiton, E. C.; J. B. Lippincott Company, Philadelphia and New York, 1973. 224 pp.

Horse Sense and Humor in Kentucky; Asbury, Dr. Eslie; The Thoroughbred Press, Inc., Lexington, 1980. 270 pp.

Horse World of the Bluegrass, The; Wharton, Mary E. and Bowen, Edward L.; John Bradford Press, Lexington, 1980. 246 pp.

International Stallions and Studs; Seth-Smith, Michael; W. Foulsham and Co., Ltd., Great Britain, 1974. 160 pp.

Judging the Horse—For Racing, Riding and Recreation; Wall, John F., Colonel, U.S.A., Retired and Jennings, Frank; The Thoroughbred Press, Inc., Lexington, 1955. 208 pp.

Lameness in Horses; Adams, O. R.; Lea and Febiger, Philadelphia, 1966. 563 pp.

Laughing in the Hills; Bill Barich; Penguin Books, New York, 1980. 228 pp.

Life and Times of Sir Archie, The; Blanchard, Elizabeth Amis Cameron and Wellman, Manly Wade; The University of North Carolina Press, Chapel Hill, 1958. 232 pp.

Look of Eagles, The; Foote, John Taintor; J. A. Allen and Co., London, England, 1969. 86 pp.

Modern Breeds of Livestock; Briggs, Hilton M.; The MacMillan Company, New York, 1958. 754 pp.

Montpelier: The Recollections of Marion duPont Scott; as told to Gerald Strine; Charles Scribner's Sons, New York, 1976. 219 pp.

Peter Biegel's Racing Pictures; First published in Great Britain by Michael Joseph, Limited, London, England, 1983. 160 pp.

Queen's Plate, The; Frayne, Trent; McClelland and Stewart, Limited, The Jockey Club, Limited, 1959. 168 pp.

Racing Breed, The; Ueltzen, Helen; Frederick Fell Publishers, New York, 1984. 233 pp.

Shoe, The; Shoemaker, Willie and Smith, Dan; Rand McNally and Company, Chicago/New York/San Francisco, 1976. 208 pp.

Stud Farm Diary, A; Finney, Humphrey S.; J. A. Allen and Co., London, England, 1959. 135 pp.

Their Turf; Livingston, Bernard; Arbor House, New York, 1973. 302 pp.

Treasury of Horses, The; Osborne, Walter D. and Johnson, Patricia H.; Golden Press, New York, 1966. 251 pp.

Twenty Great Horses; Mortimer, Roger; Cassell and Company, Ltd., London, England, 1967. 172 pp.

Veterinary Notebook; McGee, William R.; The Blood-Horse, Lexington, 1958. 179 pp.

Credits